Maid for Television

Maid for Television

Race, Class, Gender, and a Representational Economy

L.S. KIM

Rutgers University Press
New Brunswick, Camden, and Newark, New Jersey
London and Oxford

Rutgers University Press is a department of Rutgers, The State University of New Jersey, one of the leading public research universities in the nation. By publishing worldwide, it furthers the University's mission of dedication to excellence in teaching, scholarship, research, and clinical care.

Library of Congress Cataloging-in-Publication Data

Names: Kim, L. S., author.
Title: Maid for television : race, class, gender and a representational economy / L.S. Kim.
Description: New Brunswick : Rutgers University Press, [2023] | Includes bibliographical references and index.
Identifiers: LCCN 2022050700 | ISBN 9781978826991 (paperback) |
  ISBN 9781978827004 (cloth) | ISBN 9781978827011 (epub) | ISBN 9781978827035 (pdf)
Subjects: LCSH: Household employees on television. | Families on television. |
  BISAC: PERFORMING ARTS / Television / History & Criticism |
  SOCIAL SCIENCE / Media Studies
Classification: LCC PN1992.8.H68 K56 2023 | DDC 791.45/655—dc23/eng/20230413
LC record available at https://lccn.loc.gov/2022050700

A British Cataloging-in-Publication record for this book is available from the British Library.

Copyright © 2023 by L.S. Kim
All rights reserved

No part of this book may be reproduced or utilized in any form or by any means, electronic or mechanical, or by any information storage and retrieval system, without written permission from the publisher. Please contact Rutgers University Press, 106 Somerset Street, New Brunswick, NJ 08901. The only exception to this prohibition is "fair use" as defined by U.S. copyright law.

References to internet websites (URLs) were accurate at the time of writing. Neither the author nor Rutgers University Press is responsible for URLs that may have expired or changed since the manuscript was prepared.

∞ The paper used in this publication meets the requirements of the American National Standard for Information Sciences—Permanence of Paper for Printed Library Materials, ANSI Z39.48-1992.

rutgersuniversitypress.org

For my Parents

Contents

1	Introduction: The Figure of the Racialized Domestic in American Television	1
2	Domesticating Blackness: African Americans in Service in Comedy and Drama	21
3	Shades of Whiteness: White Servants Keeping Up a Class Ideal	61
4	Unresolvable Roles: Asian American Servants as Perpetual Foreigners	90
5	Invisible but Viewable: The Latina Maid in the Shadow of Nannygate	131
	Epilogue	160
	Acknowledgments	169
	Notes	171
	Bibliography	197
	Index	203

Maid for Television

1

Introduction

The Figure of the Racialized Domestic in American Television

The image of the domestic servant is both recognizable and invisible at the same time; the figure registers quickly, and then (the implication of her class, gender, and racial status) recedes just as quickly. This book pauses the process of perception, holding a view before the image fades into one's subconscious. In *Maid for Television*, we see the maid and how she tests the boundaries of race, class, and gender. The intimate nature of domestic relations risks crossing lines of demarcation, the role of the maid is to resettle anxious moments. As Patricia Hill Collins reminds us, those who stand at the margins clarify the boundaries.[1]

As I was researching—and searching for—representations of women of color on television, a pattern emerged. A maid, a housekeeper, a nanny, another maid. Often African American, they were also Asian or Latina, or, less often, ethnic white. Decade after decade, in series after series, women, and sometimes men, of color were serving white families on American television. Often they were minor characters in the story, occasionally they were major. But in all cases the television maid of color was figured and bound by gender, class, and race—that is, racialized. I came to understand that not unlike the history of race relations, the history of television is rooted in racialization, of which whiteness is a corollary. Though the racialized domestic may appear to be a person of secondary importance, this enduring figure is in fact emblematic of both television form and the history of U.S. race relations.

Maid for Television examines the intersection of race, class, and gender relations as embodied in a long history of television servants from 1950 to the turn of the millennium. Although they reside at the visual peripheries, these figures are integral, not marginal, to the idealized American family. My main intention is to redirect the gaze at television, toward the usually overlooked interface between characters, which is drawn through race, class, and gender positioning. This book also intends philosophically to redirect the gaze *of* television, that is, television's projection of racial discourse. Television does not simply represent race; rather, through both fiction and nonfiction—from situation comedies, dramas, and children's programming to news, sports, talk shows, and reality television—its stories represent race relations and support social relations in real life. Televisual and actual race relations, as text and context, function as codeterminants of racial meaning.

Maid for Television tells the stories of servants and the families they work for, in so doing it investigates how Americans have dealt with difference through television as a medium and a mediator. The topic of television servants is a unique academic inquiry, at the same time, it is one that many people have memories about. The subject of servants is at once naturalized and overlooked, a social and cultural "common sense," simultaneously, it is somewhat of an awkward topic posing a conundrum: how does having—paying and sustaining—an underclass align with our sense of freedom, opportunity, and equality? What causes moments of unease when interacting with a domestic servant, and why does television tend to erase these moments (for both the employer and the employee), supplanting them with a different narrative? It is curious that there has been so little discussion about the representation of domestic servants. This lack functions as a kind of structuring absence; relations of difference provide the architecture for much of television discourse. I think this is in part because the subject and its attendant questions (about race, class, gender roles, and equality) reside within both the televisual experience and actual life experience.

I also believe that an agreement is struck (whether it is called the status quo or hegemony) in our everyday experience of pleasure and work so that most of us exist on a plane just short of having to confront what makes us uncomfortable. It is easier to wave off these "minor" roles as superficial and insignificant by virtue of their being small or marginal. We can challenge the notion that supporting roles hold less weight, particularly in light of what I conceptualize as a representational economy in which there isn't room for "too much" difference, and harmony is afforded through the expenditure of truth about disharmony or inequality.

One of my scholarly concerns is to understand how racial discourse operates in media culture by looking at established visual-cultural practices, so that we can intervene in and innovate how race is represented and comes to have meaning. Some who may not initially be concerned about the figure of the maid or the topic of race, or who think that analyzing forms of entertainment is "reading too much into it," will gain insights from the central argument, which crosses multiple stories and case studies, that racial meaning is performative and that this performance needs to, and can, change. The goal in this examination, crossing historical and theoretical lines, is to offer formal and cultural analysis and, furthermore, to propose a critical paradigm for studying the representation of race in television culture and gauging the possibility for change.

Intersectionality and Critical Race Theory

For Bonnie Thornton Dill and Ruth E. Zambrana, scholars who have nurtured the concept of intersectionality since its inception, intersectionality constitutes "an innovative and emerging field of study that provides a critical analytic lens to interrogate racial, ethnic, class, ability, age, sexuality, and gender disparities and to contest existing ways of looking at these structures of inequality, transforming knowledges as well as the social institutions in which they have found themselves."[2] Intersectionality is not, as it is sometimes (mis)understood to be, special interest politics. One can think of intersectionality as a critical analytic lens that serves social justice; it is interdisciplinary and committed to claiming the much-neglected space of praxis. Legal scholar Kimberlé Crenshaw is credited with penning the term in 1991, to name a "heterogeneous set of practices.... More importantly, Crenshaw saw knowledge and hierarchical power relations as co-constituted."[3] There are four theoretical interventions that this method delineates: advocacy, analysis, theorizing, and pedagogy, which Dill and Zambrana argue "are basic components essential to the production of knowledge as well as the pursuit of social justice and equality."[4]

Key to an intersectional approach is an understanding of the social relations in real people's lives. In developing this theory-method, one critique of other existing approaches is that discourse analysis, for example (an approach favored in media studies), has not "garnered any substantive changes in the organizations and social institutions that continue to reproduce racism, sexism, class exploitation, heterosexism, and the like."[5] Intersectionality challenges the traditional ways that knowledge has been produced in the United States. My approach to television studies foregrounds the question, How is racial knowledge produced?

I venture to extend an intersectional approach to media studies in upholding the tenets (and optimism) that intersectionality makes "an effort to improve society, in part, by understanding and explaining the lives and experiences of marginalized people and by examining the constraints and demands of the many social structures that influence their options and opportunities."[6] Media culture and images are social structures that influence options and opportunities for people.

An intersectional approach to media studies calls for reframing and creating new knowledge. I see a parallel between the fact that "historical and systemic patterns of disinvestment in nonprivileged groups are major contributors to the low social and economic position of those groups" and the phenomenon that "representations of groups and individuals in media, art, music, and other cultural forms create and sustain ideologies of group and individual inferiority/superiority."[7] Furthermore, I argue that more than creating and sustaining ideologies, representations are themselves structures. And "representation" is both a noun and a verb; that is, representation is a discursive practice.

Critical race theory (CRT) is concerned with the ways in which race and racial power are constructed and represented. Both have to do with intertextuality, racial politics, and cultural production. CRT, founded in the 1980s, begins with a deep dissatisfaction with traditional civil rights discourse. Such is a discourse of ease, as I would describe it. As some of the founding scholars of CRT describe, "The adoption of this perspective allowed a broad cultural mainstream both explicitly to acknowledge the fact of racism and, simultaneously, to insist on its irregular occurrence and limited significance.... Liberal race reform thus served to legitimize the basic myths of American meritocracy."[8] This approach to civil rights treats the category of merit as neutral and impersonal, outside social power and unconnected to systems of racial privilege.

CRT "aims to recover the tradition of race-consciousness among African-Americans and other peoples of color—a tradition that was discarded when integration, assimilation and the ideal of color-blindness became the official norms of racial enlightenment."[9] This book, too, calls for race consciousness, particularly in a time when being conscious of race is disavowed ("I don't see color"). It also aims to clarify what racial inequality constitutes in a post–civil rights era when people think they know what racism looks like.[10] In the visions of both liberals and conservatives engaged in a civil rights discourse, *racism* has (inaccurately) come to mean the opposite of color blindness.

For critical race theorists, the project is to uncover how law was a *constitutive* element of race itself, in other words, how law constituted race. Racial power was not simply—or even primarily—a product of biased decision-making on the part of judges; it was instead the sum total of the pervasive ways in which law shapes and is shaped by "race relations" across the social plane.[11] Like law, media constructs and constitutes race: Television meaning both produces and is a product of social power.

The Racialized Domestic Servant in U.S. Television

The story begins with a jovial Black maid working for a white suburban family in the 1950s. It moves through eras in which "the help" was white and takes plot turns when African American families employ household help, signifying their own social mobility. It continues with the less controversial, though no less complex, images of Asians as servants and brings us up to date with the very contemporary issue of our society's dependence on immigrant labor from Latin America. Through television's practice of replaying old episodes and rebroadcasting characters in syndication, as well as the incorporation of the servant figure into new programs, media, and film, the story of the racialized servant remains part of an ongoing and open-ended American narrative.

It is, in large part though not exclusively, a story about women. *Maid for Television* examines the cultural significance of the racialized female domestic by tracing the maid's representational and narrative function in American television. As domestic service has been a long-standing occupation for women of color, the figure of the maid in the employer's home is a recurrent and patterned image, simultaneously enacting and revealing the nexus of race, class, and gender hierarchies in American culture. My focus is on how racial discourse works to define race and to encourage the reification of social hierarchies through the figure of the racialized domestic.

The post–World War II economic boom led to a distinct shift in employment opportunities and expectations for American women, specifically middle-class white women. Some moved into higher-status jobs, leaving the "dirty work" for women of color, and others participated in building the (image of the) perfect home as domestic managers, employing domestic workers. Second, the early 1950s saw the beginning of the end of the classical Hollywood film era and the rise of television as both an industry and a fixture in the American home, the very space in which the racialized domestic labors. As middle-class American culture became suburbanized, both the domestic servant and the television set became components of a household's status and success—a mark of upward mobility and of an idealized family lifestyle.

National television broadcasting began in 1948, and in the 1950s and 1960s numerous top-rated programs featured maids. They included *Beulah* (1950–1953), *Make Room for Daddy* (1953–1964), *Bachelor Father* (1957–1962), *Hazel* (1961–1966), *The Courtship of Eddie's Father* (1969–1972), and *The Brady Bunch* (1969–1974). Even the animated series *The Jetsons* (1962–1963) had a futuristic robot maid, Rosie. In her essay "White Flight," Lynn Spigel argues that *The Jetsons* mirrored the ideology of space exploration in the 1960s, which in turn represented the desire for a new suburbia, a metaphoric "new frontier" belonging to white Americans. Rosie is a robot instead of a racial minority—but "she" is female and her mechanical vocalization has a Brooklyn accent, giving her both a gender and a class designation.[12]

In the 1960s, the civil rights movement, the space race, the Vietnam War, and the women's movement all seemed to point toward a transformation of U.S. society. Yet even these tumultuous changes could be ignored by Americans who escaped into (tele)visions that conveniently de-emphasized storylines and characters depicting major social changes. A conspicuous number of popular prime-time television programs had a missing mother, allowing viewers to sidestep the issue of women's departure from traditional housewife roles. *My Three Sons, Family Affair, Bachelor Father, The Courtship of Eddie's Father, The Andy Griffith Show*, and *Bonanza* are examples of television programs in which the mother was dead (yet memorialized romantically). In all these programs an aunt, uncle, butler, houseboy, or maid provided a substitute mother figure. These "supporting" characters were instrumental in sustaining a notion of family from the 1950s, but their presence did not completely erase the question of women's roles in a changing household and society. In her book about 1960s television, Aniko Bodroghkozy argues, "Entertainment television could not, and did not, manage to ignore or repress the protest, rebellion, experimentation, and discord going on in the nation's streets and campuses. Prime-time programming grappled with and confronted (often in highly mediated ways) many of the turbulent and painful phenomena of the period."[13] Racialized domestics were often at the center of such mediations.

The maid was also a significant figure in the 1970s, a decade marked by an economic recession, deindustrialization, and rising unemployment. She was still prominent in the 1980s, which saw a shift from the era of women's liberation to a backlash against working mothers, criticized as "supermoms" doing and having it all. Television programs with maids included *Maude* (1972–1978), *The Jeffersons* (1975–1985), and *Gimme a Break!* (1981–1987). The decade also saw the debut of several programs with male domestics. In *Who's the Boss?* (1984–1992), *Charles in Charge* (1984–1985, 1987–1990), and *Mr. Belvedere* (1985–1990), white men took over the role of the housekeeper while the women of the household were working or going to school. Thus, during the period leading up to a postfeminist era, men sometimes replaced women as the managers of domestic life. The figure of the household servant is still present in the contemporary era among the programs *I'll Fly Away* (1991–1993), *Dudley* (1993), *The Fresh Prince of Bel-Air* (1990–1996), *The Nanny* (1993–1999), *Frasier* (1993–2004), *Gilmore Girls* (2000–2007), *Weeds* (2005–2012), *Mad Men* (2007–2015), *Supernanny* (2005–2011), and another reality series, *Flipping Out* (2007–2018). *Will & Grace* (1998–2005), a hit that still runs in syndication, boasts progressive gay male characters and also has a maid, Rosario, who is involved in a sometimes demeaning love–hate relationship with her employer, a wealthy white divorcée. (The series had a three-season reboot in 2017–2019, though Rosario, played by Shelley Morrison, did not come back.) While the white nuclear family is still the televisual norm, television increasingly reflects changes in the constitution of the American household, showing African American families as well as alternative configurations, such as blended stepfamilies and families headed by a single parent. But the figure of the domestic servant remains—to uphold ideals of the structure of work, the home, the family, patriarchy, middle-classness, and whiteness.

Racialized domestics portrayed in television sitcoms and dramas serve to idealize both family dynamics and racial harmony. In so doing, they help mythologize middle-class status and the American Dream. The figure of the racialized domestic has been particularly prominent in television precisely at times when both race relations and the structure of domestic life were undergoing profound change. My first key assertion is that while there have been a series of displacements in television history with respect to which racial group occupies the role of the servant and under what conditions of societal change, these portrayals nonetheless always serve to maintain the privilege and power of whiteness, which is as much a class category as a racial one. Programs that appear on the surface to be simply structured family situation comedies, with banal plots and thinly drawn characters—for example, *Beulah* or *The Brady Bunch*—actually have embedded in them complex performances of racial, classed, and gendered roles; when analyzed, these tell us much about the myths that Americans found and continue to find reassuring. The insertion of the maid trope into the representation of the American middle-class family helps sustain myths under siege in real daily life.

These displacements are a part of what I conceptualize as a representational economy in the portrayals of television maids. A representational economy is an operational mode whereby cultural production balances those images that challenge the status quo. That is, while a degree of difference from the white, middle-class, Christian, heterosexual, patriarchal "norm" is given moments in the representational spotlight, an ideological bottom line is always apparent. There will never be "too much" difference—too much Blackness, working-classness, female power. Hence there has been a constraint in how much difference can be represented in mainstream culture through mediums such as film and television; an economy is in place that maintains and sustains a hegemonic status quo.

The second key premise in this book is that the figure of the racialized domestic represents not only race, that is, racial identity, but also race relations—through difference—and for that matter, gender and class relations as well.[14] My analysis of racialized servants reveals that such race relations are read, understood, and experienced intertextually, and it affirms that race relations themselves are intertextual.

"Intertextuality" refers to the ways that television texts acquire meaning through their relationship to other texts: it is through referential reading that viewers understand televisual representations. For example, the maid character in *Beulah* is read in relation to the actress who played her, Hattie McDaniel, who is read as "Mammy" in her Academy Award–winning film role in *Gone With the Wind*, a role that in turn evokes literary figures, such as Aunt Chloe in *Uncle Tom's Cabin*.[15] According to some theorists, texts lack any kind of independent meaning; it is the act of reading that "plunges us into a network of textual relations.... Reading thus becomes a process of moving between texts."[16] Similarly, making meaning through television is a process involving an intertextual flow among mutually reinforcing images and ideas about race, class, gender, and social hierarchy.

Television, as an intertextual medium, historically and consistently promotes a discourse of race that is at once polysemic (open to multiple readings) and prescriptive in the way racial meaning is created and understood, and a social-racial order is maintained. The racialized servant is a negotiating figure in the discourse and discussion about race, yet the trope seals racial boundaries at the same time.

The figure of the racialized domestic in American television beginning in the 1950s engages viewers in a mode of perception about race, family, and social and individual status. Each instance of the servant character marks a particular historical circumstance through which the meaning of race is rendered. This book joins the effort of other scholarship and commentary on race to show that race affects the lives of Americans. *Maid for Television: Race, Class, Gender, and a Representational Economy* expands the study of race on television by examining the textual, social, and ideological role of the domestic servant during a period (1950–2000) when families gathered together regularly to consume stories about American life. It shows that race and racial difference are defined in structures of work, family, class, and gender through the figure of the racialized domestic, that these structures are intricately intertwined yet also rationalized.

Racialization and Racial Formation

In their foundational work, *Racial Formation in the United States from the 1960s to the 1990s*, sociologists Michael Omi and Howard Winant argue for the specificity and hence the significance of race, rather than ethnicity, in light of the vastly unequal experiences of immigrants—those who can benefit from white privilege and those who cannot. Ethnic identity becomes conflated with racial identity, the idea of assimilation becomes conflated with integration and equality. Omi and Winant conceptualize race as a particular and pervasive social formation, what they call a "racial formation," and recognize the active determination of racial categories as an "intensely political process."[17] Racial formation is unique and flexible and has immediacy in both everyday experience and social conflict. Understanding racial formation as a framework overlaid upon society allows one to see that race is a factor not only in interpersonal class and gender relations but also more materially, in the structural and systemic modes of business relations. In other words, racial formation is a sociopolitical process that shapes both individual identity and institutional infrastructures. Key to the concept and reality of race is that it is both personal and political; race is about both identities and institutions.

There are also problems with class-based approaches, whether built on classic Marxist, neoclassical, or stratification/labor market segmentation theories, insofar as they fail to incorporate race into the equation and reflect the belief that the market is unbiased or neutral. As Omi and Winant argue, "Racial dynamics must be understood as determinants of class relationships and indeed class identities, not as mere consequences of these relationships."[18] Economic institutions do not exist apart from (self-interested, racialized) individuals, and therefore such institutions are affected by racial definitions and racial hierarchies as much as they affect them.

This shaping of identities and institutions is central to the way in which I incorporate the notion of racialization. Racialization is a process of assigning a person's social and economic status according to his or her race; it is a means to express and form a social and economic hierarchy that is based on race.[19] In *Racial Fault Lines: The Historical Origins of White Supremacy in California*, Tomás Almaguer argues that the nineteenth-century expansion into the American West, solidified by the U.S.–Mexico War of 1846–1848, "forged a new pattern of racialized relationships between conquerors, conquered, and the numerous immigrants that settled in the newly acquired territory."[20] The philosophy/dictate of Manifest Destiny, which was conceived as a justification for westward expansion, separated people—white from nonwhite, men from women—according to a hierarchy in which white males were dominant and structurally located in a superior (i.e., advantageous) position. The term *racialized* implies the demarcation of race as a significant factor in one's economic as well as social status, that is, in one's class categorization.

As theoretical anchors in this project, racial formation and racialization differ in the degree to which each names oppression and specifies what bell hooks calls "white supremacist capitalist patriarchy."[21] Whereas racial formation concentrates on current and ongoing processes of racial meaning making—processes that allow for negotiation and perhaps liberation—racialization marks the way the historical supremacy of white patriarchy embedded in the rise of capitalism has profoundly shaped today's societal structure as biased and fundamentally inegalitarian.

Practically, race means racial difference. The representation of race(s), therefore, functions to demarcate social positions according to race, class, and gender, usually in a subtle or hidden manner, or opaquely, often covered by humor. Intertextuality, too, makes difficult or imprecise the deconstruction of the source of racial meaning. Because any single image can be read, accepted, and applied in multiple ways by different viewers, the meaning of race in the television text is slippery; nevertheless, an overall picture delineating social hierarchy based on race, class, and gender emerges. Racialized characters, and especially the figure of the racialized female domestic, participate in what Herman Gray calls a "discursive struggle" for racial meaning, but ultimately they reveal the limits of that struggle.[22] The figure of the domestic servant is a key demonstration of a representational economy that frames (or budgets) difference—it is an economy of difference. Further, the maid demonstrates how discourses about social change are often displaced by discourses about racial, gender, and class harmony.

Whiteness as Privilege

One meaning of the racialized domestic in American television, which has held true across different racial groups and historical periods, is that this figure consistently serves to uphold whiteness. Whiteness is at once mythical and institutional, representational and material; whiteness names a location of structural advantage, of race, class, and gender privilege in the social formation. In this way, the figure of the racialized domestic is marginalized from, yet also central to, whiteness.

In her examination of whiteness, Ruth Frankenberg looks specifically at gender and the sociohistorical construction of white women. She argues, "'Whiteness' refers to a set of locations that are historically, socially, politically, and culturally produced and moreover, are intrinsically linked to unfolding relations of domination."[23] Whiteness is a seemingly unmarked cultural space, frequently unseen and unnamed by those who inhabit it, though identifiable by those who suffer the consequences of it; it becomes normalized and naturalized as the status quo, as a form of cultural, social, political, and economic dominance. White women have a dual experience in the social praxis of racialization: they are at once dominated by patriarchy and privileged by whiteness. This has been a contradiction in feminism and also in the lives of (white middle- or upper-class) feminists who employ domestic servants who are often of a different race and almost always of a different class. Both a white woman and a woman of color are positioned within a patriarchal system, but while the white woman is disadvantaged by her gender, she is privileged by her racial and sometimes her class status within a system of whiteness.

Psychologist Aída Hurtado understands gender as being determined through white patriarchy in a way that has different outcomes for white women, women of color, and men of color. Domination is executed according to what Hurtado calls "relational privilege." She argues that subordination processes are not static, do not apply to all members of a category equally, and, by being relational, are difficult to pinpoint.[24] Nevertheless, at the center of everyone's identity positioning is the fact that "white families are organized and united around the notion of the male breadwinner's access to socioeconomic power and success; his success is the entire family's success. Therefore, gender subordination, as imposed by white men, is experienced *differently* by white women and by women of color."[25] White women and women of color gain or lose to the extent that they are able either to resist white patriarchy or ally themselves with white men.

In the early twentieth century in the United States, more women began working outside the home. Domestic work, as a paid occupation, grew steadily more racialized. "Between 1890 and 1920," David Katzman writes, "the number of white female servants declined by one-third, while black female domestics increased in number by 43 percent. In 1920 black women comprised 40 percent of all domestic service."[26] By 1930, according to Mary Romero, African American women dominated the service in many Northern cities. A similar situation existed for Mexican women: in 1930, 45 percent of all employed Mexican women were domestics.[27] Women of color did not find other professional opportunities open to them, so they remained overrepresented in domestic work. By 1950, 41.4 percent of employed African American women—ten times the proportion of whites—worked as household workers.[28] In the decades that followed, immigrant women of color joined American women of color in this low-status occupational category.[29]

Katzman asserts, "Domestic services drew less from women who chose service and more from those who due to race, ethnicity, or lack of education, or marital condition had no choice."[30] While Irish and German immigrant women also toiled as domestic workers early in the century, within one generation they were largely able to move out of such service. Industrialization in the United States from 1880 to 1920 was a driver of the mass immigration from Europe.[31] Job opportunities were available for immigrant and working-class women who were, or could come to be considered, white. Moreover, young white domestics were considered marriageable by white men; many were able to marry up and thus "marry out" of domestic service and move into privileged whiteness. This opportunity scarcely existed for domestic servants of color. Finally, with the rise of the suburban home and postwar prosperity in the 1950s, many white women who had worked were persuaded to return home to take care of their husbands and children. Accordingly, domestic service as an occupation declined for white women, but not for minority and immigrant women. As Romero writes, "For black and Asian women, for Mexican and immigrant women who were neither Anglo-Saxon nor English-speaking, domestic service was a trap—a situation of being dominated from which they could not rise and which they had to pass on to their daughters."[32]

With a domestic servant of color working for a family, the home becomes a primary site of race relations and the most intimate social space in which race and whiteness are defined, understood, and acted out.[33] In this context, "the 'servant problem' became synonymous with more general social conflicts over ethnicity, race, or religion," as Romero argues.[34] How and why the figure of the televisualized racialized domestic circumvents such a "problem" and has become a naturalized and perhaps even necessary element in the representation of American families is a central question in this book.

Themes

Four basic themes cut across the study and analysis of all the groups of racialized servants treated in this book:

1) Domestic work performed by a servant class presents a contradiction within a democratic society, and this contradiction is represented through television, a "democratic medium."
2) Capitalism and the superiority of white and nondomestic labor are materialized in a segmented labor market and hierarchical work roles.
3) Identities are formed through the Other—for example, in the relationship between the maid and the white woman who employs her, or, when the mother figure is not present, between the maid, the white employer/father, and the children of the house.
4) Controlling images have power in that a degraded and inferior status is reinforced and legitimized through cultural representation.

While such themes are present in the analyses of all groups of racialized servants, the groups have distinct and specific histories and experiences that nuance the common themes. These experiences—of African Americans and slavery, of white ethnic immigrants and indentured servitude, of Asian Americans and job discrimination, and of Latin American immigrants and migrant labor—operate at different registers within the larger history of capitalism and racialization.

Contradictions of Domestic Service, Democracy, and Television

The persistence of domestic service as a devalued occupation in the United States poses a fundamental contradiction to our nation's self-image and stated ideals. Indeed, the practice of servitude may be seen as incompatible with the nation's founding principle of democracy. Servitude, especially forced servitude, is different from domestic service, which is a paid job. But they can be compared to each other because domestic service in the American context entails exploitation based on race, class, and gender, and moreover, working in the service sector is not as much a choice as a socioeconomic circumstance based on race, class, and citizenship status. As Judith Rollins asserts, "From its beginnings, domestic servitude in this country has embodied a kind of contradiction between principles and behavior ... a contradiction between the value of egalitarianism and the actual class and caste stratification."[35] Americans want to enjoy the practical benefits of having servants and may even proudly display their servants as symbols of "success". Yet they implicitly deny that having servants reflects a system of class privilege, much less one that is exploitative. Americans proclaim, and perhaps wish to believe in, an egalitarian ideal while living a nonegalitarian reality. In the words of a white South African, "Americans ... can't seem to cope with servants."[36] The ideal of democracy fails to account for America's having a servant class.

After television entered American homes in the early 1950s, it became a part of family life.[37] Television also broadcast images of what family life was supposed to be like. The auspices under which television was introduced to the American public and the discourses that it elicited about the family and about economic prosperity and success revealed anxieties about a changing society.[38] In the postwar years, the television set became a central figure in representation and regulation of family relationships.

Lynn Spigel examines television's relationship to the family in light of the reconstruction and reconstitution of family life after the war. She asserts that "the 1950s was a decade that invested an enormous amount of cultural capital in the ability to form a family and live out a set of highly structured gender and generational roles."[39] Television was supposed to bring the family together yet also demarcate social and sexual divisions in the home. Examining the figure of the domestic draws out tensions between these two functions.

Particularly in the postwar era, television signified social and economic well-being. Acquiring a television set had implications for a family's emotional health and togetherness as well as its consumer power.[40] Furthermore, from the beginning, the television was advertised as an item that all Americans could and should afford. A television—like a maid—appeared fairly obtainable. This American family was presumed to be, and was depicted as, white. In actuality, most families did not own a television until the 1960s, nor did they have a maid.[41] Although advertisers projected the television set as fully integrated in the American home, the living rooms pictured in early television programs often did not have televisions in them. *I Love Lucy*, *Mama*, and *The Honeymooners* all featured episodes about the event of buying a television. Owning television technology (similar to accessing streaming services these days) started out as, and continues to be, a signifier of economic well-being and social normalcy.

As art and entertainment for the masses, and as a way to establish homes and reestablish families, the coming of television also opened up the possibility of a less base representation of people and characters of color. J. Fred MacDonald writes, "The historic circumstances of postwar America suggested equitable treatment of African-American entertainers, and unbiased images."[42] But he also asks, "To what degree should the new industry transmit egalitarian ideals at the expense of viewer ratings and advertiser revenue? Should TV adopt the racist stereotyping that flourished in radio and motion pictures, or could the medium establish new boundaries of ... expression and racial dignity?"[43] Those who study, and some of those who create and produce, contemporary television programming continue to grapple with these questions.[44]

Capitalism and White Supremacy

Capitalism facilitates, thrives on, and even relies on social stratification. In the United States, the justification for discrimination against immigrants and exploitation of immigrant labor came from ideological (political and religious) beliefs that helped institute a racial and class hierarchy. There was strong prejudice against particular groups of white immigrants at various points in history, for example, against Irish and Italian immigrants in the late nineteenth and early twentieth centuries by Anglo-Americans who had immigrated earlier. Jewish immigrants have suffered discrimination and intolerance from other white immigrants and native-born white Americans and faced barriers to integration into dominant American institutions. However, Irish, Italian, and German immigrants, among others, were able to assimilate as "white" before World War II, especially relative to non-whites, who were seen as inferior. The significance of race emerged within the framework of the development of capitalism in the 1800s and the ensuing competition between whites and non-whites.[45]

Though different ethnic (i.e., non-white) groups have had separate experiences and have been perceived and treated by European Americans in distinct ways, one common denominator remains—that of white supremacy. George Fredrickson defines white supremacy as "the attitudes, ideologies, and policies associated with the rise of blatant forms of white or European dominance over 'nonwhite' populations."[46] As a confluence of social, political, and religious ideologies, white supremacy has enforced and reinforced the economic practice of subordinating people of color within the social structure. Almaguer writes in his study of race and capitalism in California, one of the regions that absorbed and structured racial difference in the early period of America's development, that race and the process of racialization became the organizing principle in the state's formative stages.[47] To further solidify discriminatory or exclusionary practices, social and moral ideologies melded with political and economic ones.

In the late nineteenth and early twentieth centuries, industrialization and capitalism together ushered in a newly prosperous middle class. With the invention of new machines and time-saving devices, women's economic value as workers diminished. Angela Davis writes, "As industrialization advanced, shifting economic production from the home to the factory, the importance of women's domestic work suffered a systematic erosion. Women were the losers in a double sense: as their traditional jobs were usurped by the burgeoning factories, the entire economy moved away from the home, leaving many women largely bereft of significant economic roles."[48] Instead, industrialization brought about a new concept of the ideal woman: the housewife.

The "cult of domesticity," according to Barbara Welter, "called upon middle-class women to professionalize homemaking activity and to devote themselves to the vocation of enriching family life, thereby improving society at large."[49] The housewife's vocation ideally did not include the dirtiest or heaviest household chores; those were seen as inappropriate for the lady of the house, even when her only occupation was to keep house. The ideology of the happy nuclear family with defined and assigned roles therefore included a role for the domestic servant, who was carefully assimilated into the home in such a way as to uplift the woman of the house and uphold a gender-racial-class hierarchy. The typical housewife was a middle-class white woman; in one sense, her status was confirmed by the presence of a woman of color to serve her. That both housewife and house servant were relegated to domestic obligations provided "flagrant evidence of the power of sexism," Davis notes, but she argues that Black women working as maids suffered a double burden: "Because of the added intrusion of racism, vast numbers of Black women have had to do their own housekeeping and other women's home chores as well. And frequently, the demands of the job in a white woman's home have forced the domestic worker to neglect her own home and even her own children."[50] The servant thus enables "the lady of the house" to be one.

Forming Identities through the Other

The way in which domestic labor is performed signifies social status according to race, class, and gender. To claim high status, white women must give the appearance of not laboring, whether they actually have a maid or not. Popular television representations of the racialized domestic servant and the relationship to her white employers define white womanhood in two general representational figurations: first, the ideal wife and mother, and second, the failed or missing wife and mother. In both scenarios, the domestic servant sets the boundaries of white womanhood, either by not measuring up to it or by attempting to fill in or having to make up for it. In either case, the servant occupies an undesirable or secondary position, and it is a position of alterity. The white woman's identity is formed in direct relation to the working woman of color, the Other.

The intricacies of the nexus of race, class, and gender are based on the dynamics of deference and maternalism.[51] In defining these terms, Judith Rollins argues, "What is important about deferential behavior between non-equals is that it confirms the inequality and each party's position in the relationship to the other.... Because one's consciousness is confirmed only by that of another, one's superior position exists only in relation to another."[52] *Maternalism* refers to the unique situation in which employer and employee are both women, a mistress and servant, and to the way in which the mistress achieves her rule over the servant. Both women have been socialized to be treated as inferior to men. But with the advent of women managing servants, some women can attempt to escape sexism (or at least circumvent some of its burdens) through class and racial privilege. The white woman improves her own status at the literal expense of working women of color.

Like Rollins, Elizabeth Clark-Lewis reveals the psychological and ego-based ways in which the employer uses the servant. Her rigorous and eloquent book, *Living In, Living Out: African American Domestics and the Great Migration*, traces the history of domestic service from its ideological, racially charged beginnings.

Clark-Lewis also specifically locates the relationship between white women as employers and African American women as employees in the home. The home was the wife's stage, a space where she could strive for legitimacy. However, domestics could see that the white woman's domination of them was "a transparent exercise of the only kind of power she had."[53]

To be successful, servants discovered, meant satisfying far more than the labor requirements of the job. Employers seemed to need a self-enhancing relationship that came from having an inferior at their disposal around the clock. To their surprise, the women who came north were expected to appear more subservient than in the rural South. Velma Davis stated that "at home they was white and they knew it. Wasn't no need to be on you to make them feel more white. Up here they knew they was white too, but they seemed to need you to make-up to them to keep reminding them how white they are."[54]

In performing domestic duties, the servant also gives a social performance; she is being paid to be Black/not white, and to enhance the status and value of whiteness.

Domestic service involving white women as employers and women of color as employees, serves a function "based in rituals of deference and maternalism that are as integral to this occupation as are low pay and low prestige ... to the perpetuation of the occupation and the perpetuation of a social system of class, racial, and gender stratification."[55] Hence domestic service is both a practice and an ideology, and as such, it is situated in the home as well as on the television screen that sits within the home.

Race, class, and gender identities are also defined and delineated through the servant when the white woman, as wife and mother, is not present or does not fulfill the expected role. Television has shown families with a missing mother, a stepmother, a single mother, a working mother, or an otherwise "failed" mother; in different ways, these women refuse or are unable to conform to the performance of motherhood idealized in the emblematic American sitcom *Leave It to Beaver* (1957–1963). Examples of such programs include *My Three Sons, The Courtship of Eddie's Father, The Brady Bunch, Maude, One Day at a Time, Gimme a Break!, Who's the Boss?, Mr. Belvedere, Married . . . with Children, Roseanne*, and *The Nanny*. Some of these programs have a surrogate mother; when the racialized domestic plays that role, she takes the mother's place, though not completely or legitimately.

In these cases it is often the employer's child who measures the degree to which the maid is able to enter the family, specifically in relation to the father. The closeness and intimacy forged and expressed in the daily domestic experience between the servant and the child facilitates and regulates the servant's relationship to the employer, and by extension, the servant's position within the family. The affection between the child and the maid serves to gloss over the fact that she is an employee.[56] This apparent intimacy is countered by racialization, which establishes boundaries and sets the maid outside the family. The dynamics of the relationship between maid and child establish the racial politics as being harmonious and indicating a promising and improved future, which erases or eases the notion that race is a problem in society *today* (and relies on a notion that "things will get better on their own" without deliberate intervention). In the United States, domestic servitude conflicts with ideals of democracy, so the concept of and attitudes surrounding servitude have to be adjusted. One way of doing this is to conceptualize servants as family members. They are portrayed as happy to do the work, even at the expense of their own independence and family welfare, because of their love for or loyalty to their employers. The affection between the maid and the employer's child is an important element in making this narrative convincing.

Controlling Images

Regardless of the intimacy forged between the maid and the family she works for, "maintaining images of Black women as the Other provides ideological justification for race, gender, and class oppression," as Patricia Hill Collins argues.[57] Collins delineates four stereotypical tropes of Black womanhood: the mammy, the matriarch, the welfare mother, and the Jezebel. Although different in various ways, these controlling images are interrelated in relation to white patriarchy: all four fail to meet the standards of white middle-class womanhood.

Collins writes, "Juxtaposed against the image of white women promulgated through the cult of true womanhood, the mammy image as the Other symbolizes the oppositional difference between mind/body and culture/nature thought to distinguish Black women from everyone else."[58] The mammy is distinguished particularly by her corporeal difference from the white woman. Overweight, large-bosomed, and equally endowed in back, the mammy figure's literal figure—her body—is such an exaggeration of femaleness that it is rendered asexual in the dominant culture. She is often portrayed and perceived as matronly, beyond childbearing years. The racialized domestic is often desexualized exactly because she (or he) poses a sexual threat, that is, the threat of miscegenation. The African American female servant and the Asian American male servant are dramatically asexual. There are exceptions when stereotypical tropes, such as the "exotic" Asian female or the "fiery" Latina lover, are combined with the servant figure; ultimately, however, the maid is "domesticated" by either the man or the woman of the house or both. A caricature as well as a distorted kind of fetish,[59] the mammy's body is neutralized, eliminating any threat of her presence in the white family's home.

As discussed by Darrell Hamamoto and K. Sue Jewell, "controlling images" involve a process of objectification, subordination, and justification.[60] The objectification of subordinate groups is achieved through the application of images that help justify economic exploitation and social oppression on the basis of an interlocking system comprising race, class, and gender. The culture surrounding domestic service includes both the lived experiences of domestic servants and the representation of servants. For example, because even the most cultured and educated Asian immigrants worked as gardeners and domestics in the formative years of the film and television industry in the 1930s and 1940s, it follows in some sort of sad logic that Asian actors would get only certain kinds of acting jobs, often as servants. Evelyn Nakano Glenn argues that "their concentration in domestic service in turn reinforced their degraded status in society."[61] A concentration of people of color in domestic service, in both lived experience and representation, forms a hierarchy based on race, class, and gender materialized in the American social structure and legitimized through the American imaginary.

Organization of the Book

Maid for Television is a study of the servant figure in American television across several racialized groups. It provides a culturally and historically specific contextualization for each experience while at the same time revealing commonalities in the enduring figure of the maid across racial boundaries. This project constructs an intersectional, interethnic analysis of women of color within the frame of whiteness, patriarchy, and the idealized middle-class family. Specific case studies of the figure of the racialized domestic demonstrate how the production of racial meanings is polysemic and prescriptive, negotiating and discursive, intertextual, hyperreal, and relevant to those concerned with television as a powerful cultural medium and the people of color it "represents" or misrepresents.

The domestic sitcom remains a particularly charged staging ground; it is well suited for, and rather preoccupied with, representing and negotiating the tensions over categories of difference. Therefore, prime-time, U.S. television series comprise the majority of the selected texts.

Chapter 2, "Domesticating Blackness: African Americans in Service in Comedy and Drama," examines the television programs *Beulah* (1950–1953) and *I'll Fly Away* (1991–1993). The 1950s situation comedy and 1990s "quality television" drama differ in many respects: the first is set in the early years of the civil rights movement but makes no reference at all to this social context, while the second is set in the civil rights era and features a narrative directly concerned with impending social change. Yet the figure of the African American woman as a maid is enduring and pivotal in each of these two very different stories, and genres, where she embodies Blackness and not-whiteness. In *Beulah* she displaces racial tension through the comedic representation of racial harmony between African American employees and white American employers and their children. In *I'll Fly Away* she reveals racism, but in a way that is contained within, and limited to, the characterization of the civil rights era. This chapter introduces a concept I have formulated, retrospective displacement, in presenting the African American domestic as a post–civil rights subject. Representing racism retrospectively and as contained within a specific historical period of struggle seems to imply that present-day society is relatively free of racism, even exonerated, because the sins of the past are in the past.

Chapter 3, "Shades of Whiteness: White Servants Keeping Up a Class Ideal," discusses the function and cultural practice of whiteness as it is manifested in the televisual portrayal of family in American television. Indeed, "family" in this context has been synonymous with "whiteness," and vice versa. The structure of the family, the structure of work, and the structure of race and identity are illuminated in programs such as *Hazel* (1961–1966), *Family Affair* (1966–1971), *The Brady Bunch* (1969–1974), *Who's the Boss?* (1984–1992), and *The Nanny* (1993–1999). In this chapter, I am arguing that the meanings of whiteness and Americanness coincide, through (the notion of) family, and that the significance of the white servant in American television is that she or he affirms the class ideal as "white."

Chapter 4, "Unresolvable Roles: Asian American Servants as Perpetual Foreigners," focuses on the character of Mrs. Livingston in *The Courtship of Eddie's Father* (1969–1972). On the one hand, Mrs. Livingston represents what it is to be someone "Other" than a white woman who is "courting Eddie's father." On the other hand, her "ideal" femininity as passive femininity and as distinctly Japanese holds currency in the context of the women's liberation movement in the U.S. Gender politics and national identity are crystallized and mythified through the figure of the Japanese war bride employed as a housekeeper serving as a stand-in for the (nostalgically) missing white housewife and mother. Race is gendered, and gender is raced.

This chapter also examines the Asian American male servant, specifically the character of Hop Sing in *Bonanza* (1959–1973), a revisionist Western. This figure is shown as feminized and subservient to his white male masters. Along with a consideration of the program *Bachelor Father* (1957–1962), I analyze the gendered discourse of Orientalism: it offers some flexibility for Asian females, who are often marked by excess (as other racialized servants are like Beulah, Nanny Fine, Florence in *The Jeffersons*, and Geoffrey in *The Fresh Prince of Bel-Air*), but remains restrictive for Asian males whose characterizations are deprived of sexual/ heterosexual status, rendering them insignificant or forgettable. Asian American servants are also seemingly unable to be integrated, literally or symbolically, into the American family, a phenomenon connected to the "model minority" as a preferred race (for perceived passivity and competency) and also as resented and rejected. They are "unassimilable" despite their model minority status.

Chapter 5, "Invisible but Viewable: The Latina Maid in the Shadow of Nannygate," looks at the portrayal of Latina domestics within the context of popular discourses around Latin American immigrants and workers that emphasize the legality of their existence. Televisual representations of Latina maids perform a kind of mediation through the family, through social space, and through the law. The chapter looks specifically at the figure of the domestic worker in three situation comedies: *Dudley* (1993), *I Married Dora* (1987–1988), and *Designing Women* (1986–1993). Latina maids and nannies in nonfiction texts and intertexts are important as well. Clips of Rosa Lopez testifying in the O. J. Simpson trial are analyzed as media images that depict a maid's relation to a celebrity household in a trial about credibility and trustworthiness.

The backdrop to the discussion is the scandal known as Nannygate, in which the employment of "illegal" Latina domestics became a moral and legal transgression for public officials and implicated the Latina worker herself in a web of ethical issues. The increasing representations of *domésticas* are part of a larger discourse on immigration, criminality, and the question of who deserves inclusion in U.S. society. These representations revolve around the "violation" that the Latina maid supposedly represents: at once a violation of federal law (if she is undocumented), and a violation of middle-class family values, especially concerning the role that traditionally belongs to a mother. Thus the struggle over the legality of the Latina maid is contextualized in her position in a family as well as her place in society. Her "status"—in multiple senses—is in question.

The epilogue is a further reflection on race and genre. And while *Maid for Television* is an example of an academic expression of concern, I also set forth some suggestions in the other realms such as creative development in the television industry.

I close the book by emphasizing that the representation of race is essentially the representation of race relations and racial difference, and by raising the question about where the power for intervention—industrially, creatively, ideologically, economically, intellectually—ultimately lies. Once we have made this argument about the representation of race relations, where does that lead us? What is the potential for social change through television culture and televisual discourse?

What makes race such a powerful cultural, intellectual, and political issue is that it is also deeply personal. Race is not only represented, but also perceived: race is about how an individual is understood (or misunderstood) and about how she or he is treated (or mistreated) in society. Television plays an important role in communicating and sometimes dictating social roles and social hierarchies according to racial, class, gender, sexual, national, and religious identities. Social representation is connected to social meaning is connected to social practices. Finally, I argue that race relations themselves are intertextual. "Race" exists to the extent that individuals and institutions "read" race through a number of sources that inform each other and then proceed to form opinions and behavioral practices based on those readings. The racialized domestic is an enduring figure in such struggles for meaning, and she is integral, not marginal, to the idealized American family. As such struggles are discursive, intertextual, intellectual, political, personal, and everyday, understanding the maid can help us better understand our own positions in media culture and society.

2

Domesticating Blackness

African Americans in Service in Comedy and Drama

Domestic service as performed by African Americans for white Americans conjures a picture of the history of race relations in this country. Iconoclastic imagery presented in the earliest films, such as *The Birth of a Nation* (1915), in the first sound films, such as *The Jazz Singer* (1927), and in Technicolor masterpieces, such as *Gone With the Wind* (1939), demonstrates that Black otherness in the service of white subjectivity is a deeply established aesthetic and ideological mode of storytelling in U.S. visual culture.[1] These films were cinema's blockbusters before the term existed. By the late 1940s and early 1950s, images of Blackness migrated to the smaller screens that were set in the homes of an expanding white American middle class. Mammy herself, played by Hattie McDaniel in both *Gone With the Wind* and the 1950s sitcom *Beulah*, was transported from the movie theater to the television box, from the Civil War South to postwar suburbia.

Television in the 1950s fictionalized race relations by painting a portrait of middle-class, white domestic tranquility facilitated by the figure of the African American female domestic. This ideological brushstroke attempts to paint a cheerful grin across a stark social reality.[2] In the world of the program *Beulah* (1950–1953) and of the family that the title character served, there was no civil rights struggle. By the early 1960s, new images of African Americans involved in the civil rights movement appeared on television. The complement to the prime-time fiction show was the dinner-hour news program. They offered two significant and distinct forms of racial representation: the representation of easy race relations and the representation of contentious racism, in which the former often denies the latter. The figure of the racialized domestic in a harmonious relationship with her employers serves to argue that racism is not a problem, or to use a modern phrase, that race is "not an issue" or does not "matter"—at least not from the perspective of the white employer and the white-majority audience watching family shows with minority characters.

The representation of acknowledged, systemic racism is a rarity in U.S. popular, public culture. Racist incidents are cast as aberrations and are presented as news stories, typically sensationalized or controversial.[3] Representation of institutional racism against African Americans has been relegated to and contained within discussions of the civil rights era and the concomitant trope of "the civil rights struggle" as one that ended effectively. Like the historical memory of slavery, Black–white race relations are told as a story of past sins that have since been rectified; this already-concluded story is pervasive in American culture in general and in media culture in particular.[4] By the 1990s through the millennium, television portrayals of African Americans and whites interacting serve (or attempt) to assuage racial tension. That is, even in a laudable drama like *I'll Fly Away* (1991–1993), which depicts racial strife among African American and white citizens in the starting years of the civil rights era, the contemporary viewer can gain a sense of satisfaction or relief from the idea that these particular struggles are finished.[5]

This chapter examines the aesthetic, narrative, and ideological legacy of the figure of the African American servant as a transforming, though not yet transformed, representation of Black womanhood. Certainly the domestic is not the only character of interest in the analysis of the representation of Black women, but the maid trope is influential in determining how popular imagery of African Americans reinforces (and occasionally questions) racial hierarchies. From her inauspicious beginning as a slave to whites, even if a "sassy" slave like Mammy in an Academy Award–winning role in the melodrama *Gone With the Wind*, the figure of the Black domestic has resurfaced over the decades in programs as different as the 1950s sitcom *Beulah* and the 1990s drama *I'll Fly Away*, as a maid working for African American employers in the 1970s program *The Jeffersons*, as an ambiguously positioned housekeeper/stepmother who is unambiguously a Black woman in a white household in the 1980s program, *Gimme a Break!*, and as a butler in *Benson* (1979–1986) and *The Fresh Prince of Bel-Air* (1990–1996).

In what ways do representations of African American domestic workers in either a family sitcom or an hour-long drama produce racial knowledge? Why is there a return to a past era in representing Blackness, and Black womanhood in particular? How or why does servitude in this particular arrangement continue to mark the racial dynamic between African Americans and white Americans? Through these institutional aesthetics, whiteness is coterminous with Blackness. It is an entanglement that is unequal, manifested in ideological images. In order to untether Blackness from being in the service of whiteness, viewers must be vigilant in identifying the ways that contemporary images might capitulate to past meanings of Blackness (and whiteness).

Comforting Images, Controlling Images

The figure of the African American domestic is a nostalgic and comforting one for those familiar with the image or for viewers who adapt the idea that someone is present to provide warmth and sustenance. Even when depicted in a contemporaneous context, she is already a figure of the past. Mammy, the slave character of the pre–Civil War South, gave way to Beulah, the Southern domestic servant of the early 1950s featured in the program of the same name. A woman reminiscent of Beulah is reiterated in many cultural media texts, for example, in the unironic hit, *The Help* (which became a recommended title during the post-BLM activism and COVID-19 pandemic streaming era in 2020[6]), and also in Jordan Peele's *Get Out*, in which the tear-stricken smiling face of the maid exuded the horror of that household. The figure of the African American domestic, then, is naturalized and reassuring to some viewers in two ways: her traditional visual/filmic form affirms white superiority—or stability for whiteness—in class and social status, and at the same time, the figure caters to progressive desires to confirm that such figures no longer exist in real life.

This mode of racial representation is based on my notion of retrospective displacement. By setting and seeing race relations in the past, both producers of televisual texts and readers of them can sidestep scrutiny of race relations in the present. Racial discord and injustice have already been amended in significant and dramatic ways, so what viewers ultimately experience is the confirmation that race relations are better than before (a constantly shifting "before"). By displacing race relations to the past, we reassure ourselves that racial conflict is getting better in the present and eventually will be solved in the future. This encourages a state of contentment and passivity about race, as well as about racial representation.

The representation of Blackness is delivered in two predominant forms on television. Harmonious race relations between African Americans (e.g., as employees) and white Americans (usually employers) are most often represented in domestic situation comedies, or in feel-good stories of benevolence (usually bestowed upon African Americans, though occasionally there is a Black person, often a convivial man or boy, praised as a good Samaritan). The representation of racism, on the other hand, is typically contained within the civil rights context in nonfiction news, prime-time dramas, and public service television documentaries.

Race is not an issue in standard postwar situation comedies, whereas race is literally the issue in news and documentaries or in dramas with African American protagonists. In other words, race is either ignored or it is the central problem and source of conflict. There seems to be little in between, with the exception of the work of stand-up comedians, such as Dick Gregory, Richard Pryor, Chris Rock, and Dave Chappelle, all male performers who explicitly engage in a kind of raw, cathartic critique of racism that is mitigated through laughter. Bambi Haggins's book, *Laughing Mad*, explores such performances.[7] Such comedy can be simultaneously subversive and contained. But in presenting female characters of color in the domestic sphere, the space where most television stories are situated, television comedies tend to handle race lightly by virtue of their half-hour format and family-oriented themes, while more serious dramas tend to present racial characters as conflicted by their racial identity.

In both the "conservative" sitcom *Beulah* and the "progressive" quality drama *I'll Fly Away*, the racialized servant is a negotiating figure in the discourse about race, and yet the trope seals racial boundaries at the same time. Beulah and Lilly can each be read in ways that endow the maid character with a semblance of power: Beulah often "saves the day," and Lilly stimulates change in the family she works for, in her town, and in the larger society. While the former is more easily dismissed as a product of its (racially oppressive) time and the latter engages in a layered reception process, both programs provide examples of how African Americans in representational culture are read vis-à-vis a post–civil rights subject.

The backlash to affirmative action that began in the 1980s, featuring arguments about meritocracy and impartiality, has become a key impulse in reading race today. Voters in some states have approved legislation that reverses specific affirmative action measures, the best known being Proposition 209 in California; this suggests that a large portion of the population does not believe that broad and institutional racism needs to be ameliorated (or even exists). Yet it is impossible to literally be "color-blind." Visual, narrative, and ideological markers of race continue to signify and cue racial (and class and gender) hierarchies. The figure of the African American domestic is a starting point for excavating the ways in which fictional characters interact with lived experiences, and for uncovering how creative entertainment can have political outcomes.

In America's past, racism was not formally or morally wrong. Treating people who were not white as inferior and as holders of lesser rights was, in fact, the law. It wasn't until the late 1950s and early 1960s that this country experienced a profound racial paradigm shift. In a highly race-conscious society in which "non-whites" were a visible minority, it became illegal to segregate and discriminate. (Though what was on the books and what was in practice remained inconsistent.) In the 1980s there was another paradigm shift, and being race-cognizant came to be considered a bad act. However, the campaign to "be color-blind" remains not only disingenuous, but in its claim to combat racism it works to deny racism. To this day, the push to be color-blind, to not notice race, distorts the rationale for considering racial status (so that to introduce race as a factor becomes construed as "racist"). Michael Omi and Howard Winant elaborate on this confusion by which whites tend to locate racism in color consciousness, identifying that there are "two languages of race."[8]

The comforting and controlling image of the African American maid serves to simultaneously ensure the existence of racial, gender, and class privilege while blunting racial, gender, and class consciousness. The mode of representation for the African American domestic servant is retroactive in both *Beulah* and *I'll Fly Away*. It is intriguing that the two programs stand on either side of the abyss, before and after the civil rights movement.

The history of race relations between African Americans and white Americans has been fraught, and the creation of images showing such relations are multidimensional, generating both visual pleasure (reassurance) and ideological messaging (regulation). From the "threatening Black buck" to the "lazy coon" to the "cunning Step-'n-Fetchit" to the "ever-loyal mammy," ideological/symbolic tropes have helped regulate social dynamics between African Americans and whites in ways that have encouraged one group to maintain its dominance over the Other. The representation of the mammy figure in literature, film, and television reveals the way in which society perpetuates racial, gender, and class hierarchies. For example, Patricia A. Turner writes that during the time of slavery, "Pro-slavery writers countered charges of cruelty by characterizing slave/master relationships as warm familial ones and claiming that lively slave music and ribald humor were rampant on the plantations."[9] Then, after abolition, "By suggesting that antebellum households had been run by smiling, self-assured, overweight, born-to-nurture black women, fiction writers and journalists began to perpetuate a mythological Southern past that nearly removed all of the heinous dimensions of slavery."[10] African American women (actresses as well as viewers) have attempted to resist the boundaries set around the figure of the mammy. Can or will whites also resist? How deeply invested are whites in Black subordination?[11]

Who Is Mammy?[12]

The figure of the mammy is deeply ingrained in the culture and unconscious of America and its people.[13] K. Sue Jewell contends that though the figure originated in the South, it has been one of the most pervasive of all media phenomena (and the most pervasive image of Black women) and it has permeated every region of the country. Both Jewell and Turner take up the issue of popular representation and its effects on policy and culture. In *Ceramic Uncles and Celluloid Mammies*, Turner examines to what extent the image of the mammy is based on the realities of Southern households and asks, "What does the present fascination with mammy images reveal about contemporary culture?" Jewell's *From Mammy to Miss America and Beyond* turns the investigation to "the relationship between cultural images and the formulation, administration and impact of US social policy on Black women."[14] Her stance is aligned with the overarching

FIGURE 1 Hattie McDaniel's Academy Award–winning role as Mammy in *Gone With the Wind* (1939) with Scarlett O'Hara played by Vivien Leigh. Notably, "mammy" is a nickname for "mother" in Ireland.

argument of this book—that ideological media images affect political and economic institutions, thereby maintaining structures of social hierarchy.

Figuring the African American woman as a mammy circumvented the condemnation of slavery by portraying a character who was content with her lot in life and who had a positive relationship with the family for whom she worked.[15] The mammy also became the "antithesis of the American conception of womanhood"—which is specifically white womanhood—because of her race and class, with the underlying understanding that she is inferior because she is Black and because she labors for the white woman.[16]

The unfeminine labor that the Black domestic performed helped the white mistress achieve and maintain her own femininity. (Yet it is hyperfeminine labor when performed by the Asian woman, as explained in chapter 4.) The Black woman did this by assisting the white woman with her feminine practices, such as dressing and grooming, as well as by doing the heavy household work so the mistress would not have to sully her femininity with dirt and sweat. In this way, the white woman's femininity derives in part from the Black woman being defined as unfeminine. This is the case in *Beulah* and in numerous Hollywood films before it. Consider one of the most indelible images in Hollywood history, that of the large-framed, strong-voiced Mammy in *Gone With the Wind* (Hattie McDaniel) tying a corset around the tiny eighteen-inch waist of the coquette par excellence, Scarlett O'Hara (Vivien Leigh). As in Margaret Mitchell's famed novel, Mammy admonishes Miss Scarlett to be a lady (Scarlett's own mother is too unearthly to do so). Kimberly Wallace-Sanders writes about the novel's author: "By insisting that she knows the standard of 'white ladyhood' in the South, Mitchell mocks the racist exclusivity of the cult of true womanhood. Whatever Mitchell's intention might have been, there is something off-putting about Mammy. Her enormous size, her towering strength and endurance, her nonstop nagging often make her seem more monstrous than compassionate. These extraordinary qualities actually detract from her humanity instead of affirming it."[17]

Although *I'll Fly Away* shows a different kind of African American domestic, white femininity retains a presence in the program. There are several episodes involving Mrs. Gwen Bedford, the lady of the house, who resides at a mental hospital; for example, the family goes to visit her there, and she comes for a Thanksgiving meal in another episode. Gwen is pleasant, delicate, and loves her children, but she is oversensitive and eventually breaks down when perceived pressures overwhelm her (the children drinking out of Coca-Cola bottles rather than glasses, or the candles at the dining table burning unevenly). While fragile, she represents the ideal Southern woman who is ultrafeminine and who desires to be the best mother, wife, and homemaker she can be in genteel terms. Despite Lilly's compassion for Mrs. Bedford and despite the fact that she essentially performs Mrs. Bedford's duties, the division between them is marked visually (manner of dress), economically (employment structure), and socially (racial hierarchy). Lilly's only access to "ideal femininity" is through cleaning, cooking, and caring for children in a white woman's home.[18]

In performing domestic labor founded in slavery, Black women historically have had a tenuous relationship with, if not an outright exclusion from, the notion of femininity. In her exposition on the dilemma of the women's movement, *Women, Race, & Class*, Angela Davis argues, "Required by the masters' demands to be as "masculine" in the performance of their work as their men, Black women must have been profoundly affected by their experiences during slavery. Some, no doubt, were broken and destroyed, yet the majority survived and, in the process, acquired qualities considered taboo by the nineteenth-century ideology of womanhood."[19] Instead of being rewarded for her endurance and skill, the African American servant was exploited all the more because of her strength. In addition to creating Black female otherness to white femininity, Black female labor raises the larger question of gender (in)equality. That is, if Black women can indeed work alongside Black men and, in some instances, white men, how can it be true that women are inferior to men? As Davis writes: "Black women were equal to their men in the oppression they suffered; they were their men's social equals within the slave community; and they resisted slavery with a passion equal to their men's. This was one of the greatest ironies of the slave system, for in subjecting women to the most ruthless exploitation conceivable, exploitation which knew no sex distinctions, the groundwork was created not only for Black women to assert their equality through their social relations, but also to express it through their acts of resistance. This must have been a terrifying revelation for the slaveowner."[20] This challenge to gender ideology had to be contained and so it was: within the home. Domestic labor, as an ideology and a practice, kept both women and Black Americans "in their place."

One of the first mammy characters in American culture is that of Aunt Chloe in Harriet Beecher Stowe's *Uncle Tom's Cabin* (1851). Depicted as plump, poor, and yet content, Aunt Chloe set a precedent for mammies to come.[21] She is fiercely loyal to "her family," that is, the people she works for, even and inevitably at the expense of her own family: "Even on their own time, in their own cabin, mammies in the fictive tradition of Aunt Chloe were expected to put the needs of their white charges ahead of those of their own children."[22] The figure of the mammy is a maternal figure but not a sexual one, and while female, she is differentially not ascribed the traits or benefits of white femininity.

Black womanhood has been decidedly depicted in specific ways. Turner, among other Black feminist scholars like Patricia Hill Collins, reminds us of figures such as Sojourner Truth, a former slave and abolitionist, and Ida B. Wells, a political activist who crusaded against lynching. By the time *Uncle Tom's Cabin* was written, books had been published on the slave experiences of real African American women, such as Truth, Harriet Tubman, and Linda Brent, but they sold far less than Beecher's fictionalized work. Turner asks why the public preferred a fictional depiction to a real account. Her answer: "Dark-skinned, loyal to her master and mistress, an able cook and housekeeper, plump, asexual, good-humored, Aunt Chloe was one of the first of a long line of fictional black women whose character comforted and assuaged. Abrasive and confrontational, willing to remind her audiences of white male lust, uncompromisingly loyal to her *own* children and her *own* people, Sojourner Truth disturbed and unsettled her audiences."[23] The popularity of *Uncle Tom's Cabin*, an antislavery piece of literature, had mixed effects. On the one hand, it allowed for the denunciation of slavery, which for at least some people was an obvious evil. On the other hand, it served to deflect attention from a continuing problem—a national ideology of racism, sexism, and classism. Whereas meeting the demands of Sojourner Truth would require social upheaval, "Aunt Chloe allowed the masses to indulge in wishful thinking."[24] Mammy has been a staple and stable figure, and yet, the task I am requesting is to perceive her differently, in a nonbinary way and through a nonlenticular lens. Mammy is not simply Black, female, and working class in opposition to ideals of whiteness; rather, blackness and whiteness are coterminous. A lenticular lens, as Tara McPherson illuminates in *Reconstructing Dixie: Race, Gender, and Nostalgia in the Imagined South*, is one that only allows a view of one thing at a time; she, as I, argues that we must see multiple views and manage what Teshome Gabriel emphasized as "parallel otherness."[25]

Patterns in Depiction of Black Womanhood

Television and lived experience are not mutually exclusive spheres. Darnell Hunt argues that in today's intertextual, televisual, hyperreal mode of perception, "images routinely reference one another, creating for us a hypermediated world, one composed of signifiers that often seem more real than the signifieds. In short, the television experience has become an integral part of contemporary lived experience."[26] The social imaginary upholds and informs social practice. Controlling images are part of the practice of political and economic domination of subordinate groups. Tropes such as the mammy figure have stood in for African American women just as the "lotus blossom/dragon lady" dichotomy continues to be understood as racial and sexual prescriptions for Asian women. Other, less dramatic images also support the assumptions that Asian or Asian American women occupy subordinated roles and are passive, exotic, or petite and that African American women are employed in service positions or are bossy or big. As Patricia Hill Collins explains, "These controlling images are designed to make racism, sexism, and poverty appear to be natural, normal, and an inevitable part of everyday life."[27]

Such images hold enduring power even though race relations have changed since the 1950s and 1960s. Tropes of Black womanhood have been deeply embedded and widely circulated in American culture. Though the similarities may not be immediately obvious, there is continuity between the Black domestic servant figure and the nurturing (and sometimes intimidating) maternal figure projected onto women such as Oprah Winfrey and Niecy Nash, who has appeared as the host of the home makeover program *Clean House*.[28]

From the turn of the century through the 1950s, the image of the mammy became increasingly more common in American popular culture. The mammy's smiling face turned up in food advertising and packaging (Aunt Jemima, Luzianne coffee, Aunt Dinah molasses). She was a figure in numerous films, not only in *Gone With the Wind* but also *The Birth of a Nation* (1915), *Imitation of Life* (1934 and 1956), and others. Turner writes, "Implicit in each rendition was the notion that these thick-waisted Black women were happy with their lot, honored to spend their days and nights caring for white benefactors." Furthermore, "Mammy's love for her white employers was not unrequited. Her loyalty was matched by the white public's prolonged love affair with her."[29] The emergence of the 1950s television version of the mammy figure, Beulah, continued this affair.

In *Blacks in American Films and Television*, Donald Bogle concurs with other scholars that Mammy is a fantasy, and yet she has remained a basic element of the idealized middle-class family because "she ensured that setting's stability. Plainly, this was an old-fashioned, stale fantasy that, like so many past movies, incorporated blacks into the American dream: ... Beulah lived in a spotless, comfortable home, but of course, she had to clean it and never, in anyone's wildest imagination, would she own it. The Negro had made it into the television's cultural mainstream. But only as a maid."[30] The new medium of television carried on the filmic and literary tradition of representing African American women and men as unequal to white Americans, an image solidified in the stock character of the servant. In addition to Beulah, other television programs with African American servant characters (female and male) in the 1950s and 1960s included *The Jack Benny Show* (1950–1965), *My Little Margie* (1952–1955), *The Danny Thomas Show / Make Room for Daddy* (1953–1964), *The Great Gildersleeve* (1955), and *Father of the Bride* (1961–1962). In *Maude* (1972–1978), Esther Rolle's character spun off into her own series, *Good Times* (1974–1979). Shows in the 1980s included *Gimme a Break!* (1981–1987) and *Just Our Luck* (1983), a series in which an African American man played a genie with a white master. The Emmy Award–winning soap opera *The Young and the Restless* (1973–present) had the character Mamie (a name that is similar to Mammy); Mamie faithfully worked in the home of the drama's main family, the Abbotts, and raised John Abbott's three children until it was discovered that she was independently wealthy. Her loyalty and love as a domestic is the "common sense" explanation (ideological rationalization) for this.[31]

If African Americans did not take such characterizations as any kind of truth but were simply glad, as Bogle suggests, to see real Black faces on the screen, many white viewers were presumably gratified by television images of the happy household cared for by a figure who personified the happy slave. "For black America, 'Beulah' was television's only glimpse of a black community where blacks worked, talked, joked, lived together. For white America, however, 'Beulah' offered an ideal homogenized community in which the family unit remained secure."[32] The mammy image is not made for African Americans, then, but for non–African Americans to view, observe, and be entertained by.[33] *Beulah* was the beginning of a long trend in which the industry and audiences sought to deal with racial, gender, and class difference through comedy. In *Nervous Laughter*, Darrell Hamamoto writes, "Through narratives that assimilate social contradictions into everyday personal experience, the situation comedy has stood as an enduring sociodramatic model that has helped 'explain' American society to itself."[34]

Beulah (1950–1953)

Beulah aired on ABC from 1950 to 1953 and was the first television series that revolved around an African American character. It was joined a year later by another comedy, *Amos 'n' Andy*, which ended after two seasons because of protest by the NAACP.[35] Other programs around this time featured or guest-starred African American musical performers, including Bob Howard, Hazel Scott, Nat King Cole, and Sammy Davis Jr., whose appearances had to be defended by Steve Allen hosting *The Tonight Show*.[36] Ed Sullivan similarly hosted African

Domesticating Blackness • 31

FIGURE 2   Hattie McDaniel as Beulah, in *Beulah*.

American performers on his show, *Toast of the Town* (1948–1971). But *Beulah* was the only series written with an African American as a major figure, and it is significant that the figure was that of a mammy.

Beulah began in radio as a character in the program *Fibber McGee and Molly* (1944). The character was created by white male actor Marlin Hurt, who then spun off *Beulah* as a separate radio series. Both programs subsequently moved to television, though only *Beulah* made the transition successfully.[37] Three Hollywood movie stars played Beulah on television: Ethel Waters, who eventually quit, Hattie McDaniel, who acted in only a few episodes before she became ill, and lastly Louise Beavers, who decided to stop working despite the show's popularity. The series was not canceled, but the three lead actresses left the program during its three-year run. These enduring actresses—having paid their dues to Hollywood, having struggled to "make it" and to simply make a living—all ended their careers in the not-so-triumphant role of Beulah.

Beavers, Waters, and McDaniel were all known for their earlier roles as maids to leading ladies in Hollywood films. Beavers appeared in several notable pictures: *Bombshell* (1932) with Jean Harlow, *She Done Him Wrong* (1933) with Mae West, and *Imitation of Life* (1934) with Claudette Colbert. Ethel Waters only succumbed to the role of maid later in her successful career as a singer and stage actress, starring in *Cairo* (1942) with Jeannette MacDonald and in *Member of the Wedding* (1952). Perhaps the most famous of the three was Hattie McDaniel. She played in over three hundred films, often uncredited and most often as a maid. Beavers and McDaniel had different acting styles and were able to offer different personas even within the stereotypical stock character of the domestic. Donald Bogle writes in *Brown Sugar*:

> While Beavers was relaxed and easygoing, Hattie McDaniel was anything but. Also a large, dark black woman typed as the mammy, McDaniel was as well one of the most charismatic performers, black or white, to work in American motion pictures. In scores of movies McDaniel kept her own with some of the most famous stars of the decade: Gable, Hepburn, Harlow, Vivien Leigh, Shirley Temple, Olivia de Havilland, and Barbara Stanwyk. Boldly, she looked her white costars directly in the eye, never backing off from anyone. Her extraordinary sonic boom of a voice delivered perfectly timed one-line zingers with the greatest of ease. Sometimes McDaniel seemed angry. Although the movies never explained it, her undercover hostility, even when coated with humor, was never lost on the audience. She set her own standards and sailed through many films with an astonishing sense of self and personal dignity.[38]

McDaniel is particularly memorable in *Blonde Venus* (1932) with Marlene Dietrich, *The Little Colonel* (1935) with Shirley Temple, *Alice Adams* (1935) with Katherine Hepburn, and, of course, *Gone With the Wind* (1939). McDaniel won the Academy Award for Best Supporting Actress for her performance as Mammy in *Gone With the Wind*, becoming the first Black actress to be nominated for an Oscar.[39] Ethel Waters was the second, nominated for her role in *Pinky* (1949).

In addition to their film roles, McDaniel was a singer, and Waters was a Broadway actress; Beavers began her career as a minstrel performer. The life stories of these and other actresses of color, and a critical reading of their film and television texts, suggest that they performed with self-awareness and integrity.[40] This in turn allows for a more complex analysis of depictions otherwise deemed racist. At the same time, these film and television characters promoted distinct ideas about Black women, white women, race relations, and the social hierarchy.[41]

All three actresses faced personal challenges in their lives. McDaniel's father was a freed slave. Beavers actually worked as a maid for another actress. Waters was born to a very young mother who had been raped. Such tragedies and injustices in their off-screen lives belied the naivete and cheerfulness that their on-screen mammy characters were supposed to possess.[42] Sadness, anger, trauma were not emotional states that a domestic was allowed to show. Instead, any kind of dissatisfaction about the maid's current situation or any resentment of past injustice (including slavery) was transmuted into a classic attribute of the Black maid/Black woman: sassiness.

It is worthwhile to consider more deeply the "sass" displayed by African American women and African American domestics in particular in film, television, and literature. While understood as a humorous character, the sassy Black maid personifies a form of independence if not rebelliousness. On the one hand, sassy back talk is an appeasement, a safe (i.e., comedic) way for subordinated African Americans to release steam; on the other hand, it is a coping mechanism through which a servant can to some extent voice her thoughts and feelings (without holding the power). Both Black and non-Black (i.e., white) audiences can appreciate such a performance, though probably for different reasons. The Black maid is subordinated as a character of color, but at the same time, viewers can perceive some resistance on the part of the on-screen character as well as the actress herself. This resistance takes the form of sassiness, but it never crosses the line to direct revolt, which would disrupt the racial order. Furthermore, it is often an expected character trait of the Black maid/Black woman, part of the unspoken and perhaps unconscious bargain that is struck in Black–white racial discourse. It is not coincidental that in *I'll Fly Away*, a program in which an African American woman is taken seriously, this kind of sassy and mitigated resistance is not invoked.

Hattie McDaniel perhaps originated, and certainly personifies, the boisterous, bossy, somewhat intimidating but still lovable and loyal mammy figure—a figure that easily slipped into or became conflated with the role of the maid. In the 1938 screwball comedy *The Mad Miss Manton*, McDaniel's character tells off her employer, played by Barbara Stanwyck, and the employer's socialite friends. When McDaniel came to play Beulah in 1952, she brought an extensive intertextual history with her. In 1939 she had received the Academy Award for Best Supporting Actress for her role as Mammy in *Gone With the Wind*. Over a decade later, she played the same character type in *Beulah*.[43] Her sassy, bossy voice provided a strange kind of comfort.

Beulah, whose name conjures up images of the Southern plantation, is a character that hails from an earlier time. She is more of a caricature than a character. Her large body stands in striking contrast to the Christian Dior silhouette and tiny waist of "Mizz Alice," who graces the kitchen while doing none of the work. Beulah's gait is heavy and plodding as she labors around the house. Her low, booming voice with intentional childlike intonations and overdrawn accent is cacophonous in contrast to the "refined" codes of Mr. Harry, Mizz Alice, and even their son, little Donnie Henderson.

Also demarcating Beulah's otherness is her gesturing. The camera often cuts to a close-up of Beulah looking up or rolling her eyes. Her acting is exaggerated, her actions are pantomime-like, and the camera works accordingly (or according to the director). That is, rather than using medium and long shots as in the scenes with the family members, the camera is fascinated with Beulah and cuts anxiously to close-ups catching her "funny" faces and gestures. Her character is written in a different aesthetic language.

The figure of the maid is often taken out of the narrative and showcased as a visual spectacle; her representation is thus predominantly visual rather than textual.[44] When Beulah is the source of humor, her delivery is on a visual level. When she is with the family, Beulah speaks only when asked a question, and when she responds, she often does not answer the question but makes a joke instead. There is a lack of integration on several registers. Not only is the humor directed at Beulah rather than being inspired by her, but it also implies that she has a simpler sense of humor and a simpler intellect in general. A curious and more complex performance of the Beulah persona occurred when Hattie McDaniel performed on *The Ed Wynn Show* (1949–1950), first in character as "Beulah" and then, after the skit finished, as Hattie McDaniel, the singer.[45] These demonstrated McDaniel's levels of performance and awareness, in that both were performances of Blackness specifically for a white audience. When McDaniel sang as herself, she stepped out of the Beulah character (though not completely) and revealed her own pleasure in being on stage before appreciative fans. It was, however, a fleeting moment that is little remembered in comparison to McDaniel's popular on-screen performances in mammy mode.

Beulah is more usually a source of extradiegetic humor because her character is not fully integrated into the narrative and her humor is not part of the storyline. Often, the program opens with Beulah telling a joke in direct address. Then, throughout the show, the camera cuts to Beulah in medium or close shots as she says her lines. This is especially the case when she is in a scene with Mr. Harry or Mizz Alice. Beulah's differences are pointed out to remind the viewers of her separateness from the white middle-class family that she works for. Her lines are usually an aside or a parenthetical statement, not directly related to the flow of conversation. (She does not speak as a kind of narrator either.) She is constantly isolated within the diegesis and is thereby alienated, in fact segregated, from the story itself.

Although the series ran for three seasons, only seven of the eighty-seven (16 mm) episodes are available: three with Hattie McDaniel, two with Louise Beavers, and two with Ethel Waters. In the plots of the episodes, Beulah teaches Donnie how to dance; Beulah has to do even more work because Mr. Henderson wants to save money by firing the gardener; Beulah saves the day when Mr. Henderson and Donnie attempt to go camping; Beulah mistakenly thinks that the Hendersons are expecting a new baby; Beulah tries to patch things up for Mrs. and Mr. Henderson after their relationship seems to have lost its spark; Beulah's friend Bill has to babysit the bratty daughter of Harry's business colleague; and Beulah helps to protect the family from a burglar. In this sample of episodes, it is evident that the storylines are not about Beulah, even though she is a major character and even though the show is named for her. Her character serves the well-being and happiness of "her" family.

Beulah's African American friends are also set apart from the main story and from the accepted norm of white American life. The program makes a spectacle not only of Beulah but also of her (boy)friend, Bill, who owns the garage down the street, and the housemaid from next door, Oriole (played by Butterfly McQueen most famous for her role as Scarlett O'Hara's slave in *Gone With the Wind*).[46] The Oriole character is known for her lack of intelligence and skittishness and Bill for his freeloading, put-it-off-'til-tomorrow attitude. Always entering through the back door, Bill and Oriole are part of Beulah's entirely separate life as an African American woman. The only time we see her friends interact with the white Hendersons is when they interact with the child, a safe and socially acceptable association: the notion of African Americans as caregivers to white children follows a social code that goes back to slavery. Once, when Bill stops by to visit, he and Beulah teach Donnie how to dance. They do so in secret, thinking that if Donnie's parents knew they might not approve because they are paying for him to take ballroom dance lessons, and because of the connotations of "race music" as sexual and dangerous. (At the same time, by the end of the film, there is a certain reliance on the servants, or a handing over of Donnie's education about how to be successful with girls, to African Americans because his ability to be "cool" has made him popular.) As they dance to a record that Bill and Beulah apparently dance to on other occasions, one that Beulah says is more lively and jivin' than the "square" music in Donnie's social dance class, both Beulah and Bill are made a spectacle of through camera shots, cuts, and an elongated musical segment with little dialogue. It is a scene reminiscent of slaves performing for the master and also of another Bill dancing—Bill "Bojangles" Robinson, who plays a Black antebellum butler opposite Shirley Temple in both *The Little Colonel* and *The Littlest Rebel*, both set around the Civil War.

Beulah is probably most famous for her jolly body and ebullient smile. This expression of the maid's contentment with her job and with her lot in life serves to assuage any doubts or guilt that her employers, and the program's viewers, might have. Moreover, the representation of the smiling mammy smoothes over and naturalizes the existence of inequitable social relations, as it did in times of slavery: "The continuous displaying of teeth, in a grin or a smile, suggests satisfaction or contentment, which was important to slave owners. It was customary for slave owners and proponents of slavery to perpetuate the myth that slaves were content with their status; and therefore the institution of slavery was harmless, and even benevolent, since it provided for the material and spiritual needs of those who would otherwise remain uncivilized."[47] The African American maid on television in the 1950s served dinner with a smile for her on-screen employers as well as for the program's viewers.[48]

Like the image of the happy, dancing slave, Beulah and Bill conjure up a nostalgic past as well as provide entertainment value for viewers who individually may not have a connection to America's history of slavery but who likely share a collective cultural memory of it. Working as a paid domestic servant is not the same as being forced to work as a slave, but that they are represented in similar ways causes a conflation of the two. Whether Hollywood sets her on an antebellum plantation or in a 1950s suburban home, there has been a resistance to letting Mammy go.

When Beulah is with her friends, we see them interacting and hear them talking about their own concerns and commenting about the white characters. In this way, the servant/employee knows more than the master/employer because she is able to inhabit both worlds, the family's and her own, whereas the family members only (choose to) have knowledge of their own lives. Moreover, the servant arguably knows and sees the family better than they see themselves.

Drawing on this knowledge, Beulah works to express herself as more than "just the maid." One episode begins with Beulah speaking directly into the camera: "Everybody says I'm a girl that knows all the answers. The only trouble is, no one ever asks me the questions." She smiles broadly. As she confides to the camera, the audience becomes privy to Beulah's mild lament. But her implied complaint that the Hendersons do not appreciate her is rendered moot because at least the television viewers feel that they themselves do. The camera iris closes down on Beulah after her joke and reopens on the Hendersons eating a meal with Beulah serving them (this could be interpreted as a means to make the Hendersons the object of implied critique). Alice is coquettish, hinting that she wants to buy a new hat; her son Donnie acts as an intermediary and helps win his father's agreement. Harry then says that the family needs to economize and announces that Tony the gardener wants a raise and so he is going to be let go. They will all simply have to help out. In the following scenes, Donnie, Mizz Alice, and Mr. Harry each get out of doing their share of the yard work by coyly asking Beulah if she can do it. Of course, she has no real option of refusing. Instead she says, "Everybody keeps telling me I'm wonderful today. I wonder why?" which echoes her opening joke.

In the next scene, Oriole declares that women never should have started smoking in public; letting women smoke, in Oriole's puzzling view, set a precedent for obliging Beulah to do demeaning (and masculine) yard work. "Next, we'll have the suffrage," she says in her high-pitched voice, a trademark of McQueen's character, Prissy, in *Gone With the Wind*.[49] Her bringing up suffrage is not only ironic but also an example of displacement: "suffrage" refers to white women getting the vote in the early part of the century, while African Americans, both women and men, were fighting for the right to vote in the 1950s. (And in this scenario, there are no feminists.) Beulah asks, "I sometimes wonder if you ever learned anything." To which Oriole replies, "Oh sure, I learned a lot of things—I just don't attain 'em!" She giggles. This scene shows their reaction to being forced to do undesirable work as an almost-complaint. Neither of them directly criticizes the employer or employment.

As a consequence of Beulah's having to do so much extra work, the dinner gets overcooked. "It's spoiled, but don't blame me, it was prepared by a field hand, not a cook!" exclaims an upset Beulah. Although it is a laugh line, Beulah has made a telling point about the parallel between being a servant and being a slave. In this limited way—in the form of a joke and without confirmation that her white employers "get it"—the maid talks back.

From the famed playwright and actress, Alice Childress, *Like One of the Family*:

> Now when you say, "We don't know what we'd do without her" this is a polite lie ... because I know that if I dropped dead or had a stroke, you would get somebody to replace me. You think it is a compliment when you say, "We don't think of her as a servant ..." but after I have worked myself into a sweat cleaning the bathroom and the kitchen ... making the beds ... cooking the lunch, washing the dishes and ironing little Carol's pinafores ... I do not feel like no weekend houseguest. I feel like a servant.[50]

This kind of rebuke is not available to Beulah. The implications of her comment are glossed over in the sitcom format. The family feels sorry for Beulah and says that they will just eat cold cuts. "Mr. Harry," Beulah responds, "I'll dig the yard if I have to—I'll lay a brick wall for you—but I'm not gonna serve my family no cold cuts on Saturday night!" Thus the maid puts their well-being first because, after all, this is her role in the family, in the story, and in media culture. She is deemed successful the harder she labors for her employers. Her passing hint of discontent about racialized work is quickly redirected into a harmonious family discourse in which the maid is showered with appreciation and "love," and the situation is resolved when Mr. Harry agrees to rehire the gardener. As Beulah negotiates her responsibilities and, by extension, the role she plays as an African American female domestic employee, race relations (and her race-gender-class status) are resealed.

I'll Fly Away (1991–1993)

Two significant and distinct forms of racial representation were articulated at the beginning of this chapter: the representation of race relations and the representation of racism. *Beulah* falls under the rubric of the former, which functions to deny the latter. Forty years after *Beulah*, in a post–civil rights era marked by a cultural and legal backlash to affirmative action, *I'll Fly Away* appeared. In this

FIGURE 3 Regina Taylor as a serious Lilly Harper, in *I'll Fly Away*.

television drama, the idea of "talking back" registers at very different levels: on the narrative level it is integrated rather than being a throw-away joke, and on the ideological level the maid's words and ideas carry weight. Such a seemingly subtle difference marks a significant change in the way racial discourse can operate. In *Beulah*, the excess of a bellowing but affectionate mammy figure talking back is contained; through humor, her sass does not break or spill out of the limits of the trope and in fact becomes part of it. Her voice, however loud, is not really heard. There is no subversion. In the hour-long drama series, *I'll Fly Away*, the calm and directed challenges and protests raised by the African American domestic servant in a white, Southern household cause those around her (both Black and white) to notice, and then think about racial injustice. Her voice, quite soft actually, speaks volumes. The social critique is apparent, albeit set in the past.

Premiering in 1991, a season celebrated for launching a new age of "quality television," NBC's *I'll Fly Away* debuted alongside *Brooklyn Bridge* (CBS) and *Homefront* (ABC) as dramatic period pieces. These three programs on each of the three prime time networks arguably offered a critical engagement with the past, or at least new perspectives. *Brooklyn Bridge* was set in the 1950s, the golden age of baseball and candy shops. It presented a multigenerational Jewish American family that was living an "all-American" life but also dealing with specifically Jewish issues, such as the dating relationship between young Alan Silver and a Catholic girl. *Homefront*, too, dealt with a nostalgic period in America's past, the post–World War II years. It centered on the homecoming of "our boys," but their return was portrayed as neither easy nor successful. The series shows women being fired from their wartime jobs to make room for the returning men. Moreover, Corporal Robert Davis, an African American officer, was only able to get a job as a janitor, and he was only promoted to an assembly line job through the help of the wealthy white family that his father and mother worked for—as a chauffeur and a maid.

While representations of race and race relations in television history have traditionally avoided portraying disharmony, racial conflict has been depicted specifically within the framework of the civil rights struggle. This frames racial conflict, that is, racism, within a narrative of contrition—and forgiveness—and places racism in a historical past. *I'll Fly Away* is an example of this retrospective displacement, but it also achieves something new in its portrayal of Blackness expressing subjectivity and, simultaneously, its portrayal of whiteness as fallible and unstable, even culpable. In order for Blackness to be represented in a new way, whiteness must be represented differently. Furthermore, the signification of whiteness must be understood as coterminous to the Black experience in America.

I'll Fly Away is about an African American woman, Lilly Harper, who works as a maid for a white family in the small town of Bryland, Georgia, during the rise of the civil rights movement. In presenting the critical perspective of a maid, the program raises questions about but also verifies the intricate, sometimes difficult, and always complex dynamics of race, gender, and class. The tone and pace of *I'll Fly Away* are pensive. This engages viewers in a similar mode of thoughtfulness and allows them to experience emotions such as horror and frustration rather than finding swift release in nervous or dismissive laughter, as is usually the case when race is touched on in a comedic format. There are confrontational rather than passive moments of viewing in this series. Such confrontation is not as it is colloquially (mis)understood within the discourse of race relations, that is, as aggressive or accusatory toward whites, though white oppression is unquestionably represented. It is a program that succeeds in maintaining rather than alienating or dividing audiences because of its subject matter: racism in America.

I'll Fly Away shows race relations vis-à-vis the justice system in ways that suggest that the law has regulated race relations unfairly and unjustly. The lead male character, Forrest Bedford, the town's district attorney, must deal with changes in the laws (and perhaps promote such changes) during the period of

FIGURE 4   Regina Taylor as Lilly Harper with the Bedford Family, in *I'll Fly Away*.

civil rights advocacy. In a small Southern town, these changes are met with resistance and even violence. Viewers are able to identify with Forrest's struggles to bridge the gap between legal, institutional, and philosophical ideals and the realities of human nature. Forrest feels pressure from fellow whites in the town, and he also experiences a challenge to consciousness stemming from his own whiteness: one angry mother of a defendant shouts to him, "I know where you come from and your neck is as red as mine!" Furthermore, the program shows protest and resistance by the town's African American citizens and depicts the injustices and cruelty against them as actually unjust and cruel. Viewers can identify with Lilly's growing consciousness and courage to do what she believes is right, to "make change come," as she says in the first episode.

From the opening sequence in the pilot episode, we have a juxtaposition between African Americans and white Americans. The Black townspeople, after a church picnic, are riding on a bus that will soon crash because of the carelessness of the white driver, while the white townspeople, in church, are happily singing, "I'll Fly Away." The significance of the Negro hymn is lost on the white singers; it is a song "reminiscent of two centuries of slavery, more than 90-years of legalized segregation, the fight against this nation's Jim Crow laws, the colored waiting rooms and drinking fountains—the whole spectrum of the Black struggle in America."[51]

The camera lingers on Forrest Bedford and the Bedford children and intercuts these shots with shots of the speeding bus carrying the riders to a certain tragedy. The two scenes are linked, formally and symbolically: while privileged people are sitting in a sanctuary, a place of peace and light, a "safe haven," while Other people are being driven down a life-threatening path, their pleas in the dark ignored. Eventually, the two separate and unequal worlds collide. The first episode begins with the white bus driver, Jimmy Yates, in court and on trial for manslaughter of three African Americans who died in the crash. The series begins with whites and African Americans being forced to think about their town, their families and friends, the beliefs and opinions they hold—and being forced, along with the viewers, to choose sides.

The series also begins with the authorial direction of Lilly Harper, played by Regina Taylor, whose voice-over narration opens and closes each episode. Resembling a journal entry, her philosophical words bracket the individual episode, but they also serve to link one episode to another, pulling together an overall story of her family, her job, her town, and the social changes underway that she chooses to take part in. For many viewers, it is an unaccustomed and perhaps even curious experience to be made to identify with an African American woman as protagonist.

I'll Fly Away differs from other programs that feature African American domestics in several important ways. A first difference is in the way the figure of the maid is filmed and characterized. Unlike Beulah, this Black domestic is serious, calm, and self-possessed. A second category of difference concerns the representation of the white family: they are shown as realistically flawed characters, and the relationship between the maid and her employers is sometimes contentious, not always harmonious. Moreover, the maid is shown as having a full and complex life, one that includes her own family and even her own house. Third, race relations and the larger social world are shown as unsettled and undeniably elemental in the lives of the show's characters. Finally, the program's production strategies allow Black characters and Blackness to achieve subjectivity, and the choice of genre—a serious drama rather than a situation comedy—affords viewers time to contemplate the social issues raised.

After decades of laughable, caricatured African American women in service positions, Lilly Harper emerges as calm, knowing, and resolute. That she has a distinct personality, and a powerful one, might challenge and surprise the viewer. This personality emerges in the first dinner scene with Lilly and the Bedfords. Nathan, the eldest Bedford teenager, is sympathetic toward the Yates family, whose daughter is in his history class. When his father asks him whether he thinks Jimmy Yates ought to be held accountable for his actions, Nathan replies, "Well, yeah, okay, but her parents are really upset. They're losing sleep. Their father's missing work, it's just doing really terrible things, it's wrecking that whole family." Lilly, serving a dish, says quietly, "What about the families of the ones that died?"

There is, dramatically, no answer. The silent moment is offered to the viewer as much as to the Bedfords. Nathan is infuriated and embarrassed. Forrest comes into the kitchen to ask, "Lilly, do you have an opinion on this?" Lilly expects to be fired for sassing Nathan, though this is a very different kind of sass than expressed by mammy characters. This kind of talking back is self-assertive and challenges the presumption of white privilege. Surprised, she realizes that she isn't going to be fired. The reactions and relationships that the Bedford family members have with Lilly illustrate the complexities involved in an African American maid's presence in a white household.

Lilly's character contrasts with the mammy figure, who soothes and entertains rather than causing family members to feel uncomfortable. She works, acts, and even looks much different than Beulah does. Physically, she is not an exaggerated spectacle. Self-assured and self-aware, she has feelings, personal opinions, and political convictions. The social issues affecting her life as well as the lives of the people she works for are integrated into her characterization and motivation, this is not the case with the maid in *Beulah*.

The white family for whom Lilly works is also portrayed differently than a televisual ideal, as the Bedfords are shown to have imperfections. Forrest Bedford, played by Sam Waterston, is a complex and flawed man. He is not the overbearing white patriarchal figure that viewers are accustomed to seeing in film and television stories in popular culture, particularly of the 1950s. The children, too, have faults that are displayed and understood as unacceptable to Lilly. Lilly challenges and reprimands the children—Nathan, Francie, and little John Morgan—not only as a disciplinarian, which is part of her job, but as an African American woman who finds the children's behavior often wrong or ignorant. In contrast to the assumption in *Beulah* that the Black maid is "one of the family," *I'll Fly Away* portrays Lilly's surrogate mother position as uncomfortable and as forced by circumstance. Gwen Bedford is "not well"; she is confined to a mental hospital after having suffered a nervous breakdown and never returns home. Thus the white mother is depicted as a failure. Lilly and the Bedfords are aware of the fact that while Lilly fulfills many of the duties expected of a mother, she is not the Bedford children's mother; she is the mother of Adlaine, her own six-year-old daughter.

Perhaps the most powerful and moving relationship for viewers is between Lilly and the youngest Bedford child, six-year-old John Morgan. His innocent love for Lilly is also subject to societal pressures, transmitted through his misbehaving friend and through a racist uncle with whom Forrest eventually severs ties. These influences lead little John Morgan to say (though not yet to firmly believe) that Lilly is just the maid and has to do what he says because he is better than she is. The tension in the relationship between Lilly and John Morgan stems from the fact that she is essentially a mother to him, yet she is a servant and an African American woman in relation to a privileged little white boy. This kind

FIGURE 5 Regina Taylor as Lilly Harper, in *I'll Fly Away*.

of relationship has existed since slavery, but it is personalized through the series and, moreover, is now seen from the maid's perspective.[52]

In one episode in particular, "All God's Children," John Morgan is seen struggling to understand his relationship with Lilly, whereas she, the maid, is quite clear about her relationship to him. One morning John Morgan sees Lilly and her daughter Adlaine walking up to the house, hand in hand. He runs to greet Lilly and grabs her free hand. "Who's that?" John Morgan demands insecurely. Lilly says, "This is my daughter, Adlaine. Remember, I told you I had a daughter."

Though Adlaine and John Morgan become friends, throughout the series there are moments in which their different skin colors entitle them to severely different treatments: at the store, where Lilly gets John Morgan whatever he wants but does not have money to buy Adlaine anything; at the swimming pool on a sweltering hot day, when John Morgan shows off his diving to Lilly while Adlaine stands sweating behind the fence; on Halloween night, when Adlaine mistakenly believes she can go trick-or-treating with John Morgan, only to be reprimanded by her mother in front of everyone. The series thus shows how Lilly and her family experience a quality of life different from the Bedfords' because they are Black and the Bedfords are white.

In *I'll Fly Away*, the maid is shown as having a family life that is loving, complex, important, interesting, and rich. When the two children first meet, Adlaine tells John Morgan a secret: the next day is her mother's birthday and there is going to be a party. John Morgan is elated. The next morning he comes down to the kitchen prepared for a birthday party only to find out that Lilly has the day off. He is bewildered and crushed. When Lilly returns, John Morgan is cold and angry. Lilly asks him to tell her what is wrong. He asks where she was the day before and when she replies that she was at her birthday party, John Morgan then asks who was there. Lilly replies, "All my friends and family," to which John Morgan exclaims with pain, "But I thought I was your family."

I'll Fly Away shows that the maid has her own family and her own life, but that these often must be sacrificed so that she can do her job for her employers. In one episode, the Bedfords nonchalantly and at the last minute ask Lilly to spend the weekend; she agrees and thus misses the annual church picnic that Adlaine had been looking forward to attending with her mother. As Patricia Turner has written, "The inside/outside split was less applicable to African-American women's history. As many labor historians and sociologists have illustrated, *outside* work for African-American women took place *inside* the homes of white women. Black women left their own kitchens to take care of someone else's."[53] It is not that the Bedfords are thoughtless or callous; rather, it is the fact that Lilly works for and takes care of them for over twelve hours a day, six days a week. She is there for them, and they know that they are fortunate, but perhaps like real-life employers of maids, they do not want to acknowledge that this might come at someone else's expense.

Whether it is a lack of awareness or willful ignorance, employers need to learn about the person who gives so much of their time to work in their home. *I'll Fly Away* offers such information. In an episode that focuses on voting rights, Lilly wins against disenfranchisement despite an unreasonably difficult test and sabotage by white courthouse workers. Other episodes focus on segregation. In one, community protests and sit-ins are held at a segregated local lunch counter, and the white owner decides to go bankrupt rather than have it become integrated. In another, three African American students hold a sit-in on the basketball court because Black students are not allowed to play on sports teams or take college preparatory classes.[54] This episode makes clear reference to the history of federally forced school integration in Arkansas and other parts of the country. Still other episodes deal with racial violence: an African American man dies mysteriously after being released from jail, where he was held on false charges of attacking a white police officer; an African American war hero who was getting too much attention is murdered. One episode presents the brutal slaughter of a visiting youth from the North who, trying to impress some local boys, makes an overture to a white woman—a clear reference to the horrifying case of the murder of Emmett Till.[55]

For viewers unable to identify with Lilly's perspective on such events, *I'll Fly Away* also offers us Forrest's and Nathan's understanding of what is going on. Through the traditional identification with the white male protagonist, the viewer can experience confusion, fear, passion, and revelation. *I'll Fly Away* is about "ordinary people, living in extraordinary times," as the show's tagline reads, and the conflicts that they all experience in the face of change. It gives us the rare perspective of an African American woman living in those times, and presents fallible white men struggling to accept a changing society.

At a fundamental level, this television program is about characters, all sharply drawn social types, struggling to come to grips with social change:

- The white patriarch and literal keeper of the law
- The African American domestic servant who knows life should be better and more equal
- The privileged Southern son who begins to recognize his entitlement
- His poor white friend who inherited his father's bitterness toward Blacks
- An independent-minded teenage daughter growing up without her mother
- A little white boy who has been raised by Black maids and who represents the next generation in race relations
- A little Black girl who is denied the simple pleasures that white children automatically enjoy
- A grandfather who remembers the dangerous era after slavery
- A racist uncle who is part of the Southern elite establishment
- Reverend Henry, a character who represents the religious-political activism of Dr. Martin Luther King Jr.

Viewers of the program move between these characters, able to support and root for some of them, to judge and reject others, and to have compassion and understanding for all of them in different moments. The equality in treatment of all the characters by the writers and the production process echoes the program's main theme.

Like news or documentary genres, *I'll Fly Away* contains the representation of racism within the civil rights movement of the 1950s and 1960s. Despite this, the program is unusual and, arguably, effective because its production strategies allow Black characters and Blackness to achieve subjectivity.

The first such strategy concerns the plot structure of the program and its point of view. An episode of *I'll Fly Away* typically has three plots, but the plot involving the maid carries the narrative weight. The voice-over narrative at the opening and closing of each episode establishes Lilly Harper's authorial presence. This story about a Black maid in the American South is being told by the maid herself, and television viewers learn mainly from her perspective.

The viewpoints of African Americans more generally are expressed through dialogue between the characters, including secondary characters that give voice to people who are often ignored or unseen. Bill Cobbs, the actor who plays Lilly's father and Adlaine's grandfather, has said, "Maybe the extraordinary thing about the character is that we have an opportunity to know this man... to have an insight about this man in a way that I don't think you have [had] an opportunity to before. The man is a lot like my father. And the history of the media and communications in this country [hasn't] found my father's life very important."[56] Through such minor characters—Lilly's father, several neighbors, another maid who appears once or twice—viewers are provided a look into the experiences of African Americans living in the program's time and place. The responses, emotions, voices, political opinions, and hopes that African American characters have are presented as important.

Significant screen time is provided for the African American characters. In addition to the dialogue spoken by them, there are long monologues by Lilly or Reverend Henry, eloquently stating the conundrums of racial inequality or calmly calling for solidarity in a time of upheaval and fear. *I'll Fly Away* is unusually well suited to such speeches because of its slow pace.

Furthermore, Black and white characters in the series are filmed using the same cinematic style. The angles, distance, lighting, colors, and costuming do not in and of themselves objectify one racial group or privilege another as they do in a text like *Beulah* or in the tradition of the cinematic apparatus in regard to Blackness established by *The Birth of a Nation*, in which racial hierarchy is marked through differing aesthetics.

Ultimately, all these production strategies result in giving Black characters—their stories and their perspectives—credibility. The Black point of view, specifically on discrimination and oppression, is presented as believable and important.

The choice of genre—a one-hour quality drama—is in itself important. The program contrasts with mainstream television news programs, which almost always show conflict from the mainstream white perspective.[57] *I'll Fly Away*, although a fiction program written by white American men, provides a needed perspective on race relations between Blacks and whites.[58] The program also contrasts with the half-hour sitcom format in its length and pace, which allows for gravity and provides the televisual time for stories and characters to develop. The pensive pace, which is one of the markers of *I'll Fly Away*, invites viewers to think about the questions of justice, American culture, and national identity. *I'll Fly Away* draws out the difficult questions and allows time for them to be confronted and contemplated.

After *I'll Fly Away* was canceled in its second season, public television made the unprecedented move of re-airing a network program.[59] It also produced a new final episode to close the series, a made-for-television movie called *I'll Fly Away: Then and Now* (1994). In this final episode, written and produced to provide closure, Lilly Harper has become a successful writer. Her grandson, Lewis Jr. (named after her father, his great-grandfather), comes from Los Angeles subsequent to the L.A. Uprising for a visit. Lilly tells her grandson about their family's experience of American segregation and about the events that forced them to leave Bryland, Georgia. In this flashback sequence, a teenager named Elden, visiting from the North, apparently offends a white woman in their town. Later that night Elden is kidnapped, screaming, from his aunt's house as Lilly's elderly father helplessly pleads for the kidnappers to have mercy. The young man is found butchered in the morning. With great courage, the elder Lewis decides to testify against the white men he witnessed taking Elden; Lilly supports this decision, realizing that her family will have to escape from their beloved hometown in order to survive. After learning that an all-white jury acquits the white men, Lewis Jr. calls his grandmother, Lilly, a hero and likens the strength and courage of her family, his family, to that of Reverend Martin Luther King Jr. and Malcolm X. Lewis Jr. brings the past to the present by talking about the uprisings in Los Angeles and questioning how much has truly changed.

Herman Gray's critique about popular cultural memory of the civil rights movement is that there are two opposite approaches: noble citizens dreaming of the promises of democracy embodied by Martin Luther King Jr., and radical disruption to the establishment embodied by Malcolm X; still today, there is a tendency to (feel compelled to) choose one or the other. *I'll Fly Away* attempts to avoid such a dichotomy. The character Reverend Henry, while being calm-speaking, is also more volatile than the popular image of the strictly nonviolent Black pastor; he is more angry. Anger, expressed by any oppressed person, is a serious act and a sign of rebellion, and it is usually suppressed. Three situation comedies (from the 1970s, 1980s, and 1990s) present Black servants outside the mode of nostalgic impulse, though humor remains a cover to obscure deeper racial or class critique.

African American Men as Servants in Contemporary Settings: *The Fresh Prince of Bel-Air, The Jeffersons, Benson*

Whether one calls it the Los Angeles Uprising, the Los Angeles Rebellion, or the Los Angeles Riots, a national, racial spectacle was made on April 29, 1992. The events that preceded the civil unrest involved the "not guilty" verdicts read in a Simi Valley courthouse that afternoon for the beating of motorist Rodney King two months before; the events that followed involved police chaos, military guard, news action, moral panic, presidential commentary, multiple ideological conclusions, and transpositions into fictional scripts. John Caldwell outlines three media/ted stages of the L.A. Rebellion: "Televisual Mill," "Crisis Management," and "Containment."[60] On the night of one of largest demonstrations of civil unrest in U.S. history, one of its most popular television programs came to an end. *The Cosby Show* (1984–1992) with its politics of racial and class assimilation and "pull-yourself-up-by-your-bootstraps" individualism was accompanied by the sirens as well as the eerie silence heard in L.A.[61] Reconciling the world of *The Cosby Show* with the world of the "riots" was confusing and abstract. There was another popular program at the time, representing race and class set much closer to the epicenter of the unrest, in one of the neighborhoods protected by the L.A. police department during the uprising referred to as the "3 Bs"— Beverly Hills, Bel Air, and Brentwood (by those being ushered elsewhere in the midst of the citywide curfew). Instead of attempting to define the family as "middle class" (and downplay class hierarchy as part of achieving the American Dream) which *The Cosby Show* worked to do, *The Fresh Prince of Bel-Air* made class distinction part of its comedic universe.

The Fresh Prince of Bel-Air (1990–1996)

The Fresh Prince of Bel-Air quickly contained the area of South Central, filling the space with familiar and nonthreatening Black people who delivered the reassuring message about hard work and gratitude. In an episode that aired early in the fall season following the L.A. uprising, Will (Will Smith) visits the apartment where his now wealthy cousins once lived as part of a neighborhood cleanup project mandated by Uncle Phil.[62] Using a flashback that portrayed a rosy family picture with steely determination to move on up, the "ghetto" source of urban rebellion is repackaged as "humble beginnings" for a family who has smoothly entered into one of the 3 Bs.

The integration of Blacks and wealth is brokered by the well-liked Will (Smith), as a figure who authenticates the Banks Family's Blackness. At the same time, this is a portrayal of an African American family segregated from both whites and other Blacks; they are living on their own island. Their exceptionalism—as members of the elite Bel Air community—is not acknowledged and is taken for granted within the rather implausible (but enjoyable) plot about this "prince" of Bel Air. While different in tone from *The Cosby Show* (less educational, more "fresh") and marking a different era (representing the Bush-to-Clinton 1990s rather than the Reaganist 1980s), *The Fresh Prince of Bel-Air* ultimately loses its potential to address class mobility.

The family's domestic servant is portrayed as a British butler, thus displacing his Blackness—his racial and class otherness—onto a Britishness. His being a

Domesticating Blackness • 49

FIGURE 6 Geoffrey the Butler played by Joseph Marcell and "Master Will," in *The Fresh Prince of Bel-Air*.

British butler lends social status to the family, and at the same time, it naturalizes his butlerness. Geoffrey's being British connotes "class," that is, a reservedness and knowledge (about hierarchical social relationships) that effectively sidesteps (even trumps) American social hierarchies. In other words, the servant knows better how he is supposed to conduct himself in his job than the Banks Family, who is a half-generation away from life in the ghetto (Uncle Phil "pulled himself up"). It is Geoffrey, then, who gives credence and guidance to the family's reaching the upper class much like Will gives credence to their being Black. The aptly named Banks Family can lay claim to being both upper class and "down" with the dual presence of Geoffrey and Will.

Two additional episodes revealing, and then concealing, barriers to class mobility in the absence of a discussion about race are "Kiss My Butler" and "Geoffrey Cleans Up."[63] Both have to do with Geoffrey's personal life, and specifically, his ability or proclivity to date. "Kiss My Butler" begins on Geoffrey's birthday, and Will's gift to him is to set him up on a blind date. He also schools Geoffrey on how to be masculine. Geoffrey's demeanor, his servile and formal tone of voice, contribute to his being a little tense and awkward; he projects a queerness along with his otherness, and it is unusual to consider him in a traditional dating situation.[64] Moreover, seeing domestic servants as romantic characters is not what people are accustomed to. By the end of this episode, Geoffrey thinks that the young woman is more fit for Will and gives him her telephone number. He retreats to his position as an employee, avoiding any notion of a future and family of his own, apart from being a butler for the Banks Family.

In the next season, the possibility of Geoffrey's leaving is raised again when he falls for a woman next door who he assumes is part of the household help but turns out to be a millionairess. He has to decide whether to continue a relationship with her, and, presumably, end his work as a butler—to live a life where he and his partner can afford their own servants. However, in "Geoffrey Cleans Up," Geoffrey unequivocally states that "it's just not done"—that is, dating someone of another class, changing class positions, "integrating" with a woman of a different class (who is also Black). In England, as Geoffrey describes, the help do not mix with the lords or ladies of the house.

Here in the United States, Geoffrey is comfortable in his role working for an upper-class family who is African American; he calls Will Master William, when "master" is a term Black slaves were forced to call whites. As Maya Gonzalez argues,

> It spirits away both history and race in one word, while reproducing the structures of class undergirding American society and disguised in cultural representations of class such as this. The moral, at the end of the episode "Geoffrey Cleans Up" is that "in America," as Will assures us, we don't have class. We are beyond class identity and are allowed to "mix"—although some of us are owners and some slaves. Class thus becomes a choice and not a material condition. In America, "boys from the hood" can become aristocrats, and servants can date heiresses and still the order of things will remain unchanged. As the title of the show connotes, this is a fairy tale.[65]

In Britain, class is a naturalized category; it is something one is born into. This is applied in an all-Black caste hierarchy within the show to neutralize class conflict in regard to their having a servant. In short, Geoffrey chooses to be a butler (it is a matter of pride), and his act of choosing is represented as an American thing to do (no matter if it keeps him in servitude). The racialized domestic is shown to have freedom of choice—to remain in the class that they are in.

The Jeffersons (1975–1985)

While Geoffrey is content in his job with an upwardly mobile African American family who seem secure in their wealthy neighborhood, Florence in *The Jeffersons* is distinctly discontented (or at least steadily complaining) about being a maid for George Jefferson, who "moved on up to the East Side, to finally get a piece of the pie." While Geoffrey makes cheeky remarks, Florence really talks back—about how little she gets paid, about her boss's disposition, and in ways that equalize the relationship between employee and employer. That is, she does not see George and Louise Jefferson as much different than she is because they are all working-class African Americans; George has newfound but unsecured financial success in his dry-cleaning business, and Louise used to work as a maid, herself.[66]

The Jeffersons is significant (and differs from *The Fresh Prince*) in the way it represents both the maid and the family she works for: the domestic servant displays anger, and the family expresses anxiety over their class status. In the episode, "Moving on Down," George fears he will lose his business, and that all they have reached will be lost, that they will fall from the "penthouse apartment in the sky," which has become their home. Furthermore, race and class are present factors in the dialogue, in the humor, as key to understanding where they came from (a spin-off of *All In the Family*'s working-class neighborhood in Queens, New York, where Louise was a maid, and she has now gained a maid). The link

FIGURE 7 Florence, Mrs. Louise Jefferson (who formerly worked as a maid, herself), and Mr. George Jefferson played by Marla Gibbs, Isabel Sanford, and Sherman Hemsley, in *The Jeffersons*.

between race and class is erased in *The Fresh Prince*, and remembered in *The Jeffersons* (even haunting George's Freudian dreams).

While there are occasional visits to or visitors from "the ghetto" in *The Fresh Prince*, the program does not dwell in South Central or West Philly, and the actual work involved to move from those locations to Bel Air is not given focus or illumination. There are essentially no white people in *The Fresh Prince*, ironically, in a story about an African American family's success in white culture and a white neighborhood. In *The Jeffersons*, however, the very story is about African Americans as a minority among the people who dwell in wealthy, white culture.

Benson (1979–1986)

The lines demarcating that there is a class and race barrier are acknowledged and shown as somewhat crossable in the unique program, *Benson*. What made *Benson* unusual was not that it was a half-hour sitcom with a cast of quirky characters, but that "it was neither a Black show nor white show" as Robert Guillaume, its star, has commented.[67] The lead character was African American, and the lead actor was well regarded; the lead role was that of a butler. Emanating from a spin-off and featuring a self-assured Black male servant, *Benson* presents the butler in a setting in which he turns out to be the most competent.[68]

Benson DuBois started out as a butler on the program *Soap* (1977–1981). His employer "loans" him to her cousin, a governor and a widower. With his desk in the kitchen, Benson immediately comes in to manage the household, including a staff made up of domestic and political workers. The governor's mansion is both statehouse and family home. In an unusual but gradual turn, Benson moves from butler to lieutenant governor. Moreover, as Guillaume points out, his character moves in stages, starting out by taking night classes then attending law school, he becomes head of household affairs and then budget director. In nearly every episode he is solving a problem; the cumulative effect makes Benson's rise to lieutenant governor plausible. Though there remains the question about how his white employer, who is by all estimations dim-witted though warmhearted, could have become the governor. Benson is there to "save the day" almost every day, as domestic servants often do. In this way, he takes the common position of upholding the status of whiteness, and the program provides a way for viewers to accept Governor Gatlin as the superior and Benson DuBois as the underling. Indeed, his opportunities are cut off by a glass ceiling, here, the kitchen ceiling.

There are two types of acknowledgment: of Benson's abilities, and of Benson's structural limitations. It doesn't matter that the governor is incompetent and that Benson has to cover for him. Benson will never be in first position because he is Black. Benson is cynical; this is the source of humor in the program. It is also a

FIGURE 8 Confident and the most competent, Benson DuBois played by Robert Guillaume, in *Benson*.

mechanism for letting off steam and, furthermore, for audiences to digest the fact of the servant being "superior" to the employer. Benson also attributes his race and class—his working-class status—to the lack of upward mobility. The program promotes meritocracy in Benson's rise, yet meritocracy does not explain the privilege of Governor Gatlin and his cousin.

Benson is single, married to his work, and ultimately neutered in that, like Geoffrey in *The Fresh Prince of Bel-Air*, he continues to choose his job over having a personal life. It is true that both of the main male characters are "bachelors,"

FIGURE 9 In *Benson*, Benson DuBois begins as a butler, becomes head of household affairs, then state budget director, he eventually earns the position of lieutenant governor, and in the final season, he runs against his boss for governor; the series ends on a cliffhanger.

but Governor Gatlin had a fulfilling marriage resulting in a child, Katie, who Benson helps to nurture as both mother and father. As an employee of the governor (of California), Benson is both a domestic servant and a servant of the state; his work is never finished, and he must self-exploit around the clock. As Maya Gonzalez describes, "It is a beautiful conceit; Benson is a genius, an intellectual, a street smart, sharp lady's man, a morally standup citizen, and most important of all, a family man (however to a family which is not his own). On the other hand, he's black, and thus although in every way perfect, he still has his place.... As for the racism he endures, this is easily managed as well, by the conceit that Benson is the smartest person in the room."[69] He makes us laugh. We laugh at the racially informed irony; it is a running joke that makes the show watchable.

The World Is Still Mad: *Mad Men* (2007–2015)

A critically acclaimed show for its take on white, capitalist, patriarchal life in the 1960s and its style in portraying this life, is *Mad Men*. The cable series began broadcasting in 2007, and among its nostalgic moves is the return of the domestic. There are two maids in this series, layered over one another. The first, who has a more prominent role, is Karla, who works for the Don and Betty Draper family. The second is Viola, who was Betty's childhood maid, who was let go by Betty's stepmother. She is both a beloved figure and a specter; even after Betty has grown into adulthood and sees Viola, Viola is wearing a throwback uniform marked by her maidhood and conflating a longer past racial era with a retro one.[70] The patriarch says in the first season, "In Greek, 'nostalgia' literally means 'the pain from an old wound.'"[71]

What is problematic with *Mad Men* in the choice to be a "period piece," is that this provides an excuse to show African American women in unequal positions. White women too, are subordinated, but their plights are illuminated, and their characters are fleshed out. In being a program created in today's world representing yesterday's time, there is an opportunity to improve upon racial representation and to ignite new racial discourses by allowing the maid subjectivity—allowing more lines, a distinct perspective, a disharmonious relationship with her employer (and her job), relationships to other African American characters. *Mad Men* ventures into this territory, but it does not complete the path.

In an episode called, "Tomorrowland" from the fourth season, Karla and Betty have a confrontation.[72] It is remarkable first because of the disharmony displayed, and more specifically, the two women disagree, criticize, and fight about mothering. Both the maid and the housewife are outspoken and lose a little bit of control. Second, it is a good example of how racial discourse is almost altered, if it had pushed just a few seconds further.

Does Karla have the last word? Just because Betty is seen as a brat or a witch does not necessarily lend Karla (narrative) power. We still don't know what Karla's kids are doing, how they are. And Betty criticizes Karla's mothering in retaliation for Karla calling out Betty's inability to mother (and claims that she is the one who has been doing the job). Though through this co-dependent relationship, both women are absent mothers. Betty enters into an altercation only after being stung by Karla's giving a critical opinion. After the two women exchange emotional words—the maid displays anger too—Betty fires Karla, rather nonchalantly as she attempts to regain composure; Karla is surprised but calm and announces that she will go upstairs to say goodbye to Betty's daughter. How the scene could have been different, and in my mind, complete, would be to show Karla going into the room and saying her goodbye. It would show her character's relationship to other characters and allow her to explain what had just happened in her own words. It would be the "reverse-shot" or counterpunch to Betty's privileged ability to cut off Karla's employment.[73]

Conclusion: Letting Mammy Go

There has been a deep aesthetic value placed on the image of a dark-skinned woman holding a white child. It is what Wallace-Sanders describes as a symbol of reconciliation and redemption.[74] She also argues that Mammy can be seen as the "quintessential interdisciplinary topic."[75] There is an American cultural tendency, perhaps even a social-psychological drive, to domesticate Blackness. The form of the African American servant, and its modern adaptations, is a primary mechanism in this effort. Patricia Hill Collins writes, "Even when the political and economic conditions that originally generated controlling images disappear, such images prove remarkably tenacious because they not only keep Black women oppressed but are key in maintaining interlocking systems of race, class, and gender oppression. The status of African-American women as outsiders or strangers becomes the point from which other groups define their normality . . . because those individuals who stand at the margins of society clarify its boundaries."[76]

The racialized domestic simultaneously reflects racial hierarchies and exposes them. In a popular situation comedy like *Beulah* and in similarly constructed programs, the racial boundaries are essentially resealed, in spite of a few sassy zingers. However, in the series *I'll Fly Away*, the experiences and opinions of an African American woman who works as a domestic refuse the usual happy ending, thus redirecting both racial discourse and audience pleasure.

Despite the conscientiousness and good intentions of the producers and writers of *I'll Fly Away*, a sensitively written and beautifully acted program, a problem remains: that of how to represent an African American woman in a contemporaneous context and escape the confines of past patterns of imaging and imagining African American women vis-à-vis white class privilege.[77] Not unlike Hattie McDaniel in her day, actress Regina Taylor received recognition for her portrayal of Lilly Harper. The more famous Whoopi Goldberg also received critical acclaim for films in which she plays a maid: *Clara's Heart* (1988), *The Long Walk Home* (1990), *Corrina, Corrina* (1994). She is also noted for her roles in *Ghost* (1990), and as Guinan on the television program *Star Trek: The Next Generation* (1987–1994), in which she plays a kind of spiritual adviser. It remains difficult to break from archetypes of African American women such as the mammy, the matriarch, the jezebel, and the welfare mother.[78] But it is a possibility to be pursued.

While the term "Mammy" is specific, historical, and dated, we have modern-day mammy figures, or at least not-too-distant cousins. Nell Carter's character in *Gimme a Break!* (1981–1987) was a direct descendant. Some thirty years after *Beulah*—decades in which women of other races often occupied the servant role—the Black maid was back on television. When Carter, a Broadway performer, entered the role of Nell Harper on *Gimme a Break!*, she brought her loud and sassy voice and a body clearly marked as Black. Her racial otherness is intimidating, yet not fully threatening: there's love underneath the attitude, and moreover, her employment status blunts her assertiveness, keeping it in check. The premise of the show is that after the death of his wife, Carl Kanisky asks his wife's friend, Nell Harper, to keep house and take care of his three children (but there is no explanation of why he would presume to ask her such a thing). For

FIGURE 10 Nell Carter as Nell, in *Gimme a Break!*

the creators of the program as well as for most watchers of it, Nell's Blackness is enough to qualify her as a domestic helper and justify the reason to change her life to help this family.

Gimme a Break! is in the mold of *Beulah*, despite the power wielded by Nell Carter (whose character's name is also Nell), a Tony Award–winning performer who embodied the role of Black entertainer in the series, her power is expressed through a brash and "sassy" demeanor. Her being an African American housekeeper and surrogate mother is mediated through the social distance between her and the widower father of the family.

Nell can be lascivious, or desiring. Beulah is (and isn't) asexual; on one hand, she is not portrayed as desirable to whites, on the other hand, she and her "lover boy" Bill (an older Black man) teach Donnie how to dance, how to, essentially, be heterosexually successful with the neighborhood girls. Nell also nurtures the white child's sexual education; even though she teaches the youngest daughter and tomboy, Sam, how to fight, Sam eventually becomes a fetching Samantha. Hence Black servitude supports white femininity and heterosexuality (and the reproduction of the race). *Gimme a Break!* is not a representation of a domesticated slave (as Hattie McDaniel's persona indicates and intones when saying "yes'm"), and although a kind of a throwback, the program also poses some ruptures.

One of the key arguments in Beretta Smith-Shomade's book about the representation of African American women is that there is a "conflation of objectification and agency in television's portrayal of Black women."[79] Oprah Winfrey, Niecy Nash, and Queen Latifah have offered both fictional and nonfictional performances that restimulate memories of—and love for—the comforting, assisting, and domestic(ated) African American woman. Queen Latifah's do-ragged performance in *Bringing Down the House* (2003) is in the throwback vein of a Buckwheat character. Marketing promos for the film featured Latifah with wide-open eyes and raised hair, demanding, "Who dat? Who dere?" This filmic portrayal is utterly strange and distinctly less nuanced compared with her earlier performance in the television series *Living Single* (1993–1998), and in the film *Set If Off* (1996) about four African American women, protagonists who turn to robbing banks. Cinematic stories are often much less flexible than televisional discourses of race. In the reality program *Clean House* (2003–2011), Niecy Nash helps save people from their "crisis of clutter." Each episode ends with Nash's direct-address acknowledgment that everyone wants her to come clean their house: "Oh Miss Niecy, when are you going to come to my house?" With her take-charge demeanor and performative Southern inflection, Nash is a new millennium version of Beulah, however conscious a performance it is on Nash's part and unconscious the audience is of it.[80] "Mammy" may now be a stylish, independent spirit, but she is nonetheless tethered to a past story of race relations, of Blacks helping whiteness keep its status—and the house clean.

bell hooks writes, "In general, in this culture, black women are seen and depicted as down to earth, practical, creatures of the mundane. Within sexist racist iconography, black females are most often represented as mammies, whores, or sluts. Caretakers whose bodies and beings are empty vessels to be filled with the needs of others. This imagery tells the world that the black female is born to serve—a servant—maid—made to order. She is not herself but always what someone else wants her to be."[81] This answers the question about how the mammy figure has been made over during the twentieth century and what the continuing fascination with the mammy image reveals about contemporary society. Since the era of slavery, and largely because of it, the mammy figure has been invented and elaborated in literature, advertising, memorabilia, film, and television.[82] In a section entitled "Insidious Iconography," Turner contends that Mammy is a myth: "Mammies allow the public to indulge in wishful thinking. The idea that a selfless, sexless, black woman might want to come into your kitchen and organize your household has retained a persistent hold on the American imagination. But it is not now, and never was, true."[83]

I'll Fly Away is a progressive program about a woman of color that was created by white male producers. Joshua Brand and John Falsey wanted to explore and present the life of a domestic, not only her relation to the white family she works for but also her own life apart from them. Falsey has stated that he grew up watching *The Courtship of Eddie's Father* and that he always wondered what the maid did when she wasn't working. Where did she live? What was her home like? It takes allies, such as producers and writers, already working in the mainstream industry to support, promote, and create alternative texts, programs that communicate a nonmainstream perspective. Lilly Harper is able to speak and to be heard in her own clear and eloquent voice.

Emmy-nominated actress Regina Taylor has articulated about accepting and playing the role of Lilly Taylor: "I did have reservations about playing a maid. But in reading the script and talking to people, I felt they were interested in portraying a full human being—Lilly's a mother, daughter, sister, . . . not just the hands that serve other people. She has a voice, she has a mind."[84] The fact that the character keeps a journal, from which the actress reads in a voice-over on each episode, convinced Taylor that this maid was going to be multidimensional. "Then I knew this wasn't going to be another Mammy role," she says. "You had the sense of a woman, with her own life, her own dreams, and you had the sense of a poet and philosopher in the journals."[85]

In giving voice and visibility to an African American woman as a character, protagonist, and here, a historian, is a countereffort (Lilly is a counterimage), this is a strategy for intervention. Although it situates Blackness and race relations within a historical past when racial boundaries were even more clearly etched, *I'll Fly Away* questions rather than confirms these boundaries. Significantly, the final episode brings the story into the present, suggesting that the struggle for equality remains relevant if not urgent. Lilly's work as a maid is transformed credibly into her work as an author and historian of Black culture. She embodies both present and past meanings of Blackness, prompting viewers to see that a mammy character can be overcome.

To stage change in the representation of race, in racial discourse and its concomitant social discourse(s), a three-step intervention is needed: first, eliminate common characterizations, which is not simple or easy to do because, second, individual writers and producers in power must offer perspectives that haven't been heard and seen before, and third, casting agents along with the viewing/consuming public, need to include and accept new characters in their tele-vision.

One of the problems in discursive struggle over racial meanings, that is, in interpreting images of African Americans in representational culture, is that

African Americans are read in relation to a post–civil rights subject. The general belief is that the civil rights struggle is over and affirmative action is unnecessary and that if people are poor it is not due to structural or institutional inequalities in the society. Race tends to be read as either humorous (in the present) or solemnly impenetrable (in the past).[86] Talking about race enables a discussion about racism and how to solve racial inequality. As we listen to television maids talk back, we can ask, What are they telling us?

For more than a century, in literature and in film, on stage and on television, images of African American women have been depicted, performed, consumed, accepted, and rejected. The maid trope represents, literally and figuratively, much more than a figure to be laughed at or dismissed. Indeed, the figure of mammy says more about its creators and consumers than about the person or community it attempts to characterize. One of the goals in analyzing the figure of the racialized domestic is to direct readers and viewers to read race as culturally and personally consequential. The hope is that American television, together with its audiences, will conjure up new images of race and race relations, a new vision that has truly let mammy go.

Such a cultural departure will require a shift in viewing practices and a conscious shift in taste. Audience preferences about portrayals of African American characters are ideologically based; Blackness has historically been depicted as either threatening to a white-dominated racial order or, alternatively, as entertaining and harmless (in part to appease or deflect those fears). Beulah embodies a type of Blackness that is deployed in support of an idealized American domesticity and society. Lilly embodies another type of Blackness, one that bears witness to the injustice in American society and in that way, challenges and changes the manner in which viewers see, understand, and imagine race relations. Ultimately, this character is more engaging. African Americans and non–African Americans alike can resist watching and accepting repeated modes and tropes of Blackness in an effort to witness and advocate for equitable interpersonal relationships, on screen, and beyond.

3
Shades of Whiteness

White Servants Keeping Up a Class Ideal

Television is marked and mapped by whiteness. And television provides an intertextual, interactive production of meaning that is often more flexible than other media, such as mainstream Hollywood film, because of its immediacy and liveness. Television is a space of discursive repertoires that marks race and racial difference and also delineates class and gender roles. All three concepts—race, class, and gender—give a fuller meaning to the function of whiteness.

What is white? A color, a status? Who is white? A person of European descent, a person who assimilates to Western civilization? In her book *White Women, Race Matters: The Social Construction of Whiteness*, Ruth Frankenberg argues that race affects white people's lives even though whiteness is often disassociated from a notion of race. She writes, "Any system of differentiation shapes those on whom it bestows privilege as well as those it oppresses."[1] In this way, "race matters" because it fundamentally influences how individuals think, act, and are positioned within a social setting in relation to Others. "Whiteness purports to be both nothing and everything. It is the race that need not speak its name. *Yet it defines itself as no less than whatever it chooses to exclude.* To grow up white is to be the ground zero from which everyone else differs, the thin line around which racial plots thicken, gaining density and intensity. 'I didn't think of myself as white,' a friend described herself as a child. 'I didn't feel superior. I just felt *normal*.'"[2] How are people identified as white—through skin color, through institutions, through ideology? And why does it matter? It matters because the concept and experience of whiteness is part of what creates the concept and experience of race.

By virtue of the visual experience in which skin color is apparent and codified, figures that represent "whiteness" and "Blackness" are given cultural, historical, political, and usually unconscious meanings.[3] At the same time, there is room for movement or slippage in television; the degrees of difference are in flux within the "vicissitudes of race" (to use Matthew Frye Jacobson's phrase) in television as they are in real life.[4] This is due in part to historical shifts in social and legal structures, such as those having to do with interracial marriage and immigration. But it also reflects a kind of ambivalence—or openness—in the television apparatus. That is, while television production and productions (the act and the artifacts) are affected and shaped by political culture, television is simultaneously a medium available for telling changing stories about race (as long as there is a belief that an audience is out there). Television has clear economic imperatives; its cultural goals are secondary and are not solidly committed to or even claimed. While meanings of race have shifted during nearly seventy-five years of television broadcasting, the visual impact of racial difference remains.

Jacobson writes that "race is not just a conception; it is also a perception. The problem is not merely how races are comprehended, but how they are seen." His book, *Whiteness of a Different Color*, takes three trajectories in describing particular dimensions of race, one of which focuses on race as "a mode of perception contingent upon the circumstances of the moment."[5] I would add that race is a mode of perception contingent upon intertextual circumstances. In different eras of American race relations—for example, during the pre–civil rights period, during the military engagements with Asian countries (Japan, Korea, and Vietnam), during the ongoing era of contested immigration from Mexico and Central American countries, and in the post-9/11 conflation of "Middle Eastern" and "terrorist"—the concept of racial otherness, that is, non-whiteness, has been sustained. The general notion of race and the meanings of specific racial identities shift from period to period, but a privileged status of whiteness and a racialized hegemony has remained constant. Richard Dyer has written that whiteness is "everything and nothing" and that this omniscience is its source of representational power.[6]

The figure of the racialized domestic serves as a clue, and a cue, to the racial hierarchy in a given time period. The figure of the white servant in American television reveals shades of white and whiteness, and that whiteness is linked to yet often subsumed under class and gender. The portrayal of the white working-class servant's whiteness—which grants a sliver of access, acceptance, and integration into the family—obscures class division at the moment at which it would otherwise be most pronounced. (Just when she or he is about to be explicitly separated from their employer, they are embraced by the family.) Class differences within whiteness exist, certainly, and can move working-class whites into a category of otherness or of lesser-whiteness. This helps illustrate "white" as involved in both racial and class designation (much as "Black" is simultaneously raced and classed).

Like servants of color, white servants are racialized, with class rather than skin color emerging as the key indicator of non-ideal whiteness (or of otherness). The significance of the white servant in American television is that she or he affirms the class ideal as "white," and the idealized American family is one that can afford a maid or butler who is integrated seamlessly into the home.[7] The representation of white servants and the families they work for is part of a discourse of whiteness that functions to define the power and privilege of whiteness by equating and sublimating it to notions of "American" and "family." The meanings of whiteness and Americanness coincide, and that coincidence or collapse is rendered invisible or nearly so through the trope of family on television. That is, the discourse of whiteness navigates shades of white (class difference) and upholds a white class ideal as an American family ideal; white servants help to unify the family in a way that servants of color are not able or allowed to, the monoracial harmony helps to hide economic disparity.

Examining three programs from the 1960s that prominently featured white servants, this chapter addresses several broader questions concerning the role of whiteness as consumed in television culture and as packaged and presented in the television industry. How are whiteness, Americanness, and family interconnected? In what way does white signify a class category? In what way does the performativity of white servants differ from that of servants of color? Is white privilege still available to them?

Defining Whiteness

In using the term "whiteness," I do not suggest that there exists a generalized, monolithic culture of white people, but I emphasize the common thread of white privilege. Whiteness is a place of structural advantage, deriving its power from the fact that the links between race, class, and gender that contribute to one's status in society are rendered invisible (at least to some). Whiteness implies social hierarchy and racial privilege yet does not acknowledge it explicitly. Whereas "race" often signifies or connotes a "race problem," "white" connotes a status quo, what is "normal" or standard, often with even a positive association. Whiteness normalizes hierarchy, and racial domination as well.

In *White Women, Race Matters*, Ruth Frankenberg examines the relationship between whiteness and racial domination, focusing on whiteness as a social construction that affects white women. Her argument is that people are "raced" just as much as they are "gendered." Frankenberg outlines a set of linked dimensions of whiteness: first, whiteness is a location of structural advantage, of race privilege; second, it is a "standpoint," a place from which white people look at themselves, at others, and at society; and third, whiteness refers to a set of cultural practices that are usually unmarked and unnamed. She adds that these locations and practices are intrinsically linked to unfolding relations of domination, which means that to speak of whiteness is to assign everyone a place in the hierarchy of race relations.

Here we have the link between whiteness and race: "The very use of the term 'race' raises the idea of difference, for 'race' is above all a marker of difference, an axis of differentiation."[8] Frankenberg argues that whiteness is an unmarked cultural space, unseen and unnamed by those who inhabit it, and that rather than viewing white culture as "no culture" or as the given, we need to consider the social and political contexts in which white cultural practices mark out a normative space and set of identities. Television is such a cultural practice. However, "Whiteness, as a set of cultural practices, is visible most clearly to those it definitively excludes and those to whom it does violence.... The same is true of 'Americanness' in relation to those whom it marginalizes or excludes, and of privileged class attitudes in relation to those who are not privileged."[9] In television's depiction of family comes the privileged power of whiteness to represent what is American.

Contrary to the view that American society can or should be color-blind—believing that one's race does not affect one's privilege or lack of privilege—Michael Omi and Howard Winant argue, "Even a cursory glance at American history reveals that far from being color-blind, the United States has been an extremely 'color-conscious' society. From the very inception of the Republic to the present moment, race has been a profound determinant of one's political rights, one's location in the labor market, and indeed one's sense of 'identity.' The hallmark of this history has been *racism*, not the abstract ethos of equality, and while racial minority groups have been treated differently, all can bear witness to the tragic consequences of racial oppression."[10] This in turn brings about racial domination and hierarchy (discriminatory or unequal practices) that exist on the macrolevel through cultural institutions—politics, the economy, religion, and education, to name a few examples—as well as on the microlevel, since institutions are inevitably made up of individuals who interact with one another.

Whiteness and Television

Race is a mode of taxonomy, representing a historical set of theories about people and nations that are contested both politically and scientifically. It is at once broadly cultural and deeply personal, certain and uncertain. Such is the way that race as a concept, as a visual marker and as a type of knowledge, works in and through television.

Whiteness is opaque, though no less evident, when we look at white servants working in white families. Like the Blackness or Asianness of Other servants, the whiteness of white servants can be deconstructed. The position of the employer illuminates shades of whiteness while upholding a white ideal that ultimately is a class ideal. Such an ideal is expressed through economic and familial success. These express the American values that television projects, reflects, and sells in a constant feedback loop to the public.

What exactly does white look like? In Jacobson's study of ethnic immigrants to the United States, he argues, "An earlier generation of Americans saw Celtic, Hebrew, Anglo-Saxon, or Mediterranean physiognomies where today we see only subtly varying shades of a mostly undifferentiated whiteness."[11] His important assertion is that whites are not born; they are made. I would extend this argument by saying that being "made" white also involves being accepted as American. In the history of America's settlement, poor whites were considered American in ways that so-called Negroes and Indians were not. Accordingly, many poor whites proudly clung to their status as not-Black and not-Indigenous.

In the modern context, "white" often connotes upper middle class, marked by signifiers of an affluent lifestyle: expensive cars, a big house, designer clothing, leisure time. Furthermore, when communities of color describe someone as "acting white," they generally mean that a person values these material markers and may "talk white," that is, in a neutral dialect with the conspicuous absence of an accent. Being American is associated with living in a large home in a "nice," not particularly diverse, suburban neighborhood occupied by heterosexual married couples with children who ultimately display familial behavior that is much alike. The American family is defined even by seeming exceptions. Television programs such as *Roseanne* (1988–1997), *Married . . . with Children* (1987–1997), *The Simpsons* (1989–present), and *The Osbournes* (2002–2005), which provide alternative whiteness (blue-collar, dysfunctional, animated, British rock-'n'-rollers), are still rooted in family as the structure that gives meaning to life. These programs may have nonconformist moments, but fundamentally, the paradigm that family *is* American remains solid. And family is usually white, by skin color and by cultural connotation.

This is part of a debate about "selling out" raised by the example of the Huxtables in *The Cosby Show* (1984–1992). Becoming "white" for people of color means becoming wealthy. Similar questions are suggested by the two opposing cousins in *The Fresh Prince of Bel-Air* (1990–1996): Will, who retains his "street" personality, and Carlton, who speaks in a conspicuously "white" accent, often donning either his Bel Air private school blazer or a preppy polo shirt and Bermuda shorts. *The Cosby Show* has been studied and watched extensively, critiqued and loved simultaneously. It is considered one of the most successful television programs in history, with strong performances, edifying content, and cultural influence, as well as high ratings among African American and white viewers. The political and social complexity of the text comes in the context of reception: many viewers, while acknowledging and respecting the Blackness of the family in *The Cosby Show*, perceived this family as a model for how all African Americans not only could be, but should be. John Fiske and others might refer to this frame of thinking, which emerged in the Reagan era, as dichotomizing "good

Blacks" (the Huxtables) and "bad Blacks" (welfare mothers, gang members, and all those not fulfilling the American Dream because of their own purported deficiencies).[12] The Huxtable family was also considered admirable in their African Americanness as a matter of ethnicity rather than of race.

The Huxtables, and the popularity of *The Cosby Show*, reflected a conservative post–civil rights perspective in which race was becoming less important as a significant social and economic factor in one's ability to advance in society. The Huxtables represented an idealized African American family and an ideal American family, one that reached the standards of an upper-middle-class lifestyle—of whiteness. *The Cosby Show*, while about a Black family, was understood by many as a "white" show.[13] The program was developed by Bill Cosby and Alvin Poussaint, a psychiatrist, as a direct corrective to earlier representations of Blackness. It succeeded in bringing an elegant, loving, impressive, and funny Black family into millions of living rooms at a time when racial politics were becoming more divisive. The class elevation and the "family values" displayed in the television program brought it into the realm of acceptability, even admirability, in a post–civil rights context.[14]

In his essay "The Whites of Their Eyes: Racist Ideologies and the Media," Stuart Hall considers how ways of looking, perceiving, and understanding whiteness—ways that have been culturally taught and perpetuated—have developed into a "naturalized" racist common sense. We are not trained or encouraged to see whiteness. Hall describes the construction of race in popular literature and culture at the end of the nineteenth century, stating that racism was "so *ubiquitous*, and at the same time, so *unconscious*—simply assumed to be the case—that it was impossible to get any critical purchase on it."[15] Bringing television studies into dialogue with critical race studies works to unpack whiteness as a media-cultural concept. "Television sits in the home, both part of the furniture and part of the family ... television celebrates the ordinary; and by doing so it suggests that certain versions of family life are normal and others deviant, strange, or (by exclusion) nonexistent."[16]

In the programs analyzed in the following case studies—*Hazel* (1961–1966), *Family Affair* (1966–1971), and *The Brady Bunch* (1969–1974)—whiteness is taken for granted. By the start of the 1960s, American television broadcasting had been in operation for a little over a decade, and its broadcast of what was American had become streamlined. Preceding the 1950s, Ella Taylor wrote the following:

> As the decade wore on, television families became almost exclusively white as well as middle-class. In a period when blacks and rural whites were migrating north in large numbers, when race was fast becoming a major source of urban conflict, and when television programmers were allegedly reaching out to more cosmopolitan audiences, the "ethnic comedies" of the early 1950s were rapidly disappearing. *Amos 'n' Andy*, *The Goldbergs*, and *Life with Luigi* had all been dropped from the schedules by 1954.... To a working class divided by ethnic

tensions and by the desire of many immigrants to become "fully American," life with Beaver or Ricky must indeed have seemed inviting, though it may also have generated anxieties about not measuring up to the model they provided.[17]

The programs in the case studies do not have lead characters of color against which the white characters can be measured; whiteness is then defined through class and, to a certain degree, gender. In other settings, the meaning of whiteness becomes apparent when whiteness is viewed alongside Blackness, but in the monoracial setting that these television texts reflect, whiteness is defined by class difference. There are shades of white; the employees are not as white as their employers, but they participate in the production of whiteness nonetheless.

In demarcating whiteness, through class or racial difference, the figure of the white servant in these television programs also lays out other sets of relations, such as gender positioning and the family structure. White servants help establish an ideal whiteness, that of their employers, one that casts a leisurely, trouble-free domestic life as natural/ized and deserved or presumed. Although a subordinate, the white servant serves as a central force, as a linchpin in the organization and ideology of the white family.[18]

In a monoracial setting, whiteness still needs to be defined, and it is the working-class status of the white servant that sets middle- or upper-class whiteness apart (and above). But the servant also marks the boundaries of not-family by being of a different class, a different "shade of white." This gradation in shades of whiteness is not based on skin color per se, although Jewish nanny Fran Fine in *The Nanny* (1993–1999) and Italian American housekeeper Tony Micelli in *Who's the Boss?* (1984–1992) are physically differentiated from their respective Manhattan and Connecticut suburban employers and are deliberately meant to appear "ethnic" and non-Anglo. Class racializes the white servant in relation to the white family that employs them. The whiteness of the white servant blurs the boundaries between family and not-family, mystifying the labor that is performed. At the same time, the class line is masked by the voluntary intimacy that integrates the servant into the family. This is the core contradiction that the white servant represents.

Whiteness is "ubiquitous" and "unconscious," Hall says, but it *can* be seen, or at least perceived. This chapter's case studies feature three white servants: Hazel, whose working-class accent is loud and distinct, Mr. French, a butler marked by his British accent and his gentlemanliness, and Alice, whom we know as inseparable from the Brady Bunch. They are distinguished by their class status but are integrated in a way that servants of color are not. At the same time, though they are of the same race as their employers, their working-class status keeps them from being true family members. So in seeing whiteness, there is the need to see class.

All three programs studied in this chapter are half-hour situation comedies. There have been few American television dramas showing a white servant. The preeminent television drama featuring white servants, *Upstairs Downstairs* (1971–1975), was British-made and set in London, though it aired in the United States. Certainly the more contemporary *Downton Abbey* (2010–2015), which also aired on PBS/public television, has amassed an enthusiastic audience, and the sweeping, glamorous series has been hugely popular in the United States (with two spin-off movie versions). There remains a fascination with the servant class and their relationship with their "masters." It is easier to recognize and fetishize a class system when seen as British and exotic (and as outside U.S. culture). There has also been a steady number of made for television movies with plots involving a bachelor father and a nanny that play out a romantic scenario. The Hallmark Channel has produced such titles as *The Nanny Express*, *A Nanny for Christmas*, and numerous plots where a woman hired as support staff for an estate or castle ends up becoming the princess in the story (sometimes literally). In contrast to the Hallmark special are Lifetime Channel movies in which the nanny is often an interloper in the family, threatening to kidnap a child or kill the mother in a *Fatal Attraction* type scenario.[19] But most narrative pleasures representing an "eligible" maid (i.e., young or white) in a motherless household are based more on a *Sound of Music* mythos. The narrative drive is toward the consummation of the relationship between employer and employee, which from the beginning never quite feels like a working relationship. In this way, white domestic helpers (usually the ones who are young and female) cross the line that servants of color never do: legitimate integration (across class), ultimately through marriage. Such an American fairy tale ending where class does not matter, thus far, is for whites only. While whiteness and the romance genre are closely tied, the sitcom is a predominant narrative form in which whiteness is represented seamlessly as "American." Television's connection to whiteness, particularly in the 1950s and 1960s, established an image and an understanding of ideal family along with a sense of American success and happiness based in familial love and unity.

Hazel (1961–1966)

Within a historical context of fast-fading postwar euphoria, and at the beginning of a volatile decade of societal change, the figure of the maid was handed the task of holding a crumbling American Dream family together. She extended the image of life in a postwar boom economy, even though it was the 1960s. The ideal white American family presented in *Hazel* is modeled on the 1950s sitcom family (featured in *The Adventures of Ozzie and Harriet*, *Father Knows Best*, and *Leave It to Beaver*). Here we have a show that is not named for a husband and wife, or for the male head of household, or for the child; rather, like *Beulah*, the title foregrounds the maid. The program, however, is less about Hazel and her own life than about how her life revolves around and is central to the family for whom she works. It shows her role in maintaining the family.

FIGURE 11 Shirley Booth as Hazel, in *Hazel*.

Premiering on NBC in 1961, *Hazel* starred Shirley Booth as Hazel Burke, the live-in housekeeper for the Baxter family. For the program's first four seasons, Hazel worked for lawyer George Baxter, his wife Dorothy, and their son Harold. In the fifth and final season, Hazel went to work for George's brother and his family after George and Dorothy were transferred to the Middle East for George's work. They (incredulously) left Harold with the maid, taking him from one household to another (and from NBC to CBS).[20]

Based on a popular cartoon strip that ran in the *Saturday Evening Post*, *Hazel* presents stories of Hazel's humorous involvement in both the professional and the household business of George Baxter. The maid is characterized in the cartoon as "meddling" and as causing "misadventures" in her attempts to run the household. However, in the television series, the maid "ran the Baxter household more effectively than George ran his office. She . . . preempted his authority with alarming, though justified, regularity."[21] The father, George, is often competitive with Hazel in terms of who is really in charge. Dorothy, described by one critic as "dressing like and striking the poses of a high fashion model," is in the tradition of the glamorous television mother whose work as a housewife is done by the maid.[22] Harold, also in keeping with television tradition, fulfils the image of the all-American kid (with blond hair, in T-shirt and jeans, wearing a baseball cap and sneakers). Hazel's job is to keep order—both literal and ideological—in the house. Though seemingly innocuous, she holds the household together: the servant, in a marginalized position, is at the same time central to marking the well-being of the nuclear family.[23]

Following the pattern set by *Leave It to Beaver* (1957–1963) and *Father Knows Best* (1954–1960), *Hazel* presents a suburban American family living apart from any class struggle—and apart from race conflict and women's resistance to patriarchy, which come later in the decade and are mediated through the servants in *Family Affair* and *The Brady Bunch*. No backstory is provided to explain why and how Hazel came to work as a maid. As with numerous servants in representational culture, her obligation to serve another class is unquestioned. Like African American domestics, it is Hazel's measure against the mother figure that defines (white) femininity, her "battles" with the father figure that establish masculine authority, and her closeness with the child that gauges and guards the boundaries between her and the family.

The style and mode of *Hazel* is nostalgic in its portrayal of the family and the economy, especially in its portrayal of the ideal housewife. Dorothy is much like the 1950s Mrs. Cleaver in *Leave It to Beaver* and Mizz Alice in *Beulah*, a wife of leisure, properly dressed and perfectly manicured. She is unlike the more independent working women in contemporaneous 1960s television programs, such as Ann Marie in *That Girl* (1966–1971), and Julia Baker in *Julia* (1968–1971).[24] While a few programs offered a glimpse of changing roles for women in the family economy and the work world, *Hazel* was a throwback to an earlier era of family stability. This retrospective displacement is similar to, but in some ways the inverse of, some ethnic sitcoms that were produced in the late 1940s and early 1950s but set in a slightly earlier era. Those programs were intended to educate viewers and help justify postwar consumerism by addressing anxieties expressed by Depression-era characters. *Hazel* also gave the feeling of taking place in a previous decade, but the purpose was to redirect viewers to a period in which family and social hierarchies were relatively unchallenged, at least in visual representation.[25]

The episode "Natural Athlete," which aired on November 29, 1963, opens with Hazel asking George, whom she calls "Mr. B.," about the theory of relativity. As he begins to answer, she interrupts, saying that she doesn't mean the scientific kind of relativity, but rather the kind that ought to convince him that "relative" to their neighbors they need to get a new washing machine. This opening serves several purposes. It uses Hazel as comic relief—the joke has nothing to do with the story line of the episode, and in this sense the opening is similar to those in *Beulah*, where the maid character often tells a performative joke. It reveals her class background by showing that she is not as educated or intellectual as her employer. It demonstrates that Hazel's concerns in life merge with the domestic status of the Baxter household. Moreover, she appeals to George's sense of class competition (keeping up with the Joneses, or in this case, the Johnsons) and in this way gets something that will also make her job easier. In what Stuart Hall would call a preferred reading in alignment with the dominant/intended meaning by the producers, Hazel's manipulation would not be considered subversive but amusing. However, consideration ought to be given to how this opening would be read by different-classed viewers; to those who identify with Hazel, the class struggle would be more apparent.

On the representational level, Hazel's class difference is articulated in several ways. She is neither tall nor slender, and she moves ungracefully, which could be considered unfeminine. Her overall demeanor is awkward, suggesting a person who is unaware of the impression she makes. She speaks loudly and with a strong working-class accent, using informal language and pronouncing words brashly. (Certainly, it is associated with the city, not the suburb.) This alludes to the differentiation among "white" people, relegating whites of different ethnic origins to different positions within the hierarchy of whiteness. When her nephew comes to visit in one episode, he is suspected of swarthy business practices by George and Hazel (though in the end he—and therefore, Hazel—is exonerated). Hazel's look is plain, uniformed, and nonsexual; she has no husband or children of her own. Her characterization contrasts to the smooth and elegant persona of the woman of the house, Dorothy, whom Hazel calls "Missy."[26] Calling Dorothy by this name emphasizes not only Hazel's position as an employee but also Dorothy's double femininity.

Expected and expressed gender roles are also revealed in each character's contribution to the narrative and their relationship to consumption, that is, whether one is a consumer of goods and services or a producer of them. "Missy" does not have a job and does not have many lines of dialogue except those that support what George says or does. She mostly laughs, smiles, and looks pretty, at ease in her expensive clothing and large house. On the other hand, Hazel is employed and is not a wife or a mother. She is associated with work, selling her domestic labor to the Baxters and sparing Mrs. Baxter from any unladylike exertion. The working labor of the maid defines and distinguishes the femininity of the housewife.

The commercials that were often seen during a broadcast of *Hazel* added to the overdetermined display of idealized womanhood. The program was sponsored by Ford Motor Company and the commercials, though ridiculous by today's standards in their exaggeration and objectification of gendered roles, make a statement about the conceptualization and expectation of women in relation to consumption and in relation to men. In one commercial, a male voice-over presents Ford Thunderbird models year by year, and in each image the car is adorned by a glamorous white woman.[27] Like pin-up calendar girls, the women have no relevance to the scene in which they are situated, yet they serve as a focal point. In the final vignette, a handsome young prince type opens the door for the woman, who is dressed in a formal gown, her long silk chiffon scarf blowing romantically in the wind; he then takes the driver's seat and they literally drive off into the sunset, accompanied by the theme music from *Breakfast at Tiffany's* (1961), "Moon River."

Another commercial features a blonde white woman in a white gown standing next to a white Ford Thunderbird Galaxy. The white colors dazzle, almost blindingly. The woman is singing a song, apparently dedicated to the Ford Thunderbird. Whitney Blake, the actress who plays Dorothy on *Hazel*, also advertises the car in character as Dorothy at the end of each episode, making a sales pitch to housewives. While we might assume the outlandish display of white womanhood in the car commercials is for male viewers, it is also directed to female viewers/consumers. And whereas Hazel/Shirley Booth sells washing machines, Dorothy/Whitney Blake sells cars, emphasizing that the maid takes care of the household work while the housewife can enjoy leisure and luxury.[28] The juxtaposition of the commercials within the broadcast reinforces the presentation of white, middle-class womanhood as a desirable ideal. Like Beulah, Hazel does not match up to the woman of the house, whose beauty is remarkable and made easy and whose life and style are pleasurable to look at because of their maid's labor.

Patterns of consumption are linked to class status. Employing a household servant is a noticeable act of conspicuous consumption, yet it is contradictorily and simultaneously denied through the attempts to declare that a maid or housekeeper or babysitter is "just like" a member of the family.[29] Hazel not only stands in contrast to ideals of middle-class womanhood, she also becomes the standard for middle-class consumption. Hazel helps mark a certain class of white womanhood by doing the work that women of that class would not do. At the same time, she is still aligned with other women in relation to patriarchy; she is not a particularly "feminine" woman, due to her labor and class, but her strength and ability to take on tasks avoided by the more delicate of her gender bring little or no reward in that she remains subordinated (and deferential) to men, or at least to the man who employs her.

"Natural Athlete," ostensibly about a bowling competition, shows George trying to regain his place as head of the household as Hazel oversteps boundaries.

She does so by being the newsmaker featured in the local paper and the center of attention, by having talents other than those related to housekeeping, and, most of all, by forging a close relationship (in this instance, father-like) with Harold.[30] In the episode, Hazel becomes a local bowling champion, winning not only trophies but also Harold's admiration and respect. Hazel is loud about her success in the beginning, while George responds by mentioning that he used to be quite a bowler. Hazel is intrigued, and she and Harold both want to see him bowl. George decides to secretly take a few refresher lessons so that he can compete against Hazel in the next contest and, as he tells his wife, earn Harold's admiration. By the end of the episode the title "natural athlete" is taken away from Hazel (through subterfuge) and bestowed upon George, who wins back the affection of his son. Hazel's testing of the boundaries serves, in the end, to reify familial and class positions. Even the small glimpse of her life outside the Baxter household that we are allowed is at the bowling alley, a setting in which George intrudes. Moreover, the bowling alley owner says that Hazel would be the best teacher for George, but she is not available because she works as a maid; he also confides that she "raves" about and is "absolutely devoted" to "her family" (the Baxters).

A similar testing of boundaries is seen in the episode called "Everybody's Thankful But Us Turkeys."[31] The title is ambiguous—it's not clear who the turkeys are, the employers or the employees—and its premise is deceptive: there is a heroization of Hazel and her ability to solve the family's problems, even save the family, but she ultimately does this at the expense of her own independence.[32]

The episode begins with Hazel receiving a long-distance telephone call from her sister, wishing her a Happy Thanksgiving as she prepares the Baxters' big holiday meal. The neighbors' maid, Phoebe, stops by on her way to take the day off and says that Hazel lets people take advantage of her. Hazel displays some sadness and disappointment about not being with her own family on the holiday but states that she can't leave the Baxters. She is also worried about the neighbors, the Johnsons, who are British and who have no one to help them cook a proper Thanksgiving turkey. She ends up helping the Johnsons with their Thanksgiving dinner too. Mrs. Johnson exclaims, "There's a maid!" Mr. Johnson adds, "Yes, splendid servant. Just like the servants in my father's day: always in attendance except for Christmas Eve, when Father would let them off for church." Couched as a joke, his words nonetheless are telling, as they underscore how completely Hazel has given her life over to the Baxters. His comment also both displays and naturalizes the social hierarchy between servants and masters that is traditionally more overt in British culture. The compliment from the Baxters' British neighbors—whose standards of "good help" are presumably higher by virtue of their cultural background—reconfirms just how good Hazel is. At the same time, they are perceived as not American because Americans treat their employees more humanely (even when they have to work on Thanksgiving).

Besides solving dinner dilemmas, in this episode Hazel also helps resolve family conflict. George's sister Phyllis and his brother-in-law are "at it again," and George's mother feels unneeded. Hazel helps restore order and love by pretending to quit because the work is too demanding so that Mother Baxter will be able to prepare dinner out in the kitchen. (The characters speak of going "out" to the kitchen; there are clearly marked spaces of the house that delineate a division of work and by extension, class, according to who belongs in those spaces. The dining room is a space where people can mix, though their roles remain pronounced.) Mother Baxter enlists Phyllis's aid with the cooking, and Phyllis then asks her mother to teach her how to cook, addressing one of her husband's main complaints. In the end, Mother Baxter feels needed, Phyllis's marital squabbles are smoothed over, and all this occurs because of Hazel. Hazel has not only worked hard to provide the Baxters (and the Johnsons) with Thanksgiving dinner, but she has also solved their family crisis.

When she serves the dinner, Hazel reminds the party that they ought to give thanks; George suggests that Hazel say the prayer. She expresses thanks for the meal that they are about to eat (without her) and for family (not hers). Then, to Hazel's surprise, George invites her to sit down and join them. Hazel is tear-stricken and deeply touched. On this special day, she is seated at the corner of the head of the table between George and Harold, an honored position between father and son symbolizing her importance even above the wife and mother. She seemingly has proven Phoebe and her own blood relatives wrong: she does have a family and a place to go for the holidays, right there where she works. In convincing Hazel that she has a very important place in the family, however, the family manipulates the maid. In a strange twist, it is Hazel, the one who has done all the work, who ends up feeling thankful—thankful for being thanked, and for being allowed to assume a place "in" the family, even though on most days she remains "out" in the kitchen. Hazel is, indeed, praised for all she does for the Baxters, but this praise is supposed to be enough to compensate for all the hard work and sacrifices she has made. Being called a *good* maid is her reward. The positions of "master and servant" are carefully, stealthily maintained through a system of praise and reward for the servant by appreciative employers.

Televisual, racialized domestics are performative through the mechanism of the plot, maids and actresses of color are hired to be performative (discursively and in real life). Because Hazel is of the same race as her employers, there is a particular urgency to smooth over the class barrier that stands between employer and employee, master and servant. It seems to be more difficult with white servants than with servants of color to say just how much of a family member the servant really is, which risks crossing the class boundaries that are secretly desired and enforced. With a servant who is a racial Other, lines of difference are clearly, visibly drawn in a culture that has historically been based on racial divisions and hierarchy. Class hierarchy, however, can be more ambiguous. Americans are not supposed to have a servant class (and not one that is white, at least not in contemporary society in which there is an underclass of non-white immigrants willing to work in domestic service jobs), for it goes against the principle of democracy and equality. The fact that a servant is white presents an uncomfortable dilemma. One that, on the one hand, threatens the superiority or ideal of whiteness and at the same time reveals that there are shades of whiteness. Thus white servants, in television as in real life, are often foreign, and they are often not maids per se, but nannies or nurses instead (slightly elevated in the hierarchy of servitude).

The contradiction of being family and not-family differs from maids of color who are assumed to be help (and not a relative) because of their skin color. Although treated favorably, the white servant remains an employee and is racialized in a system of domestic labor, and capitalist patriarchy helps gloss over and naturalize the fact of a white servant.

The ambiguous racial status of a white servant in *Hazel* is also illustrated in *Family Affair* and *The Brady Bunch*. Like *The Courtship of Eddie's Father* (1969–1972), discussed in chapter 4, these programs contend with the question of what the servant's role and "place" is in relation to the family. However, unlike the Japanese-born Mrs. Livingston, whose interracial relationship with the Corbetts complicates the nexus between employer and employee in *The Courtship of Eddie's Father*, Mr. French (*Family Affair*) and Alice (*Brady Bunch*) are allowed a certain degree of intimacy with their respective families. White servants are more easily assimilated and, indeed, integrated into the narrative as well as into the family, granting them access to an American identity. Rather than race separating employee and employer, class and gender emerge as the reasons for difference, though this difference remains unacknowledged, and the family at times appears not to notice that their servant is a servant. For example, in *The Brady Bunch*, it is as if everyone is pretending that Alice is not a servant. And while the butler's Britishness is conspicuous in *Family Affair*, it lends elegance rather than subservience to his character and his role in the family. Close studies of these programs demonstrate class difference but racial "unity" through white being made the class ideal, a family ideal, and the white servant being welcomed into the American family.

Family Affair (1966-1971)

Giles French is a British "gentleman's gentleman" to Bill Davis, a successful American corporate engineer living in Manhattan.[33] A happy bachelor until his orphaned nieces and nephew come to live with him, Bill has to adjust to a new lifestyle when the children move in. As does "Mr. French," as he is referred to in the family. In Brooks and Marsh's description of the program, it is Mr. French who has the most adjusting to do, because he is the one who stays home with the three children while Bill is at work.[34] This unusual parenting arrangement, with Uncle Bill as father figure and Mr. French as a kind of mother figure, turns

FIGURE 12 Sebastian Cabot as Mr. French, in *Family Affair*.

out to be successful. (Mr. French is also a second father; there is a nonbinaryness in the male servant.)

Mr. French is integrated into the family in a way that servants of color and white female servants are not allowed. Three qualities distinguish him from Other servants and privilege his position over theirs: he is white, he is male, and he is British. Though a servant, Mr. French has upper-class airs and a reserved demeanor that set him far apart from Beulah, Mrs. Livingston (in chapter 4), and Dora (in chapter 5), for example. The deference often given to a British man keeps him from being feminized. In fact, his Britishness connotes him as in some ways culturally superior to his employer—better mannered, more refined, a proper gentleman. This is not really incongruous with his status as a servant, as he is not just any servant, but a butler. Traditionally, in wealthy British households, the butler has the highest status within a hierarchy of servants that may also include a housekeeper, nanny, valet, cook, scullery maid, driver, and so forth. Being a butler is deemed a respectable profession requiring long training and sophisticated skills, while being a maid is considered a lowly, unskilled occupation—a reflection of the devaluation of women's work.[35]

Mr. French's position in the Davis household as both a parent figure to the children and a companion to Bill is revealed in an episode entitled "The Girl Graduate."[36] High school senior Cissy wants to go away to college in the fall and also wants to attend an all-night party as part of her graduation festivities. Uncle Bill and Mr. French are concerned about both. Mr. French is included in the activities of the family, and he is represented as acting (rather than only reacting as Other servants do) in relation to the plot and the other characters. He also takes the place of the missing mother with seemingly little difficulty. There is no conflict or power struggle with the employer, as with Hazel and Alice; there is no hashing out of appropriate roles between servant and employer. Rather, Bill and Mr. French discuss together Cissy's plans to attend the party and the fact that neither wants her to go. They brainstorm about how they could prevent her from going or how they could protect her if she does go. Mr. French could act as a chaperone, for instance; that the butler rather than a blood relative would fulfill this role underscores that he is not only the family servant but also a parental figure.

Mr. French has lines of dialogue that are expected of a servant character ("Yes, sir." "Dinner will be served . . ."), but he also expresses ideas as well as his personality in a way that Other servants are not able to do. It is more than simply being opinionated—Beulah, Mrs. Livingston, and Hazel are all portrayed as having opinions. It is that he is integrated into the family, and his opinions and feelings are taken into consideration as much as those of any other family member. While his world revolves around the family for whom he works just as it does for servants of color, Mr. French is more closely involved in the family in a way that Other servants, including white female servants, are not able to be. There is an evident ranking among servants whereby a British male is granted privileges and regard above both white female servants and servants of color. And he is granted access and the possibility of integration by the text into the American family.

When Cissy goes out to the party, Bill and Mr. French worry. They cannot sleep and so they sit up together, talking and playing chess. While he starts out in his usual black suit and tie, Mr. French later is seen in his robe and pajamas as is Bill (mirroring one another), and the two sit and doze in the living room while waiting for Cissy's return, just as two parents might do.[37] This familiarity with the family's business and this level of intimacy with the employer are not reached in programs such as *Beulah* (in chapter 2), *The Courtship of Eddie's Father* (in chapter 4), or *I Married Dora* (in chapter 5). None of the servants of color in these programs would show themselves to their employers in their bathrobes.[38] In *Family Affair*, even though (or perhaps because) he is called by a formal title, Mr. French, is able to enter the informal, intimate realm of the family.

The following morning, Cissy, her younger siblings Buffy and Jody, Uncle Bill, and Mr. French are having breakfast. Uncle Bill and Mr. French are relieved that Cissy has returned home safely. Cissy replies, "The important thing is you let me do it; you trusted me." The "you" could be directed not only to her Uncle Bill but to Mr. French as well. Further, she then gets up and kisses Uncle Bill *and* Mr. French. The younger children get up too. Mr. French and Bill are left to talk proudly about what a young woman Cissy has grown to become. Later they also talk about Cissy's going off to college and all that she will do that they won't know about; they are resigned (together) to that fact.

Although presented as uncomplicated, the coupling of Uncle Bill and Mr. French elicits several complex analyses. Race and gender are established by way of class and nationality. That is, as a British butler—culturally "upper crust," the pinnacle of the servant hierarchy—Mr. French is able to escape the debasement usually associated with the work of a servant, which is often exacerbated by racial hierarchy and sexist gender-role assignment.

With the absence of the wife/white woman, Mr. French fills in for the missing mother, but unlike Hazel and Alice, he does not serve to define white womanhood. Rather, the program could be interpreted as bolstering white manhood. During the rise of the women's movement, which was implicitly white and middle class, several television programs had the wife/mother conspicuously absent (see chapter 1 for discussion of the "missing mother" theme). In the late 1980s television series *Full House*, men take over the missing mother's role and prove that they can do the job just as well if not better.[39] (Interestingly, the children in this program are all girls, which reinforces patriarchy in terms of providing all male and no female role models or authority figures.) Also, the fact that a white male servant is working for a white male employer in *Family Affair* intones the relationship with a level of seriousness and plausibility of bonding in comparison to a housewife's relationship to an even further subordinated female.[40] Though, with Mr. French as a British butler in the United States, lines are crossed that would not happen in England. (Comparatively, Geoffrey in *The Fresh Prince of Bel-Air* maintains such lines, as a British Black butler in an American Black family.)

Finally, Mr. French and his employer constitute a "queer" couple as well as a white one. Though partnered with the "manly" Uncle Bill, Mr. French is not feminized in the way that male servants of color, such as Hop Sing in *Bonanza* (1959–1973) or Peter in *Bachelor Father* (1957–1962), often are (see chapter 4). Instead, his Britishness excuses and even elevates his taking on the position of a woman. This happens specifically in the American context, however, as demonstrated in an episode in which Mr. French is ridiculed at the park by other white British butlers who disdainfully say that childcare is the duty of a nanny, not a butler. Mr. French has a momentary (lasting one episode) identity crisis in having become the children's caretaker; in the end, he maintains his dignity with the added benefit of having the children's love. Hop Sing in *Bonanza*, Peter in *Bachelor Father*, and Rochester in *The Jack Benny Show* (1950–1965) have distinctly different relationships to their employers, who are presented as white "masters." These three male servants of color are more subservient, less autonomous, and physically smaller or older than the white male characters with whom they interact. They are less "masculine" and more "feminine" in their depiction.

Like many programs of the 1960s, *Family Affair* presented an all-white world in which people of color and the civil rights movement were absent.[41] However, in an era when the actual number of African American domestic servants was still high (certainly higher than the number of white servants), and when women were becoming feminists, *Family Affair* employed a strategy of displacement in having a British white male as the servant. Like *Hazel*, the program is a throwback to an earlier time and a different political and social location—in this instance, to a time of a more strict and unchallenged class and racial order. In contradiction to the social and civil outcries against discrimination, *Family Affair* not only showed a setting free of conflict, it avoided the issue of race relations and gender relations altogether by having a white male servant.

Although there is seemingly an elision of race and gender in *Family Affair*, race and gender emerge nevertheless. In an era of radical changes pertaining to the rights of people of color and women, fictional television programming tended to avoid such issues—with women (feminists) and people of color (civil rights activists) in absentia, programs like *Family Affair* engaged in a displaced discourse on the "mastery" of white maleness with whiteness defined through class and nationality. Mr. French's shade of whiteness is quite bright, as it allows him the ability to break some class and national boundaries with an American employer and family. He is received, and perceived, with respect, not just with affection, and this respect comes not only from children but from adults as well. His level of access to and authority in the (white) American family, in accordance with his portrayal of whiteness, serves to promote the institution of television by affirming patriarchal and familial stability during a time of dramatic social change.

The Brady Bunch (1969–1974)

Of the many families in the history of television, the Brady Bunch is famous for being perfect and happy to the point of becoming a common reference and cultural joke.[42] In each episode, the Brady family experiences some kind of crisis that is always resolved through cooperation. Alice, the housekeeper, often helps

FIGURE 13   Alice is at the center of this large, lively family in *The Brady Bunch*.

solve the family's problems, whether by teaching Bobby how to play baseball, finding Cindy's Kitty Carry-All doll, or writing "secret admirer" letters to Jan. Acting as referee among the children, she carefully balances her role between that of "just a maid"—though she's never called a maid—and that of a parental figure.[43] She is a key factor in the family's success and well-being. The program aired at a time of social upheaval marked by the Vietnam War, the feminist movement, and the beginnings of an erosion of the nuclear family. It presents a family structure that could be seen as emblematic of that erosion—a blended stepfamily, formed when two parents remarried and combined their offspring from previous marriages. By presenting this blended family as a happy "bunch," the program served to stabilize and sustain the image of the ideal family.

There are moments in the series when Alice's status as a maid is drawn out because the boundaries of her role are called into question, but these boundaries soon become hidden once again within the folds of "one big happy family." As in *Hazel*, the subservience of Alice's role is mitigated by praise and love. The idealized and ideological image of one big happy family masks and suppresses the undercurrent of the feminist movement, which focused particularly on deconstructing the myths surrounding women, the home, and labor.

Alice is a working woman. While she is a live-in maid, which was no longer common by the 1970s, she is in some sense an "independent woman," more so than Mrs. Brady. Carol Brady is not employed, and though the title song implies an equal coming together of "a man named Brady" and "a lovely lady," it seems that the lovely lady and her "three very lovely girls" would not have survived well if she hadn't remarried. It is included in the backstory that Mr. Brady was a widower, evoking the motherless families of some other 1960s television shows. However, it is unconfirmed whether or not Mrs. Brady was divorced, which would have had negative connotations at that time.[44] Alice, on the other hand, though she has a boyfriend, seems to forgo marriage—which of course is beneficial to the Bradys.

Comparing Alice to Carol sets up the choice between being a working woman and being a homemaker. The irony is that the housewife's life is made desirable precisely because of the work of the maid. The fact that Alice is "like one of the family," but not quite—loved but not loved as much, unofficially a member of the family but not officially—makes it apparent that the wise choice is to be the legitimate wife and "real" mother (even a stepmother), not the maid. Carol Brady is similar to Dorothy Baxter, but more "groovy" and less formal; still, she is well groomed and is rarely shown laboring. The program provides a somewhat updated look for the housewife (moving into the style of the 1970s), but she remains idealized specifically because of her privilege of not having to do housework. Alice is needed, ostensibly, because of the large house and the six children; however, she was already employed by Mr. Brady and the three boys before the Brady bunch came together, indicating their class standing as one that can afford a live-in maid.

One episode in particular encapsulates Alice's importance to the Brady family and also demonstrates her subservient role in it. "Alice Doesn't Live Here Anymore" deals directly with Alice's place in the family.[45] In the opening scene, Alice is wiping the kitchen table and Bobby comes running in, calling for her after having fallen off his bicycle. Carol Brady enters and wants to help, but Bobby prefers Alice. Mrs. Brady's feelings are hurt, but she smiles and leaves. After a moment, Alice suddenly shoos Bobby away and directs him to Mrs. Brady. Similarly, in the following scene, when Mr. Brady asks Alice to sew a button on his shirt, she obliges at first but on second thought suggests that he ask Mrs. Brady to do it. And in the next scene, brothers Peter and Greg are having a fight over a baseball glove and Alice comes to break it up, and then sends them to their (step)-mother. Alice is able to resolve each situation but deliberately takes steps to enable Mrs. Brady to do so instead. She expresses the performative role of the maid (across all racial groups). The relationship between maid and mistress has been established: the maid must defer to the mistress. Furthermore, she works to uphold the illusion that the mother is important even though she does not do housework because she has a maid to do it. This is part of the maid's performative work.

However, there is a delicate balance between how much Alice must defer and how much she must assert. For example, though Alice takes satisfaction in making the new Mrs. Brady feel like a mother, she then begins to feel less useful as the boys start to go to Mrs. Brady with their problems, news, and joys. So what is her role, she wonders. There is a paradox in that on the one hand, she is paid to take on the role (or at least the duties) of a parental figure, but on the other hand she must relinquish the role so Mrs. Brady does not feel as if she is failing as a mother. The dynamic is compounded by the fact that Mrs. Brady is a new stepmother to the boys, while Alice has been with them for a long time. Still, Alice, who has been "like a mother" to the boys, will never achieve official status—not only because she is a servant, but because she can never be a romantic partner to Mr. Brady. What exactly is the maid being paid to do?

In "Alice Doesn't Live Here Anymore," Alice is so confused by this ambiguous role that she announces to Mr. and Mrs. Brady that she cannot stay, inventing a story that she has an ailing aunt who needs her. Yes, she has been with Mr. Brady and the boys for a long time: "seven years, four months, thirteen days, nine and a half hours—the boys will be fine . . . they have you and the girls, you're a family now," she says to Mrs. Brady. The boys' reaction is somber, different than that of the girls; as Marcia wisely puts it, "The boys have known Alice much longer than we girls have, come on, let's leave them alone."

A "battle of the sexes" is a constant theme in this series. Whether the dispute is about getting a sewing machine or an electric saw (they compromised on a television), or about who gets the attic as a private bedroom, Marcia or Greg, the battles of the feminist movement are projected onto a girls-versus-boys rivalry within the Brady family. In terms of household demographics, Alice tips the scales for "the girls" (5 to 4), yet she is often desexualized or neutralized, and she can go either way, constantly balancing the family. For example, she is tomboyish in demeanor yet always wears a maid's uniform skirt with sneakers and her hair in a bun. In family plays she often takes male roles in such a way that she appears in drag, occupying more than one gender. Moreover, she was, indeed, with the boys first.

Bobby, who at age seven has always had Alice in his life, asks Greg, "Is Alice really gonna leave? . . . I thought she was gonna stay here forever." Mrs. Brady says that things aren't going to be the same without Alice, to which Mr. Brady replies, in an uncharacteristically explicit acknowledgment of the situation, "Well, we can't make her stay. Abraham Lincoln put a stop to that." Alice is being likened to a slave, and in essence, racialized. As a white and female servant, she is constructed within a racial-class-gender hierarchy in which she is aligned with the laborer and not the taskmaster, the ruled over and not the ruler. (In comparison, Mr. French and Mr. Belvedere, who are both white, British, and literally titled as male, are never likened to slaves.[46]) In this way, Alice's position as an employee and not a member of the family is made clear. She is being granted autonomy and freedom of choice about her job (she is a "freed slave"), which only serves to reify her position of subordination and indebtedness to the family when she chooses to stay (like Mrs. Livingston and Hop Sing discussed in the next chapter, who are shown as choosing to stay in servitude; likewise, Geoffrey in *The Fresh Prince of Bel-Air*).

FIGURE 14 Alice, played by Ann B. Davis, moves through all the spaces of the house in *The Brady Bunch*.

When Jan and Marcia overhear Alice speaking to a friend on the telephone, they learn her real reason for leaving. It is rare to see Alice involved with friends, with the exception of her boyfriend, Sam-the-butcher; when it occurs in this episode, we do not actually see or hear the friend. Such involvements, when they do occur, also emphasize her class status (beneath that of the architect husband and homemaker wife) because her friends are working-class, and their activities do not include fancy parties or frivolous costume balls but rather bowling tournaments (as in *Hazel*). The girls tell their mother, after she says it is "not right to eavesdrop or tattle," that Alice doesn't really have a sick aunt and feels she isn't needed anymore. Mrs. Brady then informs her husband, and the whole clan plots to make Alice realize that she is needed; their plan is called "Operation Alice." Of course, "Operation Alice" succeeds—through family cooperation.

Carol, Mike, and all six of the Brady kids stage different scenarios in which Alice's help is vital: needing a cake, needing a ride, needing to find a tie, needing clothes cleaned immediately. Alice, about to leave and supposed to be having a day off, happily joins in the charade. It is notable that in order to make Alice feel needed, the family actually invents work for her to do; from this we deduce that the real reason they need her is not so much for her labor as it is for something else. The maid is needed to mark familial roles and domestic space and to put things in order. By being not-family and by refereeing class and gender battles, she serves to tighten and recenter the American family, which was at risk of spinning out of control due to dramatic shifts in the social paradigm—the civil rights movement, a full-swing feminist movement, the growth of the counterculture. Alice serves to naturalize, normalize, and appease uncomfortable or contradictory social relations, particularly those existing within a home and a family. She brings a sense of unity and visual clarity to the notion of family. When African American domestics might have been an effrontery (or too literal an image) in the context of the civil rights movement and when Asian American servants as subservient might have been played out as the liberalism and feminism of the 1970s was dawning, the representational economy substituted white servants in these scenarios of the American home.

In an updated "all-American" TV family (i.e., a stepfamily that is otherwise perfect), Alice serves as a stabilizing force. In fact, she is at its center: in the famed nine-square opening title image of "the Brady Bunch" that is etched into the minds of television-watching Americans, Alice pops up in the central square. She is central to the family, to its everyday operation and structure as well as its larger ideology, but hers is a bargained, contractual membership in the family. She must play her role carefully, making sure the members of the family are secure and happy, healthy, and well fed. Moreover, Alice allows the viewers a sense of stability and security—by soothing familial crises within the banal plots she is also easing a larger sense of social crisis.

The presence of white servants and the receding role of servants of color, particularly by the 1970s, was an indication not that non-white servants were no longer needed but, rather, that whiteness needed to be reasserted in a culturally sensitive time. It was not as acceptable to have a simplified Black domestic character or accommodating Asian houseboy character in the portrayal of the white American family; in these cases, the story of whiteness and Americanness was told with the help of white servants. In a television world that was specifically and sometimes literally not made "in color," a world that was free of social-racial-economic crisis, with women properly in their place (or else conveniently absent or dead), the class ideal and privilege of whiteness were broadcast through the figure of the white servant.

Conclusion: Stabilizing Whiteness and Television

Throughout television (and film) history, the representation of the American family has often been made complete by the presence of a housekeeper. The "American" family that employs the domestic servant is specifically white American, although a few exceptions have existed—notably *The Jeffersons* and *The Fresh Prince of Bel-Air*, in which African American families employ an

African American maid and a Black butler, respectively. Employing such a character in these two instances served the express purpose of marking the upward mobility.

The American family has been portrayed (and understood) for the most part as white, and the ideology of the family has been based on dominant white social values. The presence of a household servant reinforces the status, both economic and racial, of the family within society. However, when the servant is white, as in several 1960s sitcoms discussed in this chapter, their position can be ambiguous. White servants are connoted as family members, and they are able to be assimilated in a way that servants of color within a white family are not. At the same time, they demonstrate that there are "shades of whiteness." Nonetheless, while white servants may be less "pure" white due to their lower class position, they are still distinguished from servants of color. Whiteness still holds privilege, for example, the potential to integrate and move into a different class position through educational opportunities, wealth accumulation, or marriage.

Ultimately, white servants can be integrated, unlike Asian servants who are "perpetual foreigners," or Black servants who are perpetually Other, or Latina servants who are perpetually suspect (as "illegal aliens"). White domestic servants are assimilable, integrated to a stronger degree, sometimes through a sexual relationship that culminates in marriage, even if a class distinction lingers (Nanny Fine does not lose her Queens accent). White characters in American media culture are those who are in the elevated position to experience romance (not just sexual liaisons), but servants of color lose out in love (Mrs. Livingston, Hop Sing, Geoffrey), and in this way, do not fully achieve the American dream.

Contemporary programs provide nuanced or less-obvious portrayals of family servants, yet the presence of a white employee in a household still serves a function in calibrating race, class, and gender dynamics. Two popular examples are *The Nanny* (1993–1999), in which a Jewish American woman, Fran Fine, works for a wealthy British man and his three children, and *Frasier* (1993–2004), in which Daphne Moon, a British woman, is hired as a nurse for Frasier's infirm father. Unlike maids of color or white maids who are older than their employers, these household servants are portrayed as fashionable and attractive, though still a bit loud and quirky, and they play lead, not secondary, roles. More significantly, they are presented as potential mates for their employers (or the employer's son in *Frasier*). Despite the class division between employee and employer, when the servant is white there is the possibility of class mixing—while race mixing remains a line that is not crossed.[47] Both *The Nanny* and *Frasier*, along with *Who's the Boss?*, come to series conclusions with the servants ascending into the position of spouse through a wedding between employer and employee—a Hollywood happy ending, indeed. Though initially a tinged shade of white, these white servants achieve a brighter whiteness by marrying into the dominant class.

FIGURE 15 Judith Light plays Angela Bower in *Who's the Boss?* in which the woman is the boss-employer, and there is chemistry with the man she has hired to help with the household.

While servants of color are desexualized because of the threat and fear of miscegenation, some white servants are presented as highly attractive, for example, the sexy Miss Fine in *The Nanny* and the hunky Tony Micelli in *Who's the Boss?*, as well as, of course, the fetching Fraulein Maria in the well-loved film *The Sound of Music*. White servants are at a different racial and class starting point than are servants of color. For example, in the backstories of *The Nanny* and *Who's the Boss?*, Miss Fine and Tony have come to these jobs as a matter of circumstance, not of profession. There is a feeling that taking the job is a downgrade as well as temporary.[48] It is made clear that both had successful careers, though in working-class occupations, prior to their being hired as servants—Fran as a beautician and Tony as a minor-league baseball player. Moreover, being a nanny, governess, or nurse whose work involves taking care of children or the elderly is different from being a maid who labors in a hot kitchen or scrubs floors and cleans toilets (and whose kin may also have toiled in domestic service in a previous generation).[49] Daphne in *Frasier* is formally hired as a nurse, although she does more cooking and light housekeeping than nursing. White servants have access to their "masters" in a way that servants of color do not: their "masters" might just marry them, removing them from their position of service, ultimately erasing their status of servant, and rendering their work as servants as merely temporary. By contrast, in instances where women of color are sexualized, the sexual access and sexual power is usually unidirectional and gender-specific—from white male to woman of color.

FIGURE 16 Tony, played by Tony Danza, as housekeeper in *Who's the Boss?* is seen as both dominant and domestic.

In "The Possessive Investment in Whiteness," George Lipsitz analyzes both the symbolic and material meanings of whiteness in American culture. He begins by recalling Richard Wright's answer to a French reporter's question about "the Negro Problem": "There isn't any Negro problem; there is only a white problem." Lipsitz writes, "By inverting the reporter's question, Wright called attention to its hidden assumptions—that racial polarization comes from the existence of blacks rather than from the behavior of whites, that black people are a 'problem' for whites rather than fellow citizens entitled to justice, and that unless otherwise specified, 'American' means white."[50]

Whiteness is a place of structural advantage because it has material value. Whiteness is literally an investable commodity in such realms as education, the housing market, consumer lending, and employment opportunities, where

FIGURE 17 Nanny Fine, played by Fran Drescher, is vibrant and loud, her working-class background works its way into the upper-class Sheffield household and into the hearts of the family members, including that of her boss (they eventually get married), in *The Nanny*.

racial segregation and discrimination mean that it pays to be white. And it is an advantage vis-à-vis the law. Generally and globally, light-skinned people (according to a caste-bias, or colorism) are treated better when they are lighter/whiter. Lipsitz writes, "The possessive investment in whiteness is not a simple matter of black and white; all racialized minority groups have suffered from it, albeit to different degrees and in different ways."[51]

Furthermore, whiteness and racialization encapsulate and guide how whites operate in the social world. Racialization is both a process that occurs within a historical moment and one that develops over time and hence changes in meaning, for example, with the rise of capitalism and other industries as well as with the influx of different immigrant groups. But the significance of race and whiteness as organizing and structuring principles of group life remains constant.[52] If we can trace how whiteness and racial domination came about and also examine closely how they continue to develop within our social structure and cultural ideology, we will be taking a step toward preventing the continuation of racial, class, and gender oppression.

We must see whiteness, as well as the shades of whiteness that speak to social hierarchies and social barriers based on race, gender, and class. The seemingly innocuous, lovable, and sometimes even marriageable white servant in television is a key figure in studying and critiquing the intertextual discursive negotiations in the meanings and significance of race and whiteness in American culture. And, "white" is televisual. It is telegenic, it is audience friendly, it is mainstream and maintainable. Along with the rise of whiteness studies in academia, recent culture has seen a rising (though not necessarily a raising of) consciousness about whiteness on the part of whites.

Ruth Frankenberg writes as an update of her earlier work that "the notion of whiteness as unmarked norm is revealed to be a mirage or indeed, to put it even more strongly, a white delusion.... In fact, whiteness is in a continual state of being dressed and undressed, of marking and cloaking."[53] Whiteness is invisible only to some, when one chooses not to see it and, more importantly, not to see its accompanying privilege or at least its link to class and patriarchy. Uncertainty about the meanings of whiteness is not new; efforts to delineate in psychological and material terms what the status of white entails in the United States have gone on as long as racial difference has existed, from the time the European explorers set foot on the continent. But according to Howard Winant, there is a particularly acute post–World War II, post–civil rights anxiety through which there has been a "profound shift in the global logic of race . . . in racial formation."[54] In the concept of racial formation that Winant and Omi developed, representational culture and social-historical structure are interlocked: "To represent, interpret, or signify upon race, then, to assign meaning to it, is to locate it in social structural terms. It is the connection between culture and structure, which is at the core of the racial formation process."[55] Television, with its discourses of race and whiteness, is a core part of this.

It is in the very recent era that white people in mass culture have begun to see their whiteness, that "white" is emerging as an acknowledged and specific social position. Viewers and individuals are beginning to resist white as the desired status quo. Nevertheless, in televisual culture, white culture remains the basis for "American" culture. And in programs that feature a white servant, whiteness serves to stabilize television, and television works to stabilize whiteness.

4

Unresolvable Roles

Asian American Servants as
Perpetual Foreigners

Over several centuries, Western culture has broadly conceived of the contact between East and West as an encounter between the feminine and the masculine. In a history of encounters as well as a history of representation, dominance and masculinity are attributed to Westerners, obedience and femininity to Asian women and men.[1] A historically predominant trope of the Asian woman or man in American television has been as a servant. Examples include Hop Sing (Victor Sen Yung), the Chinese houseboy in the long-running program *Bonanza* (1959–1973), Peter Tong (Sammee Tong), the domestic servant in *Bachelor Father* (1957–1962), and Fuji Kobiaji (Yoshio Yoda), a Japanese POW who served as a "houseboy" in *McHale's Navy* (1962–1966). One of the top ten programs in the late 1950s and early 1960s, *Have Gun Will Travel*, had two Asian characters actually named Hey Boy (Kam Tong) and Hey Girl (Lisa Lu). And even though he fought crime in *The Green Hornet* (1966–1967), Kato, played by the inimitable Bruce Lee, donned a white jacket and black bow tie as the Green Hornet's valet, condensing and controlling the overwhelming talents of a martial artist in the form of a humble houseboy.

Perhaps the most recognized among the Asian servants is Mrs. Livingston in *The Courtship of Eddie's Father* (1969–1972), played by Hollywood performer Miyoshi Umeki. The character has an intertextual connection to the servile figure she plays in *Sayonara* (1957), for which Umeki won an Academy Award for

Unresolvable Roles • 91

FIGURE 18 Miyoshi Umeki in an Academy Award–winning role in *Sayonara* (1957). Her character, Katsumi, is in a relationship with airman Joe Kelly, but their marriage is not supported by the U.S. military.

Best Supporting Actress, the first (and still the only) Asian American woman to win this high-profile acting accolade. As with Hattie McDaniel before her, the social imagination about who Miyoshi Umeki could play was limited. Sexist racism or racist sexism continues to affect the imagery, knowledge production, and treatment (or mistreatment) of Asian Americans.

As with other servants, Asian servants articulate gender roles vis-à-vis their white employers. With both male and female Asian servants, sexuality is a primary means to define gender, race, and class identities and hierarchies. The close analyses of *Bonanza*, *Bachelor Father*, and *The Courtship of Eddie's Father*, with notes about *Twin Peaks* (1990–1991), reveal that the sexualization or desexualization of the Asian servant delimits the way in which they are able to enter the American family and the family of Americans. The representation of race as gendered and gendered as feminine for Asian Americans maintains a line of difference; it is a line that cannot be crossed, though there are discursive moments of possibility (which are ultimately sewn or sutured back into the dominant picture of the American family as white). In a discourse of belonging, Asian servants never quite belong, and their narrative presence is made useful but conditional.

Broadcast on ABC from 1969 to 1972, *The Courtship of Eddie's Father* explored differences in race, gender, and nationhood within the historical context of the civil rights movement, the feminist movement, and the Vietnam War. The series features widower Tom Corbett (Bill Bixby), who is in search of a new wife and a mother for his six-year-old son Eddie (Brandon Cruz). Although Tom Corbett never finds quite the right woman, both he and Eddie have Mrs. Livingston (Miyoshi Umeki), a widowed Japanese war bride who serves as their always-dependable housekeeper.[2] She is close to the family in that she takes care of their most basic needs in a space that is private and intimate, the home; at the same time, she is set apart from Eddie and his father by the fact that she is their employee, Asian, and a woman.

The image of the Asian woman becomes significant in relation to the image of the white American characters, both male and female, and the story of her Asianness unfolds in relation to the story of idealized American domesticity. What it means to be Asian and a woman—as well as a servant—is not completely fixed, and it is within the discourse of what I refer to as American Orientalism that identities struggle for clarity.[3] Racial identity is in negotiation within this television text through gender and nationality, in accordance with a uniquely American Orientalism that sets up a system of interracial identity formation. The process of identity formation is not a one-way projection (from "white" to "Other," for instance); rather, while upholding whiteness and patriarchy, there are moments of uncertainty. I observe and identify these as unresolvable moments, of which there are many when it comes to Asian American servant characters. And yet the Asian domestic servant experiences gendered subordination.

Orientalism: Defining the Self as Dominant by Dominating the Other

The concept of Orientalism as articulated by Edward Said in his 1978 book can be used to describe the maintenance of dominance and hierarchy through discursive images. Said begins by stating that Orientalism is a way of coming to terms with the Orient that is based on its place in European and Western experience: "The Orient has helped to define Europe (or the West) as its contrasting image, idea, personality, experience."[4] Defining the Orient is less an attempt to understand the East than to define the West. That is, Orientalism is part of the West's search for self-identity through the Other.[5]

In his introduction to the book, Said offers three definitions of Orientalism. First, it is an academic designation. Someone whose area of specialty is the Orient, whether in anthropology, sociology, philology, history, or another discipline, is an Orientalist (though the term is not preferred because of its colonialist connotations). Second, Orientalism is a style of thought, allowing writers, philosophers, political theorists, economists, and imperial administrators to make distinctions between the East and the West. And third, Orientalism can be analyzed as "the corporate institution for dealing with the Orient—dealing with it by making statements about it, authorizing views of it, describing it, by teaching it, settling it, ruling over it: in short, Orientalism as a Western style for dominating, restructuring, and having authority over the Orient."[6] It is this third meaning of Orientalism that is most relevant to the study of the Asian servant in U.S. culture as it involves the interrelation between text and context, between "viewing" and "ruling."

The United States has a long history of military involvement in Asia, either as an overt aggressor or as a purported protector. From the Spanish-American War, when the United States paid twenty million dollars to acquire the Philippines, through World War II, the Korean War, and the Vietnam War, the United States has sought to exert domination grounded in a sense of superiority or paternalism.

This military role has given rise to, and has in turn been encouraged by, a series of motivating acts and images that depict white American superiority and dominance over Asians and Asian Americans—from political cartoons, brochures, newspaper stories; to plays, poems, and novels; to television news coverage, films, graffiti, and racially specific hate crimes. How do forms of media, including television, "serve" to sustain an Orientalist dynamic? In what ways do the representations of Asians as servants demonstrate—as perhaps a preferred racial group but under the social contract of being uncomplaining and "honorary whites"—the conditional acceptance of Asian Americans? What other terms of engagement could there be between Asian Americans and white characters?

One objection to Said's formulation of Orientalism is the claim that it renders the Oriental figure a powerless victim. Some postcolonial critics, in fact, find it problematic to so rigidly delineate positions of oppressor/oppressed, dominant/passive, subject/object; they contend that to do so only reaffirms that system of power.[7] I accept Orientalism as a discourse and as a hierarchical system of representation; where I depart from Said is in adapting the concept of Orientalism for the specifics of American media culture, which can be seen as a potential space for negotiating power and identity. Though the non-Asian figure has more power, usually by virtue of their wealth, political strength, or cultural and historical dominance, the Asian figure has a presence that in moments moves beyond the prescribed racial meaning.

Mrs. Livingston in *The Courtship of Eddie's Father* is not a victim and not oppressed (though she is not shown to exert independence or a private life). She possesses moral authority in the family, especially with respect to her role in raising Eddie; her gentle opinions are considered and abided by. She exhibits a desire to be with (and somehow be a part of) the Corbett family, even as a worker or surrogate mother and wife. The series reveals cultural exchange, even if lightly done or in the form of clichés; for example, Eddie knows to remove his shoes, and he and his father eat Japanese food. Mrs. Livingston's presence in the motherless, wifeless American household destabilizes and challenges traditional concepts of the nuclear, same-race family formation. The unique framework of American Orientalism allows for such discursive activity. At the same time, the weight of social perceptions of Asian women as submissive and compliant is heavy. Such beliefs and desires, unconscious and conscious, are long-standing and continue today. There has been a conundrum about how to absorb or integrate Asians into America, socioculturally as well as in terms of screen presence.

Historical Backdrop: War Brides and Houseboys

In the three decades after World War II, an estimated 45,000 war brides came to the United States from Japan. Stranded in a foreign land, submerged in a strange language and culture, these Japanese women were not only immigrants but also female and non-white. They depended economically and socially upon their predominantly white American husbands.

The war brides encountered a U.S. labor market largely closed to them. Even the highly skilled and educated among them experienced downward mobility upon arriving in the United States. Opportunities for the war brides in many ways paralleled those that existed for issei (first-generation Japanese Americans) in the prewar period. Much of their employment consisted of traditional women's work transferred to the market (sewing, serving food), and took place within ethnic businesses (waitressing in Japanese restaurants). The war brides were disproportionately involved in private household work. In 1960, the percentage of war brides working as domestic servants was slightly lower than the percentage among the issei, but higher than among the nisei (second-generation Japanese Americans) or white Americans. As Nakano Glenn articulates, "Despite the differences [between] war brides and issei and nisei, there was nonetheless a sense of fellowship among them, if only because of the way they were treated by the dominant culture. As a result of their visible racial resemblance, all Japanese American women were lumped together by outsiders. Thus, whether they wanted to be a part of the ethnic community or not, their life chances were to a great extent determined by their ethnicity."[8]

A century earlier, in the late 1800s, many of the Chinese men in America had entered domestic service. The figure of the Asian houseboy, specifically a Chinese manservant, has its historical roots in the large Chinese "bachelor society" that arose in the United States as a result of legalized discrimination. The Page Law passed by the U.S. Congress in 1875 restricted the number of female immigrants from China, and the 1882 Chinese Exclusion Act banned new Chinese immigration outright. Darrell Hamamoto notes that "discriminatory labor practices, restrictive legislation, and immigration laws directed against Asians prevented the formation of 'traditional' families."[9]

The single Chinese male figure without a family of his own had to be managed, economically and socially. The large presence of these men in the American West (most Chinese entered through California) threatened to glut the labor market. At the same time, with no "women of their own," they seemed to pose a threat to whiteness through liaisons with white women. Fears were so high that anti-miscegenation laws were quickly passed in California and Washington during the late nineteenth century. The sexual threat posed by the Chinese man was further quelled by propagating the image of a weak and feminized Chinese male servant. The dominant society created for itself an ideological bargain, a kind of three-for-the-price-of-one: a lowly servant who was at once economically subordinated, racially inferior, and an example of failed masculinity, thereby bolstering the economic, racial, and male privilege of his employers.

Asian men effectively did the work of white women. In the process, their labor helped smooth over class tensions in white society (by occupying a servant class so whites wouldn't have to). Ronald Takaki argues, "Thus, through Chinese labor, republican virtues of industry and thrift could be promoted and the work ethic could enable men to be 'something else.' Even the wives of such men could become 'something else,' for they could depend upon Chinese house servants to lighten their domestic duties."[10] The employment of Asian servants helped usher in a new class of white bourgeoisie at the expense of Asian men and later, Asian women.

Various forms of cultural representation and discourse reinforced the perception of an inferior, racialized Other who could be justifiably exploited and abused. The notion of "the heathen Chinee" materialized in poems, cartoons, plays, and political platforms. In describing Mark Twain and Bret Harte's popular play *Ah Sin!* (1876), James Moy has written, "The process of comparison had a socializing effect on the incoming European immigrant population because its members, viewing the stereotypical representation on stage, could laugh at and deny any connection with the garish characterizations while affirming their new allegiance to America."[11] In the play, Broderick calls Ah Sin a "slant eyed son of the yellow jaunders . . . you jabbering idiot . . . you moral cancer, you unsolvable political problem."[12]

Popularized and prejudiced ideas about Chinese men continued to inform and regulate social interactions throughout the twentieth century and beyond. The figure of the undesirable, asexual, Asian eunuch remains as common a concept as the exotic, consumable Asian lotus blossom. While interracial contact is allowed between white males and Asian females, the sexist and racist double standard frowns on the union of an Asian male and a white female.[13]

Race is gendered, Asianness is feminized—women are hyperfeminine, and men are emasculated. Sexist racism and racist sexism are frames within which Asian and Asian American women and men are (mis)perceived. Twentieth-century image production regresses to nineteenth-century ideas about Asians as subjugated laborers.

In a section called, "The World the Coolies Made" in his book, *Everybody was Kung Fu Fighting: Afro-Asian Connections and the Myth of Cultural Purity*, Vijay Prashad writes,

> *Coolie* is a word that produces, among Indian and Chinese people, the same gut response as does *n*—— among blacks. It has no established etymology; some place it from the Tamil *kuli* ("hire"), others find it in use in sixteenth-century Portugal as *Koli*, after the name of a Gujarati community, still others notice that it sounds like the Chinese *ku-li* ("bitter labor") or like the Fijian *kuli* meaning "dog." One way or the other to be called a coolie is to be denigrated, and to be considered at best as a laborer with no other social markers or desires.[14]

Coolies were historically both enslaved and "free" laborers. Their social and economic status, their existence, was controlled and subordinated by white dominance. Chinese immigrant men to the United States in the nineteenth century were second-class citizens, barred from the legal rights that white men possessed (such as owning land or being able to get married or to vote), excluded from the opportunities that white men exploited and devalued as fellow human beings. Legalized discrimination has been ameliorated, and opportunities for non-whites and women have opened up. Improvement in how Asian American men are respected and valued, however, is harder to measure, as their visibility is not as dramatic on the national political stage or as prominent on film and television screens.[15] The fictional roles in which they do appear are symptomatic of particular racial ideologies and are indicative of lost opportunities to expand racial discourse through media culture. The representation of Asians as domestic servants tells a story about limited vision, potential change, and reticent creativity.

Television Discourse

Racial identity is forged on television through discursive flow. The discursive flow is hegemonic, that is, dominated by the culture of patriarchy and whiteness in which it exists, but at the same time it allows room for negotiation and for shifts in meaning. Gyan Prakash uses the term "discourse vacillating," and Lisa Lowe calls it "discourse instability."[16] Discourse is a structure that defines and demarcates race, but it simultaneously is a mechanism through which racial meanings can be challenged and resisted. Furthermore, discourse operates both textually and contextually.

Evelyn Nakano Glenn writes that "the black cleaning woman, the Mexican maid, the Japanese housecleaner, became stereotyped images that helped to rationalize and justify their subordination."[17] Such images that bolster and inform American culture are related to actual occupations for women of color. Domestic service, according to Nakano Glenn, is a "ghettoizing occupation." The persistent and patterned position of specific groups, such as Japanese American women, in a segmented labor market reveals social hierarchies of gender, race, and class. Controlling images of the racialized domestic contribute to and participate in the larger discourses of gender, race, and class, and of what—or who—is "American."[18]

The definition of domestic work as women's work marks the inherent sexism in the position of the domestic servant. At the same time, domestic work performed by a person of color marks racial and class hierarchies as well. For example, Mrs. Livingston in the position of a housekeeper does double duty: she performs the traditional gendered work of wife and mother while maintaining racial difference and lines of national identity. Domestic work in the United States and the representation of domestic work are a function of both patriarchy and whiteness, and of capitalism as well. The popular imaginary in both cultural representation and the structural economy reinvents and reinforces the figure of the racialized domestic.

The character of the Black mammy is another woman of color who "knows her place," but this image carries a different discursive and cultural resonance. Given the history of American slavery, the dynamics between African American servant and white employer are always shadowed by a racial antagonism and the fear of rebellion against the oppressor. The jovial, plump, seemingly content mammy is a smiling performance of servitude, but Black servitude was originally developed and forced through slavery; therefore, the potential for rebellion or revolution against this bond(age) creates tension between Black servant and white master or mistress. The Asian servant, on the other hand, because of the generalized perception that Asian culture is passive (even grateful), is subservient in a way that does not raise the fear or threat of resistance. Furthermore, the physical depiction of Asians has rendered them unthreatening.

When a man of color serves as the domestic, he too is subject to whiteness and patriarchy. Not only is he subordinated according to race but he is also emasculated. Even the nomination Asian house "boy" presents the Asian man as stripped of a man's status. He becomes feminized/feminine in a way that white men who labor in domestic spaces do not. (Consider the characterizations of Mr. French, Mr. Belvedere, and hunky Tony (in *Who's the Boss?*), for example.) In Tasha Oren's essay about "Angry Asians and the Politics of Cultural Visibility," she writes, "Sexuality is understandably a central filter for stereotypical representation, as many scholars have noted, following Edward Said's field-defining exploration of the orientalist impulse. But masculinity—even in its purely physical expression of power, speed, and size—functions as a complex signifier that, as Susan Jeffords has argued, speaks to contemporary definitions of nation and citizenship."[19] Like Mrs. Livingston in *The Courtship of Eddie's Father*, as men, Hop Sing in *Bonanza* and Peter in *Bachelor Father* fill in for the missing female in the family. And as part of the depiction of their Asianness, none are portrayed as angry or dissatisfied. They are polite if not naive, they are only helpful—to the narrative power of the main characters.

Three houseboys and Mrs. Livingston appeared around the same time and were among the only Asian American characters on television until thirty years later, when *All-American Girl* starring (though not written by) Margaret Cho aired. It would be twenty more years until *Fresh Off the Boat* (*Dr. Ken*, and *Kim's*

Convenience, a Canadian production available to U.S. viewers) offered Asian American and Asian Canadian faces, stories, and perspectives—fifty years after *The Courtship of Eddie's Father*, *Bachelor Father*, and *Bonanza*.

Bonanza (1957–1973)

In *Bonanza*, which was set in the 1860s but made in the 1960s, the character of the dedicated Chinese male domestic, Hop Sing (Victor Sen Yung), serves to fill the absent white woman's role (a role that was conspicuously missing in other television programs of this era as well). He is a character with whom the white male protagonists can compare and affirm themselves: Hop Sing is not white, not "masculine," and not American.[20] He, a coolie, his seeming emptiness-as-otherness is simultaneously an alterity that "projects back" something of its own—a perspective, a spirit. Despite being subordinated, Asian Others have and perform presence.

The popular genre of the Western is set in the American West during the period of white settlement, mainly in the latter half of the nineteenth century. The protagonists in a Western not only encounter Indians but also interact occasionally with Negroes, befriend people originally from Mexico, and hire Oriental immigrants as their servants. This Hollywood formula tells a particular story of the American past and facilitates nationalism through the idealization of the white male hero. Common subtexts in the Western—taking over the land and devaluing the cultures of Native Americans/Indigenous Peoples and Mexicans, avoiding newly freed Black slaves, exploiting the labor of Chinese people, all while protecting white women and white children—are carefully crafted to express the establishment of nationhood.[21]

The character of Hop Sing first appeared in 1876 as a laundryman in a play by Bret Harte called *Two Men of Sandy Bar*.[22] While the character was toned down in the television reincarnation, the character Hop Sing still incorporated the disempowered trope of being a servant. These roles emphasize a socioeconomic niche shared with African Americans. Another major television Western at this time was *The Big Valley* (1965–1969), which starred Barbara Stanwyck as a California matriarch and featured the character of Silas (played by Napoleon Whiting) as the Barkley family's majordomo.[23]

Hop Sing's Chineseness is drawn out while his masculinity is de-emphasized and diluted. His costuming consists of a traditional "Chinese" shirt with embroidered buttons fastened all the way to the "mandarin collar," flowy, wide-legged cotton pants hemmed at the ankles (in contrast to thick denim jeans with leather chaps that the other men wear), and a long, single braid (a queue). His long hair and loose clothing are asexual and foreign in comparison to the cowboy garb and hard boots donned by the Western men. Hop Sing has a thick accent and uses incorrect grammar and malapropisms, which are occasionally corrected by his

FIGURE 19 Victor Sen Yung's Hop Sing with Hoss, played by Dan Blocker, in *Bonanza*.

employers. His being Chinese, being feminized (and infantilized, which is also desexualizing), and being a servant are inextricably linked to each other.

Viewer identification is aligned with patriarch Ben Cartwright (Lorne Greene), with his beefy son Hoss (Dan Blocker), and most often with the sensitive and handsome younger son Little Joe (Michael Landon). These three form a triumvirate of goodness, morality, and justice. Many episodes in the series have to do with doing what is right and putting trust in the law. This faith and loyalty to the system, and to God, enshrouds the different positions people have in the society of the West. Not only is Hop Sing's status as a servant naturalized, but it is divinely ordered.

In the period of westward expansion, European Americans forged an identity through the distinct and specific demarcation between themselves and the "savage" Indians, "half-civilized" Mexicans, and "heathen" Chinese. African Americans, in accordance with the justification for slavery, were considered inferior. The putative superiority of whites became the core of an emerging sense of identity. Immigration and exclusion laws directed specifically toward Asians bolstered white identity. Lisa Lowe writes, "Immigration exclusion acts and naturalization laws have thus been not only means of regulating the terms of the citizen and the nation-state but also an intersection of the legal and political terms with an orientalist discourse that defined Asians as culturally and racially "other" in times when the United States was militarily and economically at war with Asia."[24] A sense of righteousness accompanied western expansion: it was "manifest destiny." Racial and economic imperatives were in operation in the settlement of, and struggle to establish, the American West.[25]

Hop Sing as the domestic figure in the Cartwright family brings together otherness and servitude. As a racial Other and like the African American domestic, his position as a servant is naturalized but also made spectacle of; and while the mammy's Blackness detracts from femininity, being Asian is linked to Hop Sing's being feminized. His work for the motherless household—cooking, serving, cleaning—is performed with efficiency. The things that concern him, as expressed by his lines and the lines that other characters speak to him, revolve around domestic duties, for example, comments on the meals and requests for certain work to be done.

As with most servants, we know little about Hop Sing's own history, his family, his friends. He seems to have no life other than the one he gives to the Cartwrights. Rather than knowing what and who he is, we know what and who he is not: a Western white hero. Hop Sing is not John Wayne. He is not the deep-voiced, commanding, economically advantaged ("best boss") Ben Cartwright. Hop Sing scurries around, fulfilling traditionally feminine household duties and thinking about how to make the people he works for comfortable. He speaks when spoken to, and then in self-effacing ways. Moreover, in his position as a servant, his race and gender are conflated and collapsed, setting him in relation to a white male ideal and naturalizing this relationship. There are only a handful of episodes in which Hop Sing plays a more prominent part, and two in particular, that focus on Hop Sing and the experience of being discriminated against—cruelly attacked, denied legal rights, and in need of protection, if not by the law, then by his employers.

There are two episodes to examine as exceptional in focusing on Hop Sing (who even speaks without an accent in one), and doing so in a way that potentially offered a new model for representing an Asian American character but which also demonstrate that this only occurred in aberrant, "one-off" scripts. "The Fear Merchants" aired during the program's first season, in January 1960.[26] The exceptional episode featuring Hop Sing's experience in Virginia City, Nevada, serves to represent racism against Asian Americans as a displacement of African Americans who, at that very time in the late 1950s and early 1960s, were agitating for civil rights. Furthermore, because the storyline has Hop Sing's relatives as the victims of racism and Hop Sing's employers as those who ultimately force some form of justice, *Bonanza* is safely positioned: it does not risk upsetting white and Black viewers in the midst of the civil rights struggle external to the television text, and it does not implicate the televisual white family in their perpetuation of social inequality. The Cartwrights are seen as indignant about the mistreatment of Chinese people, and Hop Sing's relatives in particular, while ahistorically, those delivering acts of racial discrimination are portrayed as bad and wrong (i.e., in that era, unequal treatment and abuse of non-whites was common practice and legally sanctioned).

Another ahistorical assertion on the part of the text is when eighteen-year-old Jimmy Chang (Guy Lee) is wrongly accused of killing a white woman; after a beating, he is being attended to by the Cartwright brothers who take the lead over Jimmy's own relatives in Jimmy's father's house, when a mob arrives.[27] A member of the mob throws a rock that crashes through the living room window, and he demands to take Jimmy to jail or else to "get a rope." Then Jimmy stands up to say, "Father, in America a man is innocent until proven guilty, isn't that right, Hoss?" Of course, this basic tenet did not apply to Chinese immigrants in the 1800s, or to African Americans in the 1900s. But it is a statement that the program wishes to foreground, as part of a dialectic about democracy.

The episode is also about a race-baiting mayoral candidate, who, when confronted by patriarch Ben Cartwright, retorts that Cartwright does not have a vote to cast (as presumably his Ponderosa Ranch is outside Virginia City limits).[28] Thus the Cartwrights are aligned with the politically disenfranchised though morally justified Chinese in the episode, as well as with African Americans combating racism outside the television program. In the end, when the townspeople learn of Jimmy's innocence (the viewers and Cartwrights know all along), they disband the mob and tear down the campaign posters. Jimmy is freed from the jail by Little Joe, and Hoss tells him he is free and to "go on," if he wants to go to college as has been his stated goal. Thus the good people of Virginia City do what is right within the bounds of the political system by not voting for a bigoted individual (and for not lynching a man). Individual politicians may be corrupt, but the law remains steadfast. The employers of the racialized servant are outside the system, part of the Wild West and not part of racist conspiracies; at the same time, the program affirms a sense of civil society by presenting the Cartwrights as, essentially, enlightened even beyond the historical setting.

Bonanza performs its own kind of retrospective displacement of a history of racist practices in the settlement of the West by an extradiegetic civil rights mentality, which was the context for the production of the series.

In Steven Classen's essay about television history and race, he researched *Bonanza* and uncovered that some members of the cast espoused a pro–civil rights, antisegregation stance. In "Southern Discomforts: The Racial Struggle over Popular TV," Classen analyzes the "cultural and artistic agitation" campaign carried out by student activists in Jackson, Mississippi, in 1963–1964 involving television programs such as *Bonanza*.[29] Responding to a letter by student Austin C. Moore III requesting stars to refuse to perform before a segregated audience, Dan Blocker sent a telegram that was reprinted in the local newspaper: "I have long been in sympathy with the Negro struggle for total citizenship; therefore, I would find an appearance of any sort before a segregated house completely incompatible with my moral concepts—indeed repugnant." Actors Lorne Greene and Michael Landon also withdrew their appearances. This caused rancor and embarrassment. Yet, despite a counterattack calling for a "blackout" of *Bonanza* by Jackson's (white) viewers and even though letters to the editor condemned the stars that failed to appear in their town as "immoral, unethical, untrustworthy, un-Christian, liberal, or communistic," the program maintained its popular ratings.[30]

In the opening of an episode directly about racism, "The Fear Merchants," Yung is acting with Phillip Ahn who plays his uncle; in this scene, Victor Sen Yung/Hop Sing speaks without an accent and in close-up. It is an unusual or confusing moment, not only in terms of his character's portrayal and in the dignity afforded to the Asian American actors, but also because it is inconsistent with the production. It could be considered a "gaffe," or it could be considered a moment of resistance (or at least a deliberately overlooked inconsistency on the part of the director and producers). In these few insider moments shared among Asians without the presence of white characters, it is as if viewers are being shown a different program, one that features Asian Americans as protagonists with subjectivity, emotions, ambitions. It is an example of discursive looseness, a negotiated Orientalism that pushes back against hegemony and destabilizes consent on the part of three parties—producers, performers, and viewers.

In this episode, there is a very rare figure, that of an Asian American. Jimmy is a stable-hand, representing a different life path from Hop Sing's generation of men working as cooks, laundrymen, and houseboys. He speaks and communicates in English with facility, he dresses in western clothing, and his relatives plan to celebrate his eighteenth "American birthday" with a cake and American flags.

But there is a glaring absence: there are no Asian women. Where are Jimmy's mother, sisters, aunties? He does not have a girlfriend, which would connote his romantic inclinations or possibilities (and he is constantly referred to as "boy" by both friends and foes). There is no explanation for this "bachelor society" in which the characters cook and clean for themselves, and seem to reproduce asexually as, somehow, Jimmy is Lee Chang's son.[31] What began promisingly closes with making heroes out of the white characters and not of any Chinese man. Still, the script makes the point, through Ben Cartwright, that a "tong is a protective organization composed of civilized people" rather than the presumption that it is a criminal "gang." Furthermore, Philip Ahn's performance as young Jimmy Chang's father is calm yet captivating, almost regal; there are medium close-ups of him revealing his emotions of dismay, fortitude, and knowingness. Though, he does not express anger at the unjust treatment he receives as a Chinese person, or at the dangerous treatment his son is receiving. Dressed in Chinese costuming marking visually his clear Otherness and compromising mainstream/Western notions of masculinity, Mr. Ahn/Mr. Chang, nonetheless, draws out a character that earns respect. It is a rare episode for this and several other reasons.[32] The rationale for studying an aberrant storyline shows that the program had liberal intentions but ultimately (and ironically) demonstrates that the Asian Americans are unassimilable "perpetual foreigners" who do not appear during the "normal" course of the series. Hop Sing's private life or personal experiences cannot be accommodated; rather, it is his character who is accommodating within the diegesis and beyond it as an Asian American man and actor.

Another example of a creative act that participates in redirecting racial discourse and redefining Orientalism in an American context comes in the exceptional episode "The Lonely Man." Airing in the program's last season and written by Michael Landon (who plays in the role of Little Joe), "The Lonely Man" refers to Hop Sing, who is the main character occupying every scene in this episode.

The plot of the episode involves Hop Sing taking a vacation, going to pan for gold, and meeting a woman who he takes care of and cares for; she in turn falls in love with him. The woman is white, and fragile, a runaway whose background is obscure; she is like a hungry little animal and alone in the woods. Hop Sing uses his cooking skills to feed her, he approaches her gently and intuitively (i.e., gradually over the course of what appears to be many days), until one stormy night, she seeks shelter in the small cabin Hop Sing is staying in. To escape the thunder, cold, and her fear, she even runs to the cot where Hop Sing remains facing the other direction, and while chaste, this is a clear signification of their bonding. It is also utterly unusual, both historically as well as representationally. A relationship between an Asian man and a white woman is scandalous, and ultimately, illegal, as Hop Sing and "Missy" (as he calls her) naively and heartbreakingly learn when they ride into Virginia City to get married. Not only are they denied a marriage license, they are also attacked by a crowd. What began as a hopeful outing for Hop Sing, became a joyful surprise, but ended in devastation.

This storyline in *Bonanza* is reminiscent of the silent film, *Broken Blossoms* (1919), directed by D. W. Griffith and intended to be "sympathetic" to the "yellowman," but which emasculates the Chinese man (performed in yellow face by a white actor) who holds Lillian Gish's character and whiteness in adulation.

FIGURE 20 Victor Sen Yung as Hop Sing, in *Bonanza*.

It is important to point out that this episode, "The Lonely Man," gives voice and motivation to Hop Sing apart from his life as a houseboy, and it contradicts the cinematic impulse established at the birth of visual culture/visual cultural practices in a piece like *Broken Blossoms*. In the end, however, he is made to be alone in this land, which is supposed to be made into a home.

The conclusion of the episode presents a two-fold ending. While clearly sympathetic to Hop Sing and an example of another episode engaging with an antidiscrimination sentiment, the result is that Hop Sing is even more deeply entrenched in his work—his life—as a servant. He states as much; when Ben

Cartwright expresses that he and his family are very sorry for what happened, Hop Sing brushes him off saying it's no matter, he's back where he belongs, taking care of the Cartwrights. The last words in the episode are delivered by Hop Sing. He has never spoken so much in the series, or expressed a personal, even political sentiment until this moment: "Missy gone home, Hop Sing back at Ponderosa, no law broken ... ah, Mr. Hoss hot biscuits. Missy happy. Hop Sing happy. Then people and law spoil everything. Not first time Hop Sing been kick[ed] and punch[ed], for Hop Sing, is no matter; for Missy, is very bad. Missy say she want to stay, Hop Sing tell her "Go Home." Hop Sing say "He no want her here" ... Hop Sing very big liar." Yung's acting is poignant and affecting. But in the last line, Hop Sing takes the blame for pushing Missy away, who in the previous sequence desperately and touchingly declares that she wants to marry Hop Sing, saying they could stay in the woods together, then suggesting that they could move to China. Hop Sing, while not sexualized, does take a dominant role in making a serious decision—for him and his love to be apart (he sends her back to her parents), and for him to remain alone.

Victor Sen Yung was born Sen Yew Cheung on October 18, 1915, in San Francisco. He started working at age eleven, as a houseboy. He attended Berkeley, studying animal husbandry and earning a degree in economics. He portrayed Charlie Chan's number two son twenty-five times in the late 1930s and 1940s, and he was reduced to playing middle-aged roles, such as houseboys, laundrymen, valets, clerks, dock workers, and waiters, in the 1950s. One of his most familiar roles is that of Hop Sing in *Bonanza*. But he also had a recurring role in the final season of the series *Bachelor Father*, as Peter Fong, the cousin of Peter Tong. Yung was an accomplished cook (in real life) and he wrote *The Great Wok Cookbook*, which has a cover image of him in an outfit similar to the coolie shirt and cap he wore in *Bonanza*. He capitalized on his intertextual star discourse as a domestic worker whose skill in cooking was his form of livelihood. Ironically, and sadly, Yung died in 1980 by accidental asphyxiation after turning on a faulty kitchen stove for heat. He was poor, and alone.

Bachelor Father (1957–1962)

Bachelor Father, which ran concurrently with *Bonanza*, takes the Chinese houseboy a hundred years forward in time, without any sign of change in the interracial dynamic. The character, Peter Tong (played by Sammee Tong), serves as a surrogate wife and mother to Bentley Gregg (John Forsythe, of *Charlie's Angels* and *Dynasty* fame) and Bentley's niece (Noreen Corcoran). Like Hop Sing in *Bonanza*, Peter is subject to a process of feminization and desexualization, particularly in comparison to the figure of the white patriarch.

During the rise of the civil rights movement in the late 1950s, when *Bachelor Father* was created, the figure of the Asian male servant stood in for, and in comparison to, the African American servant. As the figure of the African

FIGURE 21 Sammee Tong as houseboy Peter Tong, in *Bachelor Father*.

American mammy lost prominence, the Asian servant emerged to replace her. The Asian servant was portrayed as (more) loyal to his employers and (more) content with his position in society, while African Americans who once played this role were now rebelling against unequal social stratification.[33] This is a key politic in the emergence of the model minority myth: Asian Americans as a pliable minority and African Americans as refusing to conform. Part of the function of the model minority myth that arose in the 1960s was to praise Asian Americans for being skilled and passive exactly when African Americans were rebuked for being resistant and malcontent. Here is how the representational economy exchanged Black servants for Asian servants.

When Chinese men first immigrated to the United States, they were likened to African Americans in several ways and for several ideological reasons.[34] In what has been described as a process of "Negroization," Chinese men were conceptualized as threats to free labor, just as the newly freed Blacks were.[35] They were condemned as a "depraved class" not only because they were supposedly morally inferior, savage, and heathen but because of their physiognomic similarities with African American men. As Takaki writes, "Their depravity was associated with their almost Africanlike physical appearance. While their complexions in some instances approached 'fair,' one writer observed, their whole physiognomy indicated 'but a slight removal from the African race.'"[36] Chinese men were similarly accused of sexual depravity and lustfulness, thereby feeding the ideology of the "purity" of white womanhood and its endangerment by men of color. The irony and paranoia of such thinking now seem transparent, but during the time of westward expansion such (mis)characterization was part of the racialization process. It was a way for "white" European Americans to cope with newcomers by distinguishing themselves from them, which in turn laid the basis for economic, social, and political domination. Therefore, as "enemies to republican and free labor" and as threats to white women, Chinese men, like African American men, had to be carefully controlled in terms of their livelihoods and in terms of their images.[37] These Asian men in the West were condemned for their proximity to Negroness or Blackness.

Though likened to African Americans, the Chinese were also deemed to have qualities that made them in some ways preferable to Blacks. For example, they were viewed as intelligent, not ignorant or brutish, and as quiet rather than uppity or sassy.[38] Most of all, they were praised as "hard-working," a label that has stuck for over a century and that still generates divisions and tensions among people of color. In such early conceptualizations are the seeds of the "model minority" myth, which does not benefit Asian American communities but rather aligns them superficially and conditionally with whites ("white adjacent"), and alienates them from other communities of color.[39]

Understood as agreeable and subservient, Peter's two predominant characteristics are humor and passivity. This kind of compliance can lead to conditional acceptance.[40] "My houseboy, Peter" as Bentley Gregg calls him, works faithfully to take care of the lawyer-employer's Beverly Hills home and his teenage niece, whom Peter calls "Niece Kelly." Wearing black pants, white jacket, and bowtie, which also looks like a waiter's uniform so doubling the air of servitude—the inimitable Bruce Lee was costumed like this in his role as Kato, a manservant in *The Green Hornet* (1966)—Peter, like Hop Sing, makes sure that his employers and their friends are well-served, fed, and comfortable.

There are a few points of departure between the characters of Peter and Hop Sing. Peter is a major character while Hop Sing is not. Peter has a fair amount of lines and screen time, and he is more involved with the family's activities.

FIGURE 22 Sammee Tong in *Bachelor Father*.

(In promotional images, the three of them are featured: Bentley, Kelly, and Peter.) Still, the family and their friends often refer to him in terms of his service work, for example, by praising his cooking abilities. The greatest point of similarity between the two Chinese servants is that their "foreignness"—their speech, mannerisms, and physical appearance—is made a spectacle. Peter does not appear to be as foreign as Hop Sing, perhaps because the genre and format have shifted into the twentieth century: he has an English name, his dress is less Oriental though no less conspicuous, and he has relatives in California (which has a history of a strong Asian American population). Nevertheless, his Chineseness is made into a spectacle. For example, he, like Hop Sing, will spout off in Chinese when he is upset. His difference is emphasized as a source of anxiety through humor.

FIGURE 23   Bruce Lee as Kato, the houseboy, in *The Green Hornet*.

As a Chinese male servant, Peter suffers emasculation and desexualization. Both Uncle Bentley and Peter are older men, but Bentley (a solid and British-sounding name associated with luxury) is portrayed as a dashing eligible bachelor, whereas Peter is left generally asexual. There are hints in the series that Peter might have crushes on women he meets in the grocery store or in English language class, but ultimately these come to nothing. Like other television servants,

FIGURE 24 Bruce Lee as Kato, chauffer/superhero sidekick while masked in *The Green Hornet*. Producers wanted to ensure that Lee's Asian physiognomy was covered, especially during action scenes.

Peter is content to remain with "his family" (of employers) in lieu of having one of his own.

As with other servants, notably Beulah, the way that Peter is shot, often in close-ups held for several seconds, emphasizes his exaggerated facial expressions. This kind of camera work both objectifies Peter visually, drawing him out as different, even odd, and objectifies him narratively, as these moments of making jokes or being made a joke of stop the storyline for a beat. However, unlike Beulah, who seems to have some authority in the narrative as well as within the family, Peter is consistently portrayed as less of a man than Bentley. (Unlike

Mr. French's camaraderie with his employer, Uncle Bill in *Family Affair*, a bromance is not possible.) One example in particular illustrates this point. In the episode "The Haunted House," in which the three major characters end up spending the night in a supposedly haunted house, Peter is scared and emotional while Bentley is cool and rational. (Niece Kelly is also frightened, and Peter is often aligned with her, as both feminine and childlike.) There are several shots of Peter—eyes wide, mouth agape, speechless, though grunting in fear. This image hearkens directly back to the way African American actors were filmed as the "coon" figure who is ruled by emotions rather than rationality.

Though made similar to African American characters in some ways, the Asian houseboy is fundamentally different from the image of a big, threatening, Black male servant/slave. While male slaves were feared because of the possibility of rebellion, Asian male servants were depicted as not inclined to resist, as unable to challenge their situations because of their generally smaller physical stature and their perceived passive temperament. In this way, Asians are portrayed as both less than and "better" than African Americans, at least as better servants for those who wish to employ them.

The image of Asians as quiet, uncomplaining, and hardworking seals perfectly their suitability to the servant role and to the ideologies of racial hierarchy. In a volatile time of changes in race relations in the late 1950s and early 1960s, the image of Asians in America is compared and contrasted to the image of African Americans. Thus we have the image of the Chinese houseboy, Peter, who portrays the ideal servant: hardworking, loyal, and above all, not protesting for civil rights. There is one episode, "Bentley and the Time Clock,"[41] in which Peter bands together with other Asian domestic servants in an effort to "unionize." The Benevolent Society of Chinese Houseboys turns out to be a disaster: the employer meets Peter's demands (for an hourly wage, punching in and punching out), but Peter himself does not like the new system. The show thus presents the servants' attempt to improve their conditions as unnecessary and ridiculous and makes clear that the servants themselves realize this. African Americans and the African American male in particular are displaced, in favor of the Asian male servant who is safer, soothing, and "quiet."

The Courtship of Eddie's Father (1969–1972)

Whereas *Bonanza* displaces the civil rights discourse through a storyline about racism against Chinese men, *The Courtship of Eddie's Father* uses the figure of the racialized domestic as part of discourses about changing gender roles, shifting national identity, and race relations. These texts are examples of race being gendered, and of the servants being subordinated through the conflation of Asianness and so-perceived femininity. *The Courtship of Eddie's Father* was the first and remains one of the few prime-time American television programs to feature an Asian or Asian American in a leading role. Warranting a close study, it

FIGURE 25 Miyoshi Umeki as Mrs. Livingston, in *The Courtship of Eddie's Father* with Bill Bixby, "Mr. Eddie's Father," and Brandon Cruz, who played a kind of surrogate son, Eddie.

shows that representing Asianness or Asian Americanness is difficult and unresolved. The series ran from 1969 through 1972, tumultuous years in which women's liberation, the Vietnam War, and the civil rights movement changed American life.[42]

The position of the Asian servant in a television program must be figured in terms of several axes, namely, gender, race/nationality, and the family. The premiere episode of *The Courtship of Eddie's Father*, "Mrs. Livingston, I Presume?" sets up three major issues that are articulated, represented, and worked through in the series. First is the issue of gender difference and gender roles. Debuting at the end of the 1960s, the program reacted to the women's liberation movement, which was, for the most part, a white women's movement, by proffering

Mrs. Livingston as a feminine ideal. In contrast to the "women's libbers" represented on television in both news format and fiction, Mrs. Livingston provides a traditional model of womanhood that is linked to her Asianness. Second, with respect to the issue of racial difference, Mrs. Livingston's Japaneseness serves to highlight everyone else's whiteness, or, more specifically, their Americanness. Third, and in some ways the most telling, is the issue of how Mrs. Livingston is (or is not) integrated into the family, though she is part of the family unit. She serves as a surrogate mother and performs most of the functions of a wife, but her character is kept from taking these positions officially (or romantically). It is through a romantic, sexual relationship that a woman can gain official entry into Tom Corbett's life and family, but in this episode (as in all of the episodes) Tom remains a bachelor. Mrs. Livingston remains a mother and a wife figure—in the figure of the maid—without being romantically involved with Tom.

The opening scene takes place at Tom Corbett's office (in Santa Monica, California), where he works as the editor of *Tomorrow* magazine. Also in the office are Tina, a pretty, young, free-spirited secretary, and Tom's photographer and friend Norman (played by the producer of the series, James Komack). Norman is "working" with two beautiful white women who are models: they have long hair, lots of makeup, and flirty outfits. Norman, blatantly chauvinistic, suggests that he and Tom go out with the two models—"they're sisters," he says. Tom declines. There is a cut to Mrs. Livingston speaking softly to herself in Japanese, and a switch from the laugh track to soft but noticeable flute music. She wears little makeup and a simple bun, so her hair appears short; her clothes are plain and modest (her hemline is below the knee in an era that invented the miniskirt). She is mending Eddie's pants like a servant, but also like a mother. These two scenes establish her in contrast to the three women we have just seen working outside the home in Tom's office.

Tom comes home, hugs Eddie affectionately, and says hello to Mrs. Livingston. She says hello, calling him "Mr. Eddie's Father." This manner of speech identifies Mrs. Livingston's Japaneseness as funny. Although it is polite in many Asian cultures to call people by formal titles or to identify them as someone's mother or father, it is a source of laughter for a contemporary non-Asian audience. It also indicates Tom's elevated status and Mrs. Livingston's subordinated status by making her seem like a child respectfully addressing the father of a friend. And significantly, Tom Corbett doesn't call Mrs. Livingston by her first name, as is the practice with other employers and their maids of color, and calling her "Mrs. Livingston" keeps a formalized divide between them.[43] This distance is furthered by the fact that, for both, their names actually describe them to belonging to someone else: Tom to Eddie and Mrs. Livingston to Mr. Livingston.[44]

Mrs. Livingston comments that Eddie has grown taller, but Tom repeats what Eddie said just a few minutes before: "No, Mrs. Livingston, I think it's the way you wash his pants—they shrink." Mrs. Livingston is slightly insulted: "Oh, is that why. Good. In my country we have an expression, . . ." and she begins to speak in Japanese. This retreat to Japanese sayings occurs many times throughout the series, often to the confusion of Tom and usually as a source of humor. Moreover, it emphasizes the communication and cultural gap between Mrs. Livingston and Mr. Eddie's Father. This is another underlying tenet of their relationship. They are an almost-couple (like Mr. French, not quite like Peter); Mrs. Livingston and Tom behave as if, together, they are parents to Eddie, which serves as an underlying problem in the series. Thus their "coupling" must be strictly contained by racial, class, and gender lines. Theirs is not one in which the Asian female is consumed sexually; rather, the consumption is based on her exotic-yet-idealized femininity, and her ability to provide the duties of a mother. The retraction of Mrs. Livingston's sexuality, she is neither the partner to Eddie's father nor to any other man, creates a space for her to take part in an American white family, though within a limited frame.[45]

In this first episode of the three-year series, Eddie and his father go to MGM Studios to spend some quality time together. Eddie begins his quest to find his father a new wife. He meets a pretty young woman, Dolly Daly, who has big round eyes and wears a short skirt. She falls prey to Eddie's charm and his story about his lonely father; he doesn't mention anything about Mrs. Livingston. The camera objectifies Dolly's body, her legs, chest, face, and hair. There is a humorous yet also sexually flirtatious exchange between Tom and Dolly (which sounds like "darling" whenever he says her name). Tom agrees to take her home because she is new in town and in desperate need of a job.

Back at the apartment, Dolly jumps up on the fireplace mantle and begins to dance. She moves her body enticingly, "showing her talents" in a supposed audition for a modeling job at the magazine. Norman stops by with the two women from the office (explaining to them that Tom is a little "square"), and they find Tom, his shirt unbuttoned and tie undone, admiring a sexy woman dancing in his living room. "Mrs. Livingston, I presume," says Norman, and then the three walk back to the elevator.[46]

The following morning, Mrs. Livingston enters the apartment (she has her own key), announced by vaguely (pseudo) Asian-sounding flute music. She is puzzled by the sleeping woman on the couch, whose legs are exposed. She goes into the kitchen and finds Eddie drinking orange juice. As she puts on an apron, she politely asks about the young lady. Eddie responds in a humorous, jumbled-word way, and Mrs. Livingston begins to mumble in Japanese, clearly dismayed. When Tom comes in, Mrs. Livingston appears angry and disapproving. Eddie is hungry because he only had a candy bar the night before. "No dinner?!" Mrs. Livingston exclaims. Tom replies that they had no time, that he wanted to get home early, to which Mrs. Livingston replies, "I know...I saw her." Mrs. Livingston starts to prepare eggs, but says that there are not enough eggs for Dolly. Tom says that she is "going too far," to which Mrs. Livingston replies, "Then fire me." Tom protests that that is not what he meant by the words "go far." Eddie chimes in, "Uh-huh, Dad, if she speaks Japanese, that's what it sounds like." Mrs. Livingston starts to say, "In my country..." when Tom interrupts loudly, "... you have an expression, ..." and the bowl of eggs falls to the ground. Mrs. Livingston speaks softly to herself in Japanese and walks out of the room. Eddie cries, "Dad, you have to go after her—she left us!"

Dolly then comes into the kitchen and asks what has happened. Eddie says, "That's our Mrs. Livingston, she left us!" Dolly says that she can clean up the eggs, implying that she can replace Mrs. Livingston. Tom grabs Eddie and shakes him, telling him that he can handle things, that he doesn't need "just a six-year-old boy" telling him what to do. Eddie runs out. Tom says to Dolly, "He's upset, Mrs. Livingston has been his housekeeper for a long time." Dolly offers to be the new "housekeeper."

This brief exchange is significant in its demonstration of how Tom's feelings for Mrs. Livingston are displaced. First, Eddie is the one who expresses feelings of being alarmed and upset that Mrs. Livingston has gone. Tom displaces his being upset onto Eddie by scolding him (for being too young to discern his—meaning Tom's—needs). Second, Mrs. Livingston is referred to as "*our* Mrs. Livingston" and then as Eddie's housekeeper. This indicates the Corbetts' ownership of her as their employee, but it also links her to Eddie and to Eddie's being upset, though presumably not to Tom's feelings.

Tom's struggle over his feelings about Mrs. Livingston's leaving represent a man's dilemma about what kind of woman he must choose, a theme subsumed in the narrative. When Dolly offers to take Mrs. Livingston's place as housekeeper and, perhaps, as mother and wife, Tom quickly dismisses the idea. Though she is an "ideal" female—young, fecund, spontaneous—she is not an ideal wife. Tom seems to want to marry a more traditional woman, which Mrs. Livingston is, but the text will not allow such an interracial marriage.[47]

Tom's possibly affectionate feelings for Mrs. Livingston are further revealed, though veiled, in the next scene. As Tom escorts Dolly to the door, sending her down to his office for a job, Mrs. Livingston returns. Tom rushes to explain things to her, following her into the kitchen: "Mrs. Livingston, ah, Mrs. Livingston. This ... whole thing is really so simple." (There is a close-up shot of the eggs still on the floor, a sign that Mrs. Livingston is needed and that Dolly did not clean up the spill.) "Well, you can see for yourself that the girl is gone," he says as almost an apology. He says that he and Eddie were afraid that Mrs. Livingston left for good. No, she just went to get eggs, she replies, and the audience laughs. She says that's what she had said in Japanese; what we had thought was a strong statement of protest, even anger, then, turns out to be one of subservience and forgiveness. Mrs. Livingston and Tom have an exchange about their "language barrier," which could be interpreted as a metaphor for a communication gap between a couple. Mrs. Livingston says that Eddie is learning Japanese so that she can understand Eddie and that she goes to English class three times a week so that she can understand Tom. She calls for "more communication." Eddie comes running in and hugs Mrs. Livingston and tells her that he loves her.

He makes Tom repeat after him, "I love you, Mrs. Livingston," and "she's sweet, kind, intelligent, and beautiful." The exchange and, more specifically, the exchange of glances is between Eddie and his father, not Tom and Mrs. Livingston. Mrs. Livingston looks down the whole time, perhaps blushing. Eddie suddenly asks, "Then why don't you marry her?" Tom diverts the idea to Eddie: "Well, he's all yours, Mrs. Livingston, he speaks your language." The pilot episode reveals and reseals the love that cannot be.

Mrs. Livingston tells Eddie that he needs to get dressed. As they leave the kitchen, Mrs. Livingston pauses in the doorway, turns, and says to Tom, "I think you're very nice man." Though she is, ironically, direct with her statements (ironic because Asians, especially Asian women, are portrayed as unassertive unless they are characterized as a "dragon lady"), Mrs. Livingston's feelings for Tom are also displaced, funneled through her concern for Eddie's well-being. Tom says "wakata," meaning "I understand."[48] Like the intertextual characters she has played in Hollywood films, such as *Sayonara* and *Flower Drum Song*, here too Umeki's character is an innocent and nurturing Asian female whose sexuality is channeled into a subservient, passive demeanor.

Not only do the Corbetts want to keep Mrs. Livingston, Mrs. Livingston (somewhat inexplicably) wishes to stay in this arrangement, in which her status as beloved housekeeper is a conditional kind of acceptance or belonging. She is not allowed to become a member of this American family, except through employment and polite deference.

Throughout the series, we have Tom and Eddie looking for a wife for Tom and a mother for Eddie, even though they already have Mrs. Livingston. This is the show's dilemma. In the three-year run of the series, dozens of women are presented as potential wives for Tom, but ultimately, they prove not to be mothers for Eddie. "Liberated" (white) women who have positions in law, business, and politics are intriguing candidates and interesting characters.[49] However, the usual pattern in Tom's relationships with these impressive women is that "boarding school" is eventually brought up, and soon the girlfriend is out. The idea that Mrs. Livingston could be the new wife and mother is an impossible one on prime-time television, despite the fact that in many ways she is already both wife and mother. This is what the pilot episode establishes as well as displaces. Each episode closes with a voice-over dialogue between father and son, usually in an effort to add closure to a particular storyline. In this first episode, Tom asks Eddie what he wants to be when he grows up. Eddie says that he wants to be a sweet, kind, intelligent, good guy like his father. The description is the same one he gave of Mrs. Livingston. He wants to be like both Tom and Mrs. Livingston, like father . . . and mother. The fact that Eddie understands the two as having the same qualities implicitly brings Tom and Mrs. Livingston together, but the program, mediated through a child and constrained/contained by the premise, keeps the two characters apart.

In the tradition of television's endless deferment, Tom never does choose a new wife, despite Eddie's constant prodding. Television texts are open narratives that involve continuing storylines and characters. Televisual pleasure in these never-ending stories is more often about the weekly anticipation and experience of each episode than about getting clear narrative resolution. Under this narrative structure, questions about Tom and Mrs. Livingston—as well as about racial identity—are deferred weekly.

As set up in the premiere episode, the series continues to negotiate gender, racial, and national identities by displacing the direct questions of gender relations, racial positioning, and national status. For example, the fact that a Japanese character appears on television during the Vietnam era displaces upsetting images of the Viet Cong and a controversial war with the image of a passive and quiet member of a defeated Asian nation, Japan, in the position of a servant. Literary theorist and critic Lisa Lowe has written, "Throughout the twentieth century, the figure of the Asian immigrant has served as a "screen," a phantasmatic site, on which the nation projects a series of condensed, complicated anxieties regarding external and internal threats to the mutable coherence of the national body: the invading multitude, the lascivious seductress, the servile yet treacherous domestic, the automaton whose inhuman efficiency will supersede American ingenuity."[50] In this way, "stereotypes can be studied as indices of national anxiety."[51] Similarly, we can look at racialization as a process of identity formation, particularly in the midst of diversity and change.

Racialization can be defined as a process of assigning a person's social and economic status according to their race. In *Racial Faultlines: The Historical Origins of White Supremacy in California*, Tomás Almaguer discusses the significance of race as it emerged with the development of American capitalism. He argues that white expansion into the American West, specifically California, in the nineteenth century forged new racialized relationships—between conquerors and conquered, between white immigrants and people of color.

Lowe states that "racialization has been the site of the contradiction between the promise of political emancipation and the conditions of economic exploitation."[52] This is a consistent theme throughout much of the scholarship on Asians and Asian Americans in America. Lowe, Darrell Hamamoto, Gina Marchetti, and Ronald Takaki all examine the contradictions between the promise of democracy and the reality of social inequality.[53]

Interracial interactions are how individuals mark and gain a sense of identity. The United States has a history of race-based discrimination and a history of enslaving and exploiting non-white peoples in order to rationalize the specificities and complexities of the diverse race relations in the United States. Where there are multiple lines of power beyond the master-slave dyad, knowledge and power are distributed differently than in a colonial context. Edward Said acknowledges as much: "Orientalism is not . . . representative and expressive of some nefarious 'Western' imperialist plot to hold down the 'Oriental' world. It is rather a *distribution* of geopolitical awareness into aesthetic, scholarly, economic, sociological, historical, and philological texts; . . . it is, above all, a discourse that is by no means in direct, corresponding relationship with political power in the raw, but rather is produced and exists in an uneven exchange with power."[54]

Racialization is a process that operates both within texts and beyond them; that is, the television text racializes, and television as a cultural medium racializes. Television programs are not merely "symptomatic texts" but instead are symptomatic and determining of the relations of production themselves.[55]

Mrs. Livingston's position—her status as a woman and as an Asian, as an employee and as a "member" of the family—can be closely examined in several of the episodes of *Courtship*. The series aired during a time of social upheaval, just after the peak of the civil rights movement, at the beginning of the women's movement, and in the middle of the Vietnam War. Mrs. Livingston displaced anxiety about all three. She was Asian, a "model minority," quiet and uncomplaining and not protesting against racial and economic injustice. She was traditionally "feminine," domestic, serving and not demanding change in the relations of inequality between women and men. And as a Japanese war bride, a post–World War II figure, she was not a menacing "face of the enemy" who might remind viewers of America's ongoing and losing war in Vietnam. *Courtship* was part of a popular television trend to temper, contain, and normalize the dramatic—and for some, traumatic—changes that were taking place in the decade of the 1960s. The "liberated woman" was treated in television, for the most part, by negation, by absenting the woman from the scene. Besides *Courtship*, other series with a missing mother included *Bonanza*, *Bachelor Father* (1957–1962), *My Three Sons* (1960–1972), and *Family Affair* (1966–1971). The mother's absence effectively erased the woman and women's issues from the home and commented on changing roles for women without allowing them to speak on their own behalf.

Courtship presents a split between the traditional 1950s housewife and the mod(ern) 1960s woman, in this case embodied respectively by a traditional Asian female and the various "liberated" American women that appear (Tom regularly goes on dates with eligible bachelorettes). It is a split that remains unresolved, as sexism merges with racialization. The program presents a shift in gender roles, using race and sexuality to make sense of it. The sitcom format provides a strategy for containing the issues: tradition is racialized and the modern is sexualized, and Tom cannot decide between the two.

The series had the task of managing both race and gender, and it did so through the characterization of nationality. In an episode entitled "Gentleman Friend," Mrs. Livingston must decide whether to accept a marriage proposal and move to Japan. Mr. Sato (played by George Takei, popularly known as Mr. Sulu from *Star Trek*) announces his intention to marry Mrs. Livingston to Eddie and his father. There is a struggle to demarcate Mrs. Livingston as not the mother and wife to Eddie and Tom, as well as not "American," by giving her a Japanese husband. Mrs. Livingston has to choose whether to become the wife of a Japanese gentleman or remain where she is, with Eddie and Tom in an unnamed, unofficial family.

The episode sets up a test of Mrs. Livingston's allegiance and belonging to either Japan or the United States. Furthermore, her consideration of marriage to her "gentleman friend" is a pronouncement of her sexuality and her ability to establish her own family. By rejecting the marriage proposal and sacrificing the opportunity to have her own children, she acknowledges her adoption of and by the Corbett family. But because of her racial and cultural otherness, her position in that family officially remains that of a servant, even if the characters—and the audience—tacitly see her as more than that. It is this tension that participates in the endless deferment of both narrative and racial resolution. This episode parallels Hop Sing's exceptional episode in which he gives up a chance for happiness. Further, Mrs. Livingston, Hop Sing, and Peter do not have offspring, so no future for them (for a family line) is implied.

The opening voice-over dialogue, a regular segment in each episode, has Eddie and his father walking along the beach. Eddie asks his father three questions. "Why do people hold hands?" "Because they love each other," the father replies. "Why are Mrs. Livingston's eyes different?" "They aren't," says the father, "*our* eyes are different." (Though showing respect for Mrs. Livingston's differences, this interchange between father and son also solidifies differences and defines love as endogamous.) "Is Japan far away?" "Yes," affirms the father. "Then when Mrs. Livingston gets homesick," Eddie declares, "she gets a big homesick."

The first scene begins with a shot of birds singing in their nest then the camera pans to a close-up of Mrs. Livingston's smiling face as she tends some flowers. In voice-over we hear Tom tell Eddie that it is the first day of spring. Mrs. Livingston acts a bit dreamy and absent-minded this morning, and Tom says that "springtime does very strange things to people." Eddie asks his father why Mrs. Livingston is "acting so goofy" and Tom himself is very curious. He calls Mrs. Livingston: "Mrs. Livingston, uh, look, I don't want to pry but . . . how are you?" He then asks about her gentleman friend. Tom appears jealous, or at least extremely curious, about the fact that a(nother) man holds the attention and affection of Mrs. Livingston.

This episode portrays Mrs. Livingston as more physically attractive than at other times in the series. She is made pretty and youthful by the camera and lighting, by her makeup, and by the clothing she wears. Moreover, she is connoted as desirable by her involvement in a romantic relationship with a man. For the first time, Tom seems intently interested in Mrs. Livingston's personal life. His questions are both sweet and humorous, and they indicate his interest in her, or at least his desire that she not marry someone else. Tom and Mrs. Livingston talk about their personal lives and feelings for the first time, but the conversation does eventually turn back to Eddie, about the prospect of her "leaving him" or wanting to stay because of him. Framing this discussion is the question of whether Mrs. Livingston belongs with the Corbetts or with Mr. Sato, in America or in Japan.

One particular scene represents Mrs. Livingston's negotiation of her Japaneseness and the extent of her Americanness. The scene begins in a Japanese restaurant with Japanese music playing on the soundtrack. Mrs. Livingston and Mr. Sato are speaking to each other in Japanese (there is no translation or subtitles, so their conversation is made natural and private). When Tom and Eddie arrive, Eddie instructs his father to take off his shoes. Mrs. Livingston introduces "Mr. Eddie's Father" and Eddie to Mr. Sato. Eddie bows.

Eddie acts as a translator and liaison between Japanese and American cultures, between Mrs. Livingston and his father. He wants to continue to bridge the gap; he wants to have both cultures in his life (both his American father and his Japanese maid and mother figure), and he does not want Mrs. Livingston to leave. He treats Mr. Sato with respect but also with suspicion, as he sometimes does with the women his father dates. Eddie tells Mr. Sato that they know how to eat "Japanese-style" because Mrs. Livingston taught them; she teaches them many things. "Mrs. Livingston is neato," Eddie declares. Mr. Sato asks what "neato" means; Mrs. Livingston begins to translate, but then appeals to Tom. Tom says that it means that Eddie is very fond of Mrs. Livingston. Mr. Sato responds that he, too, is very fond of her. Eddie competitively replies, "not as fond as me and Dad are." Mr. Sato calmly counters, "perhaps in a different way, then." Mr. Sato proposes a toast: "To Mrs. Livingston, who has consented to be my wife." Eddie is surprised and crestfallen. "Your wife? Did you hear that, Dad? His wife—that means Mrs. Livingston is going to leave us." Tom: "Yes, that's what it means, Eddie." Eddie: "But gosh! Are you sure you want to marry Mrs. Livingston?" Mr. Sato says yes. Tom tells Eddie to make a toast, which he reluctantly and dejectedly does. He wishes them a long and happy life together "even if you are leaving us and not taking care of us anymore." Mrs. Livingston looks down and says nothing; the men politely smile; Eddie frowns. There seems to be a polite stand-off between the two men, with Eddie standing in for Tom. It is left to Mrs. Livingston to make the decision.

There is a cut to a second scene of Mrs. Livingston and Mr. Sato approaching one another on a bridge, which echoes the romantic scene from the beginning of the episode. They speak in Japanese in a long shot, then walk away from each other in opposite directions. In the next shot, we see Mrs. Livingston watering flowers as in the beginning to the sound of flute music (connoting Asianness or foreignness yet also springtime). Tom asks about Mr. Sato's leaving.

TOM Mrs. Livingston, I hate to ask this, but I have to ask it. Did you change your mind because of Eddie?
MRS. LIVINGSTON No. I think that I have changed my mind because I realized that homesickness is not the reason to get married. I think . . .

TOM You know what? I think it's harder for you to get married—and for me—than it is for most other people.
MRS. LIVINGSTON Why is that?
TOM I think because we did it so well the first time.

Eddie's father makes a statement that he and Mrs. Livingston would never marry one another (and perhaps not anyone else, either). So Mrs. Livingston has chosen her life in America with Tom and Eddie with the knowledge that she will never be a "legitimate" or official wife and mother. She and Tom will never be a formally interracial and intercultural married couple on-screen. This is contrary to the Orientalist fantasies of white Western men acquiring Asian mail-order brides. (Or worse, sexually consuming and subjugating them.) This episode is an example of a more traditional kind of orientalizing—the exotic display of Japanese culture—while at the same time it demonstrates how the two cultures can come to a meeting point, that point being the figure of Mrs. Livingston. And while a lotus blossom type (soft-spoken, pleasantly foreign), Mrs. Livingston differs from her filmic counterpoint, Katsumi, in the film for which she won an Academy Award, *Sayonara*. She does not give Tom back rubs and hot baths; rather, in their working relationship within the intimate space of the home, they share a closeness and a mutual respect (much due to the performances of Miyoshi Umeki and Bill Bixby). Given that the program performed well enough in the ratings to continue for another two seasons, Mrs. Livingston's decision not to marry is not a surprise.

In the closing voice-over dialogue, Eddie asks his father about being a bachelor. He then says, "Is the bride the same as a wife?" His father responds, "Not exactly.... A bride is the girl that you marry. But a wife is the woman that you live with." Eddie: "Oh. Is it okay if I don't understand that, Dad?" Father: "Sure."

"The Littlest Kidnapper" is another episode that struggles with a fundamental dilemma in the series: Mrs. Livingston cannot be a mother and wife to Eddie and Tom, but neither can she have a family and child of her own. In the first scene, Eddie says that he saw something on television: bees flying from one flower to another. He asks his father, "Why don't you pollinate Mrs. Livingston so she can have her own little boy?" Mrs. Livingston speaks in Japanese, then says, "I think I should leave two man alone."

TOM Well, it's different with people than it is with flowers. People have to be married.
EDDIE Good! Why don't you marry Mrs. Livingston? (He raises this question every so often in the series.)
TOM Eddie, I've talked to you about this before. We love Mrs. Livingston, but not like we love somebody we're going to marry. (He uses the term "we," again displacing his individual relationship to and feelings about Mrs. Livingston.)

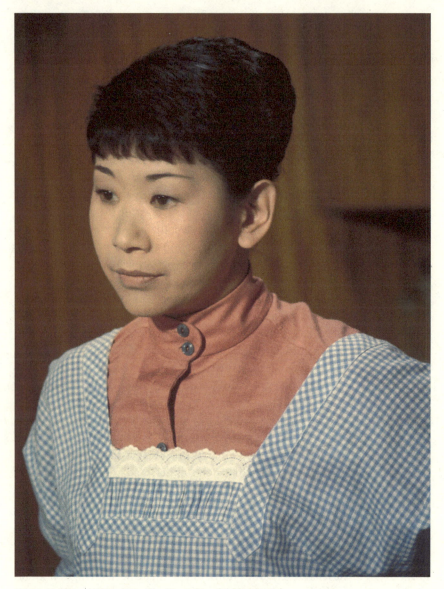

FIGURE 26 Miyoshi Umeki in *The Courtship of Eddie's Father*.

Eddie goes to the living room where Mrs. Livingston is cleaning and then heads out the door to school, still upset. Throughout the scene Mrs. Livingston says very little, even when Tom and Eddie are talking about her in her presence. At the close of the scene, Mrs. Livingston simply tells Tom not to worry, she is not alone.

The next scene shows Eddie on the school bus, returning home. There is a long, bizarre intercutting between various children on the school bus, which gets progressively faster. It becomes clear through the continued return to the image of an Asian American boy that Eddie is focusing on him—to bring him home to Mrs. Livingston! The two enter the apartment as Mrs. Livingston sits mending a suit jacket. "Hello, Mrs. Livingston. This is Frank." Mrs. Livingston smiles. "Do you like him?" Mrs. Livingston says, "Yes, I'm so glad you brought your friend home to play." Eddie repeats, "Do you like him?!" Mrs. Livingston again says yes. Eddie then exclaims, "He's yours! Now you don't have to be alone anymore. I'm giving him to you, he's your son." Mrs. Livingston, startled, says that Eddie can't just give this boy to her. Eddie leads Frank into the apartment to show him where he's "going to live." Oriental music chimes in.

This episode is significant in terms of how it represents race and racial difference, the Other as an object, and the conundrum of how to integrate Asianness. On the one hand, it shows an awareness of the distinction between a Japanese American and a Japanese immigrant to America, especially in the scene when Frank's parents come to pick him up. At the same time, the way that Eddie presumes that Mrs. Livingston needs a boy who "looks like her" to be her son, as well as the way that Frank is objectified, is curious and a little troubling (though it is possible that the producer wanted to represent it as a naive child's mistake). Through Eddie, we have a discourse on the biological versus the social construction of the family.

Furthermore, Mrs. Livingston's maternity is deflected. She both is and isn't physically a mother, we do not know of any children she may have given birth to, we do know that she nurtures and is helping to raise this boy. In writing about Mammy's maternity, Kimberly Wallace-Sanders iterates that "focusing on the mammy's body, and by extension her maternity, means seeing the body in a metonymic relationship to personhood, and essential component of recasting the mammy as more than a turban and a smile—as a transitional object for a nation moving from one development stage to another."[56] This could apply to the Asian maid in terms of Mrs. Livingston being the transitional object between two eras of national identity, before and after civil rights, before and after the feminist movement. She is maternity embodied in a maid.

When Tom comes home and asks what is going on, Eddie says happily, "He's for Mrs. Livingston. I picked him out all by myself.... His hair... just like Mrs. Livingston. And his eyes... just like Mrs. Livingston.... I found him at school," Eddie concludes matter-of-factly. Frank just smiles. Eddie, and the program, are grappling with difference.

Tom asks Mrs. Livingston to intercede. She speaks Japanese to Frank, to which he responds, "What'd she say?" Eddie says, "She wants to know your last name, Frank." While Frank does not speak Japanese (he scarcely speaks at all), Eddie is able to move easily from English to Japanese. One's language is linked with one's race, identifying a person as belonging to a certain nationality or racial group. But there is confusion because Eddie looks American and speaks Japanese while Frank looks Japanese and speaks only English.

When Frank's parents, Duke and Kendis, arrive to pick him up, Frank's father also does not speak Japanese. While Frank becomes speechless, Duke is overly gregarious; both disorders seem to stem from their looking Japanese but not speaking Japanese—which can be understood as their Asian Americanness, which is not comprehended by the text (or the audience). Duke (played by Pat Morita) is groovy and not-Japanese in an overdetermined way: "Kendis would dig some sake—she makes that whole Oriental thing.[57] Scotch and water is fine with me." He then leans over to confide, "fourth-generation American." He criticizes his wife: "I'm sorry honey, you don't have scotch with tonic." To Tom: "Nice chick, but very—square." Mrs. Livingston graciously takes over by speaking Japanese to the woman and making her feel welcome. Tom asks what they are saying. Duke says that he doesn't know, it's something about tea: "Is that old world or what? We call 'em Uncle Tom-a-sake's." Duke then makes another bad joke about eating Japanese food and being hungry again a half hour later. They continue talking, and Duke commiserates about divorce and getting stuck with a kid. Tom corrects him, noting that he is widowed, not divorced. Duke and Kendis, it turns out, are separated.

This display of Duke's Americanness is in many ways a demonstration of his un-Americanness and his self-loathing use of stereotypes. He comes across as trying too hard: his modish clothes, oversized shades, and casual attitude are not only a spectacle but slightly annoying. He makes fun of his own cultural heritage by invoking other cultures, first in making the joke about being hungry after eating, which is a joke about Chinese food, not Japanese food, and second by using the phrase "Uncle-Tom-a-sake" in reference to his wife.[58] The latter is a strange twist on the concept that evolved out of Harriet Beecher Stowe's story and one that links Asians to African Americans, as it is more Duke than Kendis who seems to have abandoned his culture to serve another. He is portrayed as unwittingly tied to another cultural heritage while at the same time disparaging and deprecating it.

Duke's status as a would-be-divorcé places him in a morally inferior position to Tom. Tom loves his child and wants to do right by him, whereas Duke talks of "getting stuck" with a kid and did not even notice that his son was missing until he received a telephone call from the police. Not only has he failed as a husband, he is an inadequate father as well. The program portrays an Asian American who falls short: he is questionably American, despite his claims and despite his family's having lived in America for four generations. Furthermore, while his otherness is discomforting, his Japanese wife, Kendis, is revealed as a more stable person, polite and quiet, comfortably Other.

When it is time for Frank to go home, he must choose between his parents; he cannot, and says that he wants to stay at Eddie's. Duke hollers at Kendis, who becomes upset. Ironically, this family of "model minorities" is shown as a dysfunctional Asian family, or perhaps their dysfunction comes from their trying to be an American family. However, in the closing sequence, as

Eddie and his father talk in voice-over, Eddie tells his father that Frank's father is learning Japanese now and that his parents are getting back together. Here we have another formulation of tradition as racial/ethnic and modern as white.

Eddie then says, "Maybe I got no mom, and dad has no wife, and Mrs. Livingston has no son, but we all have each other and that's what's important." He goes off to bed and Mrs. Livingston begins to clean up. "Mr. Eddie's Father, I'm a . . ." she starts. Tom interrupts: "Mrs. Livingston, you are a thing of Oriental beauty and of magnificent calm." "Domo arigato," Mrs. Livingston replies. "Wakata," Tom says back. Despite their happy togetherness, Mrs. Livingston is still with the Corbetts as a maid, not as a mother to Eddie, not as a wife to Tom, not even as a mother to her own child. The episode is unable to resolve this dilemma and upholds the television series format of endless deferment.

Mrs. Livingston functions as a signifier of femininity and a marker of race and racial lines for whites. Being a woman and a servant compounds her Japaneseness, her non-whiteness, and her position of subordination. *The Courtship of Eddie's Father* displays the struggle over how to deal with the figure of the Asian woman. On the one hand, she is safely contained in the position/status of a servant; at the same time, she can and does fill the role of the mother and wife. However sweet the performances are, this becomes an unresolvable problem.

Persistence of Vision: *Twin Peaks* (1990–1991)

An inability to resolve the "problem" or dilemma of the fact of and intimate presence of an Asian/Asian American appears again forty years after *Courtship*. One of the few television programs with an Asian or Asian American character in the two decades following *The Courtship of Eddie's Father* was the cult hit, *Twin Peaks*. The character of Josie Packard, played by film actress Joan Chen, represents the power of sexuality of the Asian female and the precipitous fall when she no longer plays the prototypical dangerous dragon lady. Two scenes from separate episodes illustrate these opposites. In these scenes, Josie Packard interacts with two white characters: Harry, a man who is her lover and the sheriff of the lumber town, and Katherine, her sister-in-law, a spurned business partner who has now become Packard's boss. She is presented first as a highly erotic and masterfully manipulative dragon lady, then as a taciturn, defrocked, desexualized, passive female slave.[59]

The first scene begins with an exterior shot of a storm lighting up the Pacific Northwest sky. To the sound of crashing thunder, there is a cut to the inside of a living room in a cabin-like house. It is dark, and there is an extreme high-angle shot of Harry the sheriff (Michael Ontkean) looking down pensively. From the almost bird's-eye view, only Josie Packard's bare legs are seen as she saunters into the room, modeling her new negligee. The camera swoops down and zooms as Harry's eyes move upward, following her intently until she reaches his lap. He

FIGURE 27 Joan Chen as Josie Packard (from businesswoman to maid), in *Twin Peaks*.

nods his head and says that he approves. There is a quick peek at her breast as she turns, and her full leg is exposed as she sits. From the moment she walks in, she solicits Harry's gaze and desire.

She is scantily dressed in black while Harry is fully clothed from ankle to neck in light beige. They are in close proximity as they speak: Josie whispers in a childlike voice while Harry expresses his confusion and resistance to her in his direct questioning. At every serious question Harry asks—about Josie's possible lying, sabotage, even murder—Josie deflects his masculine seriousness with performed feminine sweetness, talking about shopping and being afraid. She acts as a vulnerable, delicate female needing his protection, but we understand her to be a dangerous woman who can betray or bring harm due to her ambition.

In comparison to this figuration, the second scene marks the loss of the one power Josie held, her sexual allure (to white men), and it repositions her as a servant, a status that the narrative implies is deserved. The scene begins with a close-up shot of a photograph of an older white man. Josie's voice-over is heard as she confesses to Katherine (Piper Laurie) that this man, Katherine's brother and Josie's husband, was killed by another Euro-American man who was Josie's lover. Josie tells her story of being taken in by Thomas Eckhardt before she married Andrew Packard, who brought her to the United States. We have the common scenario of a white knight "rescuing" the Asian female and facilitating her life in a new country. When the series begins, Andrew is dead, and Josie has acquired a third white man/mentor/master, Harry. Now that the relationship with Harry is over and she has lost control of the mill because she does not have men to "do business with," Josie is radically reduced from a rich widow and beautiful mill owner to a desexualized, humbled servant.

Joan Chen's look and style have changed completely. She is differently made up and no longer wears gorgeous and expensive clothes but rather loose pants and an undefined, long-sleeved chemise in brown. Her hair, once fashionably coiffed, is now short and markedly unfeminine. When she stands to leave at the end of the scene, she looks like a Chinese houseboy. This gender switch to Asian male status is an added component to the disempowerment.

The camera no longer objectifies her sexually. Katherine's voice is stern and steady, like Harry's in the previous scene, while Josie speaks quietly and haltingly. Josie does not know what to do and in essence begs for mercy. Katherine says that she will tell her what to do: "From now on, you will work for me, here, at the house . . . as a maid." Katherine's position of superiority is conveyed through the narrative as well as through camera technique. Her maternalism is expressed when she scolds Josie and sends her to her room (which is no longer the master suite but the servant's quarters); at the same time, she is delivering a serious punishment, a punishment ordered from the position not of a mother but of a white employer. The series has transformed Josie from a wealthy, desirable, powerful, and skillfully articulate woman into a lowly servant at the mercy of her mistress, bereft of any money or property, who now can only stammer out "yes, I understand" and "thank you" (the very same words spoken in Japanese in *The Courtship of Eddie's Father*).

Like many of the characters on *Twin Peaks*, Josie portrays an extreme; moreover, with Chen's skilled performance, she goes from one extreme to another. Even if creator David Lynch's intent is a kind of parody, the Asian/Asian American woman remains locked into dichotomous archetypes—evil and powerful or helpless and passive—and both are linked to her sexuality. Josie Packard came to the United States as a prostitute, which is an ideological and disparaging fantasy; she became a capitalist, successfully surpassing her white sponsors, which is an ideological threat; and she finally was forced to become a maid, which is an ideological (economic, political, social, psychological) strategy for achieving patriarchal white identity and dominance.

Karen Eng sums up the fantasies many men hold about Asian women: "The fantasy Asian is intelligent yet pliable, mysterious yet ornamental . . . perpetually pre-pubescent–ageless and petite . . . high-pitched, girly—while simultaneously being exotic and wise. . . . She comes from a culture where women traditionally serve men."[60] Josie fulfils this fantasy of servitude, sexually, socially, and economically. And then, her transformation into an unpaid maid, a slave, transitions her into the hands of a female master. The conflation between houseboy (in costume) and maid (in word) signifies the gendered subordination of Asians; that is, whether man or woman and whether serving men or women, Asians are portrayed and perceived as subservient. There is often a sexual component, as well.[61] So-perceived Asian femininity is often pitted directly against feminism, as Mrs. Livingston is proffered as an alternative to liberal/liberated white women.[62] Hop Sing and Peter are "natural" figures in domestic space, undisruptive, suitable for facilitating domestic efficiency and harmony.

As Kent Ono and Vincent Pham point out, it is important to consider representations of Asian women in media as part of an ambivalent dialectic, two contrasting portraits that appear to be opposite but in fact function together to represent women, that is, the lotus blossom–dragon lady (Mrs. Livingston–Josie Packard). Furthermore, Ono and Pham argue that representations of Asian and Asian American men and women work in concert: "One reason Asian and Asian American men and women have been represented differently, and interrelatedly, has to do with the history of colonialism. Colonial logics have been fundamental to the ways people of color have been represented in Western media."[63] Representations of Asian and Asian American men and women are interlinked; none reach the standard of American (white) male, and one avenue to access that power is to forge a relationship with the white male figure, whether "romantic" (sexual), or through a sort of sponsorship.

Conclusion: Possible Solutions and Interventions

In thinking through the gendered subordination of Asian American characters in the media, there can be room for hope for change. Racial meanings are not fixed. For example, in the representations of African American domestics set in the past, there is an opportunity to proffer a corrective, to not offer Mammy or perhaps to offer a completely unexpected image altogether (a Black doctor, a Black philosopher, a Black scientist, etc.). Similarly, a corrective to the portrayal of Asian characters could begin with imagining and supporting Asian American roles (perhaps as an athlete, or a police officer, a dancer). They have Asian physiognomy, they may display some cultural traits or values, they demonstrate confidence and assertiveness, they are American and also of Asian descent. There can be diversity among the portrayals of Asianness in terms of ethnicity, occupation, degree of separation from the immigrant cohort, and they can demonstrate a departure from mainstream notions of feminine and masculine. It is because of controlling images that the notion of "Asian American" as separate and distinct from "Asian" has yet to be made effectively in media representation or, for that matter, in the larger social imaginary.[64][65]

The Courtship of Eddie's Father, while having moments of self-reflexivity and openness, ultimately comports to the trend of handling issues such as gender and race through narrative, visual, and ideological displacement. Even with producer-writer James Komack's deliberate efforts to foreground the talents of Miyoshi Umeki, whom he admired from her previous film work, the racial discourse was unable to move beyond a general "liberal" sentiment and portrayal of racial tolerance.

Another program that ran at this time, *Julia* (1968–1971), also struggled to proffer a woman of color as a main character. The difficulty was in creating and writing a television program that would appeal to and satisfy several audience groups: African Americans, whites, women, and men. Producer Hal Kanter has said that he created the show as a kind of apology for *Beulah* (for which he was a writer) in light of Newton Minow's 1961 "vast wasteland" speech and the NAACP's challenge to the television industry. *Julia*, which starred Diahann Carroll, featured a widowed, middle-class nurse raising her son alone. Her husband had been killed serving in the military, and some viewers objected to the show's failure to present a whole, nuclear Black family. In her essay on *Julia* and its production history, Aniko Bodroghkozy argues that the program ultimately could not manage the issues of both racial and gender equality; therefore, though "positive" in its portrayal of a Black woman in an integrated setting, it remained rather unprogressive in its portrayal of gender and gender relations.[66] Racism was addressed at the expense of sexism.

Roles for Asian Americans in some ways have not changed significantly since Miyoshi Umeki's day in the golden age of Hollywood over fifty years ago. Unlike African Americans, few Asian Americans have roles as leading men or female protagonists in American film or television. The image of Asian Americans might be updated—they speak English without an accent, dress in Western styles, and have attained a certain financial (and qualified social) standing—but in other ways the representations have changed little. Although Asian Americans are often termed a model minority, this group has progressed the least in terms of representation. There are no Asian American "stars" in the mold of a Will Smith or a J.Lo, who played a maid, in the Cinderella tale, *Maid in Manhattan*, directed by one of the first and most important Asian American filmmakers, Wayne Wang. In this instance, the woman of color got the fairy tale ending, in marrying a ("WASP") Republican politician and entering an upwardly mobile hotel management program—and in being portrayed by a huge star. American culture has not yet rallied around a vision of Asian Americans as star-worthy.[67]

Margaret Cho, who has name recognition after over three decades of work as a comedian, actress, and activist, relays, "The only thing that was sort of Asian [as a role model] was *Hello Kitty*. I don't want to model myself after *Hello Kitty*. She has no mouth."[68] More sobering is the racial hatred, and the violence, which can come from such presumptions about women of Asian background: "We who are Asian or Asian American women have our own lives and agency, but to American White supremacy, we are hypersexualized dragon ladies and young brides to be sold. And to the shooter, objects tempting him to sin. . . . There is another narrative arc. For those of us who live and love in this country, and are told we are never fully American. . . . We know this is who this country is, and who we are to it: the perpetual foreigner."[69] Reverend Laura Mariko Cheifetz wrote this in an essay after the Atlanta spa shootings, the killings of Asian immigrant women and others. In it, she beseeches for change.[70]

The Media Action Network for Asian Americans has created a document about restrictive portrayals of Asians in the media and how to balance them. In "A Memo from MANAA to Hollywood: Asian Stereotypes,"[71] the organization offers to-the-point guidelines for those writing, producing, casting, and directing in Hollywood. Here is a selection of the suggestions:

> Portraying Asians as an integral part of the United States.
> More portrayals of acculturated Asian Americans speaking *without* foreign accents.
> Asian Americans in diverse, mainstream occupations: doctors, lawyers, therapists, educators, U.S. soldiers, etc.
> More Asian and Asian American lead roles.
> More Asian men as positive romantic leads.
> Asian women as self-confident and self-respecting, pleasing themselves as well as their loved ones.
> Virtually any project—especially one with a contemporary setting—can make room for Asian characters. And just because a part isn't explicitly written as Asian doesn't necessarily mean that it can't be cast with an Asian actor.

How to integrate people of Asian descent into the American narrative landscape, how to accept Asianness, is a main conundrum in the television texts discussed in this chapter. I see that there is discursive looseness (in the aberrant episodes or in moments of fond emotions and connection), but the discursive looseness is ultimately not liberating. There is liberalism on the part of the productions of *Bonanza* and *The Courtship of Eddie's Father*, but the roles themselves for the Asian Americans in them remain subservient ones. A key goal worth pursuing is to move from an emphasis on portraying foreignness to representing Asian Americanness, and to move from conditional acceptance to belonging.

5

Invisible but Viewable

The Latina Maid in the Shadow of Nannygate

We recognize "Maria" when we see her. The Latina maid is made viewable, though we do not often know (or ask) who she is; the details of her experience are usually invisible and untold. She appears as a character in prime-time television programs and daytime soap operas and in popular Hollywood films, such as *Maid in Manhattan* (2002), in which Jennifer Lopez's growing star power made possible her character's ascent from hotel maid to hotel manager to wife of a prominent (white) Republican senator. The Latina maid figures in newspaper stories, televised news segments, and documentaries about immigration, citizenship, and domestic labor relations (and occasionally about the legal indiscretions of politicians and celebrities). In many of these media contexts, she lacks both voice and individual identity. Her voice is heard obscurely, if at all, often accented or in Spanish or in translation. Her identity may be concealed to protect against job loss or deportation. Rather than speaking for herself, she is spoken about and represented in economic, legal, and political discourse. She stands in for something more than a private employee. As Chon Noriega writes, "Latinos cease to be 'represented' by their own image. Rather, Latinos become overt and coded images for politics by other means."[1]

From the Chinese Exclusion Act of 1882 to California's Proposition 187 in 1994 to the Patriot Act passed by Congress and signed into law after the September 11, 2001, attacks,[2] to the more recent "Build a Wall" rhetoric there is a history of anti-immigrant discrimination sanctioned by the government and taken up in cultural conversation. This discrimination against people perceived as not belonging in our country has targeted different nationalities at different times (usually visually marked as Others). In the contemporary period, the volume of immigration from Latin America, some of it undocumented, means that popular culture particularly associates Latin Americans with surreptitious border crossing and an "illegal" presence in the United States. While the controversy over U.S. immigration policy is beyond the scope of this chapter, what we can focus on is the representation of Latina domestic workers, which signals and triggers racial and legal anxieties.

The Latina Maid as Signifier

The Latina domestic worker is a symbol of wealth and a cause for racial anxiety at the same time. She is both viewable and invisible (both hired and disavowed). And while employment and tax laws contract both employer and employee, it is the domestic worker who lives in precarity. One of the most common jobs for a Latina worker, both in real life and on television, is that of a domestic. As African American women steadily exited domestic service starting from the 1960s, immigrant women, many from Mexico and Central America, took their place. Today, the Latina maid or house cleaner is ubiquitous in many U.S. communities (and in California, the home of Hollywood), particularly in upper-middle-class urban and suburban neighborhoods. While widely present, she is invisible, both socially and economically. And paradoxically, though she is invisible, she is nonetheless unignorable. Her labor and her role—in a family, in society—serve as reminders of a classed, raced, and gendered economy.[3]

In this chapter, I argue that the Latina maid is invisible yet viewable as a kind of structuring absence.[4] She is a figure signifying class and familial achievement while simultaneously, her labor and sometimes her personhood need to be hidden, particularly from the law. Legality is a frame for understanding the representation of the Latina maid in that there is hyperscrutiny and the stakes are high(er) for the immigrant/woman of color who is working to make the American home an ideal one.

The Latina maid is the most current, recognized, and yet naturalized form of the racialized domestic both in media culture and in society. The number, quality, and range of roles for characters of color have been expanding; for example, African American women and men appear in professional occupations, including those with authority (surgeons, judges, politicians). At the same time, the burgeoning Latin market in the United States has attracted the attention of U.S. producers, advertisers, and investors. One may wonder why, then, the Latina maid remains a stock character. Why and how is the Latina maid an actively signifying image? What is the main function of the representation of the Latina maid?

Televisual representations of Latina maids have worked to mediate the family, social space, and the law. Mediation, here, means a mechanism to deal with difference, otherness, and an American nation that is changing demographically. Television functions as a medium and a mediator to enable Americans to deal with difference, and the television representation of race is, essentially, the representation of race relations. An analysis of racialized servants reveals that such race relations are read, understood, and experienced intertextually and that race relations themselves are intertextual, prompted by what a person thinks they know about another person by what they have absorbed through image culture. Such a study enables us to think not only about the Latina house cleaner but about race, class, gender, citizenship, the politics of immigration, and the underground economy. The figure of the Latina maid triggers a political unconscious.

While the Latina maid stimulates a discourse about otherness, citizenship, and belonging, she also raises and sustains ongoing questions about women's roles in relation to the workplace and the family. These questions apply to both employer and employee: how to raise a family, how to make a good life for oneself and loved ones, how to succeed, how to survive.

Housework and the Family Economy

In *Maid in the U.S.A.*, Mary Romero argues, "As domestic service becomes increasingly dominated by women of color, particularly immigrant women, the occupation that brought women of different class backgrounds together in the woman's sphere is now bringing race relations into the middle-class homemaker's home."[5] Domestic service is a complex compound, derived from a chain of interrelated elements: gender and familial roles, public and private space, personal and political/legal biases or ambivalences. Kathleen Anne McHugh states, "Housework is supradisciplinary, as it includes many disparate tasks and crosses over delineations of leisure, labor, and love; while responsible for setting clear boundaries, it also exceeds them."[6] In *American Domesticity*, McHugh argues that "in Hollywood melodramas focused on female protagonists, housework is consistently rendered *invisible* as labor and transformed into emotional, sentimental acts."[7]

The invisible-but-viewable tasks that Latina maids perform are also transformed into politicized, discursive acts. These acts help to confirm and affirm that maintaining an underclass produces happy families along with clean houses and to allay doubts or guilt (for the middle and upper classes). Distinctions can be made between the work that middle- and upper-middle-class women (mostly but not exclusively white) participate in and the work done by working-class women (of color, immigrant, sometimes including white). In the late 1980s and 1990s, scrutiny of working women and mothers began to crystallize with the appearance of a maid (usually a woman of color) who prompts questions about whether the working mother is lacking in parenting duties due to cultivating a career and whether she is faltering in domestic duties because a maid is covering them for her. (Such questions are not raised about men who employ domestic help.) Domestic workers are needed, perhaps necessary, in dual-career households, and yet they are often disavowed (their presence quiet or even denied)—"the elephant in the (clean) room," a structuring absence.

A look at the figure of the Latina domestic worker in four television texts can help us understand how televisual discourses on race, class, and gender participate in the cultural production of meanings about immigration, Americanness, and the family economy. (It also prompts us to think about how else Latinas and Latinos can be represented and can have a presence in American media/culture.) In the network situation comedies *Dudley* (1993) and *I Married Dora* (1987–1988), the Latina maid is employed by middle-class white families to care for their children, touching on the same absent/failed mother trope that was often seen in shows with African American, Asian, or white servants. In the series *Designing Women* (1986–1993), the Latina maid is unseen and unheard, represented by her white employer and impersonated by her white employer's African American assistant at the employer's request. The fourth text examined is not a situation comedy but real-life courtroom footage. The Rosa Lopez hearing, broadcast in February 1995 as part of the live televised coverage of the O. J. Simpson murder trial, featured testimony by the Latina maid who lived at the estate next door to Simpson. In the Lopez hearing, as in *Designing Women*, the issue of racial legitimacy/legality vis-à-vis immigration is heightened. The representation of the Latina maid who is embedded into an American home is suspect by virtue of a tenuous tension: her placement is both intimate and silent, she is both depended upon and disposable by her privileged, economically advantaged employer.

Displaced anxieties are worked through in a domestic setting in *Dudley* and *I Married Dora*, in the workplace in *Designing Women*, and in the legal arena in the Simpson trial. However, in all three venues, gender, race, class, and citizenship status are mediated by the law, by legal status. Framing representation of the Latina maid in the 1990s was the Nannygate scandal, set off by revelations that President Clinton's first two nominees to the post of U.S. attorney general, both women, employed undocumented immigrants in their homes. The affair received saturation coverage in the print, radio, and televisual media and managed to demonize three groups at the same time: immigrants, working-class women, and professional women. In this context, the Latina maid represents a violation of federal law, opening up a larger discourse on race and national identity; at the same time she embodies a violation of middle-class family values by trespassing in the role that traditionally belongs to a mother. Thus the struggle over the legality of the Latina maid revolves around her position in the family as well as her place in society. In both senses her status is called into question.

Since "illegal immigrant" in the public imagination and public discourse so often means (or is code for) illegal immigrant of color, the public images surrounding immigration policy and law are directly linked to race and ethnicity. From television fiction to local news to political campaign commercials, the figure of the Latina domestic—who is often assumed to be an illegal immigrant—embodies an unspoken fear of a changing American portrait.

Racial Themes and Images in Public and Private Life

Like other cultural images, the television image of the Latina maid marks and maintains beliefs and myths. As Marlon Riggs expresses in his film *Ethnic Notions* (1986), images "mirror and mold" social dynamics, affecting how people treat each other. In "New Ethnicities," Stuart Hall argues, "How things are represented and the 'machineries' and regimes of representation in a culture do play a *constitutive*, and not merely a reflexive, after-the-event, role. This gives questions of culture and ideology, and the scenarios of representation—subjectivity, identity, politics—a formative, not merely expressive, place in the constitution of social and political life."[8] The purportedly undocumented domestic worker has a "constitutive" role in the American ideologies of capitalism, freedom, equality, nationhood, and belonging. The Latina maid expresses as well as forms scenes of social conflict and contradiction.

The racialized domestic is an outsider—who is inside someone's home—and yet this dramatic gap is naturalized. As Juan Flores and George Yúdice argue, in order to understand the dynamics of race we need to look at both the public (racially diverse) and private (homogeneous) spheres. These authors proffer a "new social movement" approach to understanding Latino identity based on the premise that both the "melting pot" theory of the early twentieth century and the "new ethnicity" theory of the 1950s and 1960s have been insufficient. The former fails to account for the persistent significance of race in an immigrant group's degree of assimilation into the American culture and economy; that is, it does not recognize the fact of racial stratification. The latter theory, criticized as neoconservative and postmodernist (and thus, relativist), fails to acknowledge that the economic system does not exist separate from cultural values and prejudices. Flores and Yúdice define new social movements as "those struggles around questions of race, gender, environment, religion, and so on, which cannot be fully encompassed under the rubric of class struggle and which play out their demands on the terrains of the body, sexuality, language, etc., that is, those areas which are socially constituted as comprising the 'private' sphere."[9] Race, gender, and class together affect one's standing on both the individual and the institutional levels. Flores and Yúdice identify capitalism as sustaining this process of racialization, and they look to other social practices, such as language, education, policy, self-identity, and self-expression, as ways to understand the status of Latinos in the United States. These practices are intertextual and contribute to racial formation.

In understanding where the Latina maid belongs—within the private and public spheres, within the family as well as in society—language becomes key. The notion of language as a signifier of allegiance is one of the contested terrains that stretches between the public and private spheres. How language is used— how it is spoken and spoken about—permeates external and internal domains, real lived and represented cultures. Flores and Yúdice discuss the activity of "self-formation" in this context: "Self-formation is simultaneously personal and social (or private and public) because the utterances and acts through which we experience or gain our self-images are reaccentuated in relation to how genres have institutionally been made sensitive or responsive to identity factors such as race, gender, class, religion, and so on."[10] They argue that ideology is discursive and is "open to modulation." This discursivity that is "spoken" through television representation is the focus of this chapter and its case studies. Closely analyzing scenes with Latina maids reveals the projection and perception of boundaries of identity and how these scenes express yet displace anxieties about the fact of facilitating an underclass. Racial formation is happening in one's home.

Kathleen McHugh writes in *American Domesticity*, "Housework. Domesticity. Though related, the two words considered independently conjure up extremely different sets of associations and values. Housework is trivial, dull, stultifying labor, work only a woman in love or impoverished would willingly do, repetitive, strenuous, endless, infantilizing. Domesticity, by contrast, refers to home, family, maternity, warmth, hearth, to the creation of a private place where we can be who we really are, to a set of experiences, possessions, and sentiments that are highly symbolically valued in our culture."[11] Domestic service further marks distinctions between experiences in social standing, racial positioning, and measures of femininity.

Latina/o Characters and Media Hegemony

In close analyses of the four television texts, we will see how language marks the literal displacement of the Latina maid from her native home and her symbolic displacement from the home where she now works. In *Ethnic Labels, Latino Lives*, Suzanne Oboler points out the role that language plays "in constructing representations about what constitutes an 'American' national identity."[12] She questions "the role that ethnic labels such as 'Hispanic' are playing in challenging or reinforcing the social and political positions of the populations they encompass in U.S. society."[13] The analysis of television texts raises and responds to a similar question about how representation forces and reinforces social hierarchy and social praxis: how representation affects people who affect policy, and how policies and people in turn affect representation. "From the perspective of the dominant society," Oboler argues, "Hispanic ethnicity is perceived as welfare-ridden, AIDS-ridden, drug-ridden, dropout-ridden, teen-age-pregnancy-ridden—hence, 'Hispanics' become a 'social problem.'"[14] The representative label defines a group of people even as it contributes to a complex discourse about them.

There is a common theme across different racialized servants, whether African American, Asian American, or Latina—that they are considered a problem. "The Negro Problem," the "unsolvable political problem," a "social problem"—the employer/employee power dynamic in domestic service is a way to address the real "problem": the fact of diversity and the fear of a non-white majority.

The notion of Hispanics as social problem is the crux of Chon Noriega's writing on Hollywood narratives about Mexican Americans. He examines how Mexican American characters are portrayed and contained in films made during the reign of the Production Code Administration and the Good Neighbor Policy.[15] "Between 1934 and 1968 the Production Code Administration (PCA), or Hays Office, served as the self-regulatory, institutional mechanism between Hollywood films and the moral and political *status quo*."[16] Noriega argues that though issues related to race are dealt with directly through the narrative in the genre of the social problem film, "in the end, these films must still resolve these social contradictions and situate the Mexican American within normative gender roles, sexual relations, social spaces, and institutional parameters."[17] So, while there is a space to present subject matter dealing with people of color and their relations to America, strict lines are drawn as to where and how a Hispanic person can exist within the culture. Moreover, the supposed social problems are such issues as immigration, miscegenation, and citizenship—that is, the very presence of people of Latin American descent in America.

In *Shot in America: Television, the State, and the Rise of Chicano Cinema*, Noriega offers an innovative methodological approach to combining ethnic studies, cinema studies, and television studies. His goal is to "situate identity within the matrix of both social movements and social institutions."[18] Taking up the issue of ethnic, specifically Chicano, stereotypes in media representations, Noriega conducts a case study of the Frito Bandito figure. The Mexican bandit was featured in a television advertising campaign for corn chips from 1967 until 1971, when he was retired due to pressures and a lawsuit by advocacy groups. The campaign shined a light on the contradiction inherent in the purpose of the mass media, which provide a basic infrastructure serving the public interest even as they are financed by and serve private interests. "Beyond the question of the positive or negative images of an ethnic group, then, the critique of stereotypes exposed a set of power relations reinforced by and existing within mass communication."[19] Noriega shapes a history of the Chicano cinema movement as part of the Chicano civil rights movement; television was both an outlet for Chicano films and part of the struggle for political power and representation. Part of the movement's work was to win recognition for Mexican Americans as a consumer group rather than only a political constituency. Mexican Americans wanted to be categorized, counted, and considered as consumers, because consumers often have more power than community members or citizens.

Furthermore, the protests against Frito Bandito were against derogatory stereotypes and employment discrimination as well, as people demanded more job opportunities in the media. Noriega writes, "The struggle over content masked a more profound demand for access and control over the means of representation and communication. The irony resided in the fact that Chicano media reform groups sought to replace negative stereotypes with positive images through consumer rights and equal employment, and by becoming producers themselves."[20] In Noriega's book, image culture is linked to civil rights. Contemporary examples would be the Atlanta spa shootings and the killing of George Floyd in terms of how ideological representations and meanings of Asian women or Black men informed the killers and how social activism and protests understood the connections. (Race relations are intertextual.) There are grass roots political organizations (e.g., the National Domestic Workers Alliance) that focus on the welfare of domestic workers, with the understanding that maids of color are high in number and that people who are involved in the "care industries" are invoked in political speeches as well as popular culture. In some ways, while not specific, the symbolic Latina maid is invoked—a structuring absence that defines and nevertheless exposes economic exploitation and social inequality.[21]

Similar to how African American and Asian American racial representation has taken form, comedy is the main genre in which the Latina Maid appears. Three of the four television case studies are situation comedies (*Dudley*, *I Married Dora*, and *Designing Women*). Steve Neale and Frank Krutnik state, "It is hardly surprising that comedy often perpetuates prejudice, or draws uncritically on racist or sexist stereotypes, since they provide a ready-made set of images of deviation from social and cultural norms."[22] They theorize the concept of "comic verisimilitude," which has its own decorum and conventions, able to evoke a certain suspension of disbelief. Thus, when we engage with the comical, we are able to suspend or dismiss certain characterizations of people (and concepts) on the one hand, but we must accept them on the other. Neale and Krutnik note that "if the comic always involves a 'transgression of the familiar,' it also always involves a 'familiarization of the transgression.'"[23] Hence the programs' different representations of the Latina maid and the discourses tied to her—a rhetorical engagement of social issues in *I Married Dora*, and a serious legal matter made into a joke in *Designing Women*—serve to exaggerate and defy verisimilitude, but they also end with the status quo.

In the texts analyzed in this chapter, the Latina maid is constructed as a suspicious figure. In examining the attitudes Anglo Americans hold toward Mexicans as reflected in popular literature and film, Arthur Pettit identifies two general types: the half-breed harlot, a "Latina lover" who wants to trap a white man, and the decaying *doña*, a once-beautiful woman whose beauty and desirability are fading.[24] These two sexist tropes, originating in literature and developed in film, have mutated into television form. They can be seen in the figures of Latina women as domestic servants for white American households—for example, the single and attractive Dora in *I Married Dora*, and the made to appear matronly Marta in *Dudley*. However, the Latina maid is portrayed first and foremost as a foreigner and an employee. Thus gender and race are subsumed within the framework of a class barrier, specifically the employer-employee relationship, which tends to veil any sexism or racism. Furthermore, these two programs demonstrate how classism is naturalized through the familiarity (family-arity) that is forged between employer and employee, particularly when children are involved.

Dudley (1993–1994)

For the Latina maid in *Dudley*, the displaced discourse on what it means to be American pivots upon work. Questions about what kind of work she does, whether it is good work, whether she is working out, all gauge her worth and worthiness to be an immigrant striving to become American. The question of her work with the child in the household is most important. If Marta (Lupe Ontiveros) is successful in relating to the child, she can gain access to the family and maintain her job. The child mediates her success and her position in the household, particularly in relation to the father, as the maid becomes a surrogate mother.

The premiere episode has two plotlines. The primary one concerns Dudley's son Fred, a troubled teen who is brought to Dudley (Dudley Moore) by his former wife. In the secondary plot, Dudley humiliates a U.S. senator during his nightclub act and is pressured by his employer to apologize. While not directly integrated into or affecting these storylines, Marta, through humor and in Spanish, evokes a discourse on difference, work, the family, and where she fits in. Marta's moments on screen are short, lasting the duration of her lines, but they invoke issues not dealt with directly in the narrative.

Marta's racial and cultural differences are portrayed as both ridiculous and annoying to Dudley. It is ironic though not surprising that the cultural identity of Dudley, who is British and white, is never questioned. Somehow he is more American than Marta, despite (or perhaps because of) the fact that he is British and, like Marta, speaks with an accent, though a preferred one. Unlike Marta, Dudley can "mess up at work," as he describes the incident with the senator, without risk of being deported. The only time attention is called to his cultural difference is when he makes comments about having spent "half my life not even knowing what the hell a burrito is"; he now hates burritos, the only dish that Marta seems to serve. Food marks the Latina maid's difference and provides justification for the white employer's rejection of his employee.

Dudley's problems with Marta are also with her language. Marta's inability to speak English is the diegetic source of humor: her lines are delivered in

FIGURE 28 Lupe Ontiveros as Marta, in *Dudley*.

Spanish with subtitles and, not unlike Beulah's, are parenthetical jokes.[25] The jokes are presented as miscommunication because of a language difference, but this is ultimately a metaphor and an excuse. As Flores and Yúdice assert in "Living Borders/Buscando America," language is a signifier of difference or belonging, and Marta's language difference is something to be scoffed at. For example, in the 1993 pilot episode, Marta says in Spanish, "I think I broke your washing machine," and Dudley says, "Thank you!" and waves. In another brief segment, Dudley asks Marta to get some fruits and vegetables because she serves burritos too often:

DUDLEY ... the starch, is killing me. Do we have an understanding?
MARA (subtitled) Ah, I gave a bunch of your shirts to charity.
DUDLEY Thank you, thank you, bless you.

When he says "thank you," the audience is cued to laugh. This renders the interaction between employer and employee a joke, but it also demonstrates that the employee is not fulfilling the requests made of her and thus that the employer has nothing to be thankful for. Though Dudley is also an object of humor, ultimately the maid is made out to be doing a poor job. In this way, the language barrier is reduced to job performance instead of cultural difference and miscommunication. The examples of miscommunication are negative consequences to hiring someone who doesn't speak your language; a language barrier is deemed not only unfortunate but, in actuality, a barrier between a legitimate household and those who have proven they do not belong in it.

But the child in the household is able to understand the language of the maid, and as in several other television series featuring maids (*Beulah, The Courtship of Eddie's Father, Family Affair, The Brady Bunch*), it is the child who gains the servant entrance into the family. The son mediates linguistic, cultural, class, and gender differences between the maid and the father. He is situated as a potential agent of social change in a diverse society, as a progressive inheritor of the status quo, and as a point of identification for the audience. Through the work that she does for and with the child—both literal domestic work and more symbolic, interpersonal, emotional labor—the maid is integrated into the family. As the maid raises the child, he enters into a close relationship with the Other and becomes able to relate to her. He will presumably carry these skills with him when he goes out into the world. Unlike his parents, who seem to be confused and unaware, Fred has a sense of coolness and control.

Fred entered the household when Dudley's former wife Lorraine showed up at the door one day bringing their son from Los Angeles back to New York. She says that she called three times: "I spoke to a Spanish woman, didn't she tell you?" Dudley responds facetiously, "In her own way, I suppose she did." Lorraine confesses that she is a failure as a mother and that their son is a "menace to society." Fred is a distinctly white, upper-middle-class version of troubled, whose "menacing" behavior includes skipping school and body piercings. Lorraine begs Dudley to take over the parenting or she will have to send Fred to a military academy.

Fred and his father have problems communicating. The only person Fred seems to regard without hostility is the maid. In fact, it is through her character—as Fred translates between Dudley and Marta—that some semblance of coherence is brought to the household.[26] She turns out to be the magical maid who saves the day, day after day. The Latina maid emerges from the shadows (or the kitchen) to help restabilize the family, or at least to reconcile father and son. Dudley and Fred communicate through Marta; the son has nothing to say to his father but will speak in order to translate. In one scene, Fred plays a joke on his father, telling him that Marta will quit unless she receives a raise. Dudley offers her more money; she is ecstatic and spouts off several *muchas gracias* in Spanish for his generosity. Thus the white male child wields the power and exercises control in the family through the maid. But Marta also has an active role as a mediator between father and son.

Like Beulah and Mrs. Livingston, this Latina maid reunites child and parent, but unlike Alice or Mr. French, she is not invited to become a part of the family. The maid brings unity and security to a frazzled family—a belligerent father in midlife crisis, a distracted and insecure mother, and an awkward adolescent—because she is the one person who is fulfilling (and staying in) the appropriate role. Marta helps remind the family on television and the family watching television of the American Dream. And she helps them achieve it, through her literal and symbolic labor.

Dudley is not the first production in which Lupe Ontiveros played a maid. She has taken the role over 150 times during a thirty-year career as an actress. She has done so with consciousness, giving nuance to different maid roles in films that include *As Good as It Gets* (1997), Steven Spielberg's blockbuster *The Goonies* (1985), and Gregory Nava's eye-opening *El Norte* (1983), and in the NBC sitcoms *Veronica's Closet* (1997–2000) and *Leap of Faith* (2002). An American born in El Paso, Texas, she often puts on an accent in order to play a maid: "When I go in there and speak perfect English, I don't get the part."[27] Further describing her experience, "You say, you want an accent? Oh, yeah, well, we prefer for you to have an accent. And the thicker and more wobbly it is, the more they like it. And this is what I'm against, really, truly. I said Beverly? Her name is Beverly? I'll do it. I don't care what the script is about because her name is Beverly. It wasn't Maria Guadalupe Conchita Esperanza."[28]

Ontiveros has had the opportunity to work in non-maid roles, winning a special jury prize at the Sundance Film Festival for her acting in *Real Women Have Curves* (2002). In this film, she stars as the mother of a Mexican American teen (America Ferrera) who aspires to go to college but who feels pressure to stay and work alongside her family in a Los Angeles sweatshop. Ontiveros also played an unexpected role in the film *Chuck and Buck* (2000), as a theater manager, a part

FIGURE 29 Emmy-nominated, and winner of Alma, Sundance Film Festival, Independent Spirit awards, actress Lupe Ontiveros played a maid over 150 times.

she performed without an accent; for this she won the National Board of Review award for best supporting actress. She played the mother-in-law to Eva Longoria's character in the nighttime soap opera *Desperate Housewives* in its first season (2004–2012). And she narrated the documentary *Maid in America* (2005). Ontiveros has stated, "I'm proud to represent those hands that labor in this country. I've given every maid I've ever portrayed soul and heart." And, she added, she has never hired one.

I Married Dora (1987–1988)

In the social context of the 1980s and 1990s, maids and nannies are needed because mothers are working, but a working mother is often portrayed as an inept mother. The maid in *I Married Dora* fills in for the missing/failed mother even though she is supposed to be "just a maid." This pattern of the maid filling in for a missing or failed mother, seen in the late 1960s and early 1970s and then again in the 1980s, represents a textual economy in generating an ideal mother in a postfeminist televisuality. That is, though the racialized domestic takes on this privileged role, it is also in some way a suspect construction of motherhood/womanhood. The underlying question represented in this show is whether a maid could or should fill in for the missing mother. Though this series ran before Nannygate broke, it is a precursor to the 1990s backlash against a decade of working supermoms. Moreover, it is an example of the contradiction inherent in the representation of the Latina maid as on the one hand indispensable, and on the other hand posing a threat to the "traditional" family unit (of same-race mother and father with a couple of kids living in a suburban home). This program handles the dilemma by absorbing the racial, classed Other into the television family through marriage. However, this resolution also coincided with the cancellation of the short-lived series.

FIGURE 30 Elizabeth Peña as Dora, in *I Married Dora*.

I Married Dora foreshadows Nannygate as it deals with the legalities of employing an immigrant as a domestic servant. Dora Calderón (Elizabeth Peña), a woman from El Salvador, works as a maid for Peter Farrell (Daniel Hugh-Kelly), an architect in Hollywood Hills. When Dora receives a letter from the Department of Immigration informing her that she will be deported, Peter marries her in order to legalize her status and keep her as a maid. Issues of U.S. immigration policy and law are raised and questioned through the actress's performance as well as in the script. Although this program's awareness of politics differs from the subtextual or displaced discourses on race and American citizenship seen in other media representations of Latin American immigrants, its method of negotiating and articulating the meaning of race remains the same. The relationship that the racialized domestic has with her white male employer and, more specifically, with the children in the home sets her position vis-à-vis Americanness.

The character of Dora is feisty and temperamental. She readily expresses her emotions and opinions; when angry, she unleashes rapid-fire Spanish. Dora is a young woman, close enough in age to Peter to be a spouse but also young enough to relate to his two teenage children. There is a physicality to her character: she wears tight-fitting clothes that highlight her curves, her long hair is loosely tousled, and she speaks in a low, raspy voice. She is characterized as a sexual woman and one that is specifically available to Peter, her employer. While Dora is portrayed as sexually exciting, Peter is a somewhat straitlaced, upper-middle-class man. Nevertheless, there is chemistry between them.

The sexuality of the maid is of course a long-standing trope. In many films, television programs, and other stories, maids, nannies, and babysitters have been portrayed as tempting the males in the household. At the same time, Latina women in general have been sexualized and eroticized in popular American culture. The confluence of these two tendencies renders the Latina maid the frequent victim of hypersexual stereotyping. A 1959 manual entitled *Your Maid from Mexico* absurdly warns white women that their Latina maid will be "the sexual initiator for the young males in the family" and "the object of the fantasies of the more mature males."[29] In real life, by contrast, it is rarely the maid who acts as a temptress and far more often the males in the employer household who engage in sexual harassment and abuse of maids. But that reality only reinforces the perception of Latina sexuality as openly accessible.[30]

Elizabeth Peña, who plays Dora, had her first professional break playing the maid in the film *Down and Out in Beverly Hills* (1986). As Carmen (a name with strong connotations of sexual licentiousness due to its operatic fame), she has an explicit sexual liaison with the man of the house. When she is not helping prepare food or cleaning a room, her character is primarily there for erotic purposes, narratively and cinematically.[31] Carmen's character reveals a degree of independence, it seems she enters into this relationship of her own will and desire. She demonstrates her displeasure at being kept waiting when Dave attends to his wife, although this may be more an inflection of Peña's performance than of the role.

FIGURE 31 A "green card" marriage, in *I Married Dora*.

She at times displays the demeanor of a mistress rather than of an employee. Nevertheless, the portrayal of the maid remains sexist. Furthermore, when Carmen grows impatient, she takes a new lover, the family's houseguest, thus demonstrating that she is sexually accessible to the men, plural, in a household, including its guests.

The premiere episode of *I Married Dora* sets up the subject matters of race, racial difference, gender roles, and sexuality as embodied within the frame of employment. After exhausting all legal means to keep Dora from being deported, Peter is resigned. But his children have a solution: he should ask Dora to marry him. In fact, they've already told her that he will. If Peter marries Dora, she can stay in the United States and work for the Farrells. This mutually beneficial marriage/job arrangement would provide each "spouse" with something—child care for him and a place of political refuge for her.[32]

Peter goes to Dora, who is packing her things in her bedroom. Though able to speak English, Dora often speaks it without pause or breath and without breaking up what she is saying into sentences. This manner of speaking aligns her with the children, who can understand her and, when necessary, speak on her behalf. In the discussion of Dora's fate, Peter attempts to understand her situation, inquiring about her personal life for the first time. What will she do when she goes back to El Salvador? Dora answers that she plans to be an orthopedic surgeon. Taking the perspective of a stereotypical white American male, Peter acts very surprised and, inadvertently, condescending. Dora replies, "Yes, really, doctors in my country don't have to speak perfect English." The irony is pointed: in El Salvador, Dora is qualified to work as a doctor, but because of the political circumstances she must be a maid in America.

She is no longer excitable, animated, or breathless. She begins to tell Peter about the injustice and tragedy that her family has experienced, using Spanish phrases, such as *desaparecida* (disappeared) and *escuadrón de la muerte* (death squad). She translates her Spanish for Peter, as well as for the television audience. When Dora finally begins to cry, Peter rushes to the bathroom and brings out a roll of toilet tissue which trails from the bathroom, relieving the seriousness of the scene with laughter. Moreover, this gesture re-creates his offer of a roll of paper towels to his wife in the opening scene, as she was leaving the family because she felt she was not a good mother. As Dora explains her situation for a naive Peter and a naive audience to hear, Peter unwittingly brings her into the position of wife/mother.

When Peter realizes that the United States will not grant her amnesty and that deportation will place her life in danger, he asks her to marry him. Dora declines graciously. "It's not you, it's *us*. We don't talk, we don't touch, we're virtual strangers." To which Peter responds, "My parents were married 50 years under almost identical conditions!" However, even as he tries to convince her to marry him, he casts their coming together as a work arrangement: "It wouldn't be like you were really my wife. I mean, well, you would still cook and clean and take care of the kids, but you would sleep here—and I would sleep *way* down there—I mean nothing would change! You wouldn't want to leave Kate and Will... would you?" The marriage would revolve around her taking care of the children and her relationship with them, not her relations(hip) with him. The proposal is not motivated by romance or love.

Nonetheless, Dora marries Peter, placing herself in the position of surrogate mother to the Farrell children and wife to Peter Farrell. But while she falls comfortably into the role of mother, her role as wife is much more tentative—at times flirtatiously close, at other times a politically loaded joke. Before the wedding scene, a title appears on a black screen: "*Warning*. Marrying an illegal alien to avoid deportation is a federal offense punishable by fines and/or imprisonment." After a pause, the next title reads: "Do not try this in your own home." The relationship that the employer has with the employee—one that breaks racial and class lines and addresses the problem of the need for a mother—is declared illegal. Still, the characters on the show defy this law. By displaying the disclaimer (as ABC was required to do), the program acknowledges federal law while also poking fun at it.

It was a final, closing joke. Unlike other television series that ended with the marriage of former employee and employer, such as *Who's the Boss?* and *The Nanny*, *I Married Dora* did not offer the typical happy ending. The last episode had an absurdist tone, almost winking to the audience; it was not intended to be taken seriously and was in some ways a parody of the proverbial happy ending.[33]

Political Context: "Nannygate"

By the 1990s, the disclaimer that *I Married Dora* humorously offered was no laughing matter. Anti-immigrant and nativist sentiments were on the rise in the early part of the decade. Against that backdrop, Latina maids suddenly became a heated political topic.

In January 1993, Zoë Baird, President Clinton's first nominee to the post of U.S. attorney general, was forced to withdraw from consideration after it was disclosed that she employed an undocumented Peruvian immigrant as a domestic and failed to pay taxes on her wages.[34] The explosion of media coverage in newspapers, on television, and on radio talk shows set off a chain of legal investigations and threw tax law, immigration law, and female work into the public spotlight. Two weeks after the Baird affair, Clinton's second nominee for attorney general, federal judge Kimba M. Wood, withdrew her name after stating that she had hired an undocumented worker as a nanny for her children (even though she had hired the woman before the Immigration Reform and Control Act of 1986 made such hiring illegal).

What came to be known as Nannygate set the figure of the Latina domestic squarely in the realm of policy making. Initially seen as an issue of compliance with tax law, it quickly spiraled into a much larger controversy concerning immigration and employment law.[35] Just as Nannygate cast professional working women as perpetrators of a crime, criminality also came to rest upon the shoulders (and backs and hands and feet) of the immigrant workers themselves. Writing in the *New York Times* about the anti-immigrant backlash set off by the Zoë Baird affair, Lynne Duke set forth the position of activists: "When attorney general–nominee Baird was forced to withdraw because she had illegally hired two undocumented workers from Peru, Clinton officials should have used the setback as an opportunity to clarify labor and immigration laws on the firing of workers who are not citizens. . . . Instead, "hysteria" set in . . . and the issue became clouded with anti-immigrant sentiment and misinformation about immigrant labor."[36]

The issues became larger still as the morality, legality, and ethics of working women in all walks of life were called into question. Nannygate, which in its very name is gendered female, entailed public scrutiny of both the undocumented woman worker and the professional woman who employs her. In many ways, the scandal was used as an attempt to publicly discredit the Clinton administration (and Hillary Rodham Clinton, a professional woman and a mother) in the name of "family values."

Many male politicians and cabinet members also employ domestic help, and in an age when most domestic servants are immigrants, it seems likely that some of this help is undocumented. Yet powerful men, unlike Baird and Wood, are seldom called to account for the immigration status of their domestic workers. Is this because managing a household staff is traditionally seen as the domain of wives, so the men would be held blameless? A professional woman seeking public office is seen as encroaching on what was once strictly male territory and as neglecting her feminine duties in the process. Her supposed dereliction in employing and not paying taxes for an undocumented immigrant serves to highlight her failure as a wife and mother. Although Bobby Ray Inman, whom Clinton nominated for secretary of defense in late 1993, also had undocumented workers in his home, he was never linked to Nannygate (he withdrew his name for other reasons). And when California governor Pete Wilson and California senatorial candidate Michael Huffington were found to have illegal immigrants in their employ, public scrutiny was quickly and easily deflated.[37]

Nannygate implicated Latina domestic workers in a web of legal, ethical, and moral issues. This environment of scrutiny and potentialized wrongdoing was the setting for two Latina maids represented on television in the early 1990s. The character of Consuela Valverde in *Designing Women* is unwittingly involved in an attempt to defraud the government, while Rosa Lopez's role and representation in the O. J. Simpson trial was ultimately about her credibility and trustworthiness as an immigrant worker. The ideologies of Americanness and citizenship are interrogated in the portrayals of these two Latina maids.

Designing Women (1986–1993)

In *Designing Women*, Consuela Valverde is neither seen nor heard. Her employer, Suzanne Sugarbaker, comes into the Atlanta-based, women-owned design firm each morning and shares stories about her maid with the other characters. The Latina maid is spoken about and spoken for. As Ella Shohat and Robert Stam state in *Unthinking Eurocentrism*: "By speaking for marginalized communities, Hollywood indirectly block[s] their self-representation."[38] Consuela is a disembodied figure: she is not only Ralph Ellison's metaphorically invisible (wo)man, she is also literally invisible.

The character of Consuela serves as a structuring absence. A ghost of a figure, she allows the other characters to raise ideological questions about being and becoming an American citizen. The fact that she is unseen and unheard means the discourse and negotiation can take place with no intervention or objection on her part, even when she is the subject of discussion and even when her civil status is at stake.

In the episode ironically entitled "Foreign Affairs" (April 3, 1990), Suzanne has received—and opened—a letter from the Immigration and Naturalization Service addressed to Consuela, stating that the maid is subject to deportation. Although Suzanne does not appear particularly concerned about Consuela's well-being, she does not want to lose her maid. She coerces Anthony, an assistant in the office, to impersonate Consuela during a meeting with an immigration officer. An African American former convict, Anthony has loaded cultural baggage of his own. And like Johnnie Cochran, Christopher Darden, and O. J. Simpson in relation to Rosa Lopez, Anthony acting as Consuela displaces the direct involvement of whites.[39] The fact that Anthony is an ex-con saddles him with a negative stereotype and also lends criminality to Consuela, whom he literally embodies. There is a conflation of "lesser"/lower-class figures into a theatrical character who is simultaneously an imposter and a "Latina maid."

In this scene, Consuela's absence allows for the issue of illegal immigration to be played out and played with. The acts of false representation and fraud are subordinated to the comedy; there is an absence of seriousness in considering the consequences of breaching immigration laws. Nevertheless, the hierarchies of race, gender, and class remain and are mitigated by the humor. Several things are made funny and fun of. One is the maid herself. Suzanne describes Consuela as short-tempered and highly emotional, and as doing voodoo on occasion. She is the punch line to Suzanne's stories. But because her character is not physically portrayed by an actress, it is harder to call it a racist or stereotypical portrayal. Instead of a visual portrayal evoking the power of a controlling image, the troubling construction of Consuela is accomplished through dialogue, which better escapes critique.

Having Anthony take up the role of Consuela can be seen as another attempt to dodge criticism. Suzanne's sister and business partner, Julia, describes him as "a six-foot tall Black man dressed like Hazel." The escape from criticism and responsibility takes place at two levels. First, it is an African American man who impersonates a Latin American (Afro-Latina) woman. Because racism is usually understood as coming from whites, this makes it harder to locate racism in the episode even though the role-playing by Anthony is ordered within the narrative by Suzanne as well as outside the narrative by the writers, producers, and directors. Second, the portrayal of an African American man as objectified and a spectacle in drag sidesteps criticism because it is set up as a performance and farce.[40] It is a federal offense, punishable by fines and/or imprisonment, to falsely represent oneself to a government agency, as Julia warns. Regardless, Suzanne lightly, and quite conveniently, pushes Anthony into this. Furthermore, the legality, and precarity, of Consuela's presence in the United States is secondary to Suzanne's desire to have a maid.

In *Reconstructing Dixie: Race, Gender, and Nostalgia in the Imagined South*, Tara McPherson finds "a certain elitism in *Designing Women*: first, a privileging of gender can make the examination of other categories like race and class difficult, if not impossible; second, a tendency toward a certain "middle-classness" blurs the importance of other issues. For example, the relationship between masculinity and race is a constant problem for the sitcom."[41] Several episodes code Anthony as gay. The implication is that "Anthony is not a real man, and therefore it is safe for him to hang out with these white Southern women, whose

FIGURE 32 Anthony acts out Suzanne's requests, in *Designing Women*, played by Meshach Taylor (seen here with Delta Burke).

attitude toward him is sometimes subtly patronizing, especially early in the series. What is less clear is if Anthony's nonthreatening status is a result of race or sexuality, and the series has difficulty dealing with both issues."[42] Instead, in this episode he occupies the position of an invisible, undocumented Latina maid (who actually gains the flirtatious favor of the African American male judge presiding over the immigration meeting). And in many ways, Anthony takes the role of a subservient assistant in the series in general: "Spatially, he is both inside and outside of the group, often present within the 'main' room, mingling with the women, yet sometimes off in the 'the storeroom,' separate and apart.... Anthony's culturally specific position (as both African American and implicitly as gay) allows him to function within the group without disturbing its nonpatriarchal networks of power while simultaneously foregrounding the relationship between races, classes, and genders."[43] The Latina maid is simultaneously harmless and potentially someone who could bring a great deal of "trouble" to a situation by revealing information about their employer. However, this is not a position of power, for if the law starts to impose on the situation, the maid becomes the focus of blame. She may not be responsible for the employment arrangement, but she is held culpable; the consequences for an informal/illegal employment arrangement are far harsher for the maid.

The Rosa Lopez Hearing (1995)

Another dubious alliance between a brown housekeeper and a Black man can be studied in the Rosa Lopez hearing as part of the O. J. Simpson trial. Rosa Lopez, an immigrant from El Salvador, was the housekeeper in the home of O. J. Simpson's neighbors. Her early statement that she saw his white Ford Bronco parked outside his house at the approximate time of the killings of Nicole Brown Simpson and Ronald Goldman raised the defense team's hopes that she would be a key witness providing Simpson with an alibi. She became an instant media star, seen as frail and vulnerable but also as cold and inscrutable. Called to testify, and panicked by the press attention, she made a desperate attempt to flee the country but was persuaded to return before crossing the border. The questioning of Lopez on February 27, 1995, took place in front of a video camera and not before the jury, though it was broadcast on television. Her testimony was not conclusive, the tape was not played to the jury, and she left for El Salvador before the murder trial was over.[44]

In the hearing, it is as though Rosa Lopez herself is on trial. In a court, there are agents of the law (the lawyers and the judge), those who are testifying (Rosa Lopez in this instance), and those who pass judgment under the law about right and wrong, about who should be vindicated or punished (such as the jury, the spectators in the stands, and the viewers of the television broadcast). As lead prosecuting attorneys, men of color and white women along with an Asian American male judge presiding, act as executors of the law while white men can sit by, having set up the structure. Although she is physically present in the courtroom on this occasion, the Latina maid is absent from this scenario in two important senses.

She is absent, first, from the television coverage, both visually and aurally. In one sequence, prosecuting attorney Chris Darden questions Lopez about her attempt to file for unemployment.[45] For the first forty seconds we see him standing at a podium, directing his gaze out-of-frame toward Lopez. We hear the answers to his questions via the court translator; Rosa's voice is a soft mumble.

The camera eventually pans to Lopez, who sits uncomfortably, wearing an expression of nervous agitation. The translator (who acts as an intermediary) is prominent in the foreground, and Lopez appears to be almost hiding behind the translator's body as well as her words. This pan from left to right sets the boundary between those who are agents and evaluators of the law and Lopez. Though the court stenographer is in Lopez's half of the space, the camera is positioned so that it only catches the top half of the stenographer in view as it pans. Judge Lance Ito is also in this space, but his bench is far above Lopez, so only the side of his desk and part of his left arm can be seen, and he looks down at her. When the lens zooms in on a close shot of Rosa Lopez, her fuchsia sweatsuit stands in contrast to the subdued browns of the wall, the judge's bench, and the witness stand. The camera rests barely twenty seconds on Lopez before panning up to Judge Ito, who moves quickly away from her to the right side of his bench to meet the attorneys at sidebar.

In the latter half of this sequence Rosa Lopez is even more displaced. KTLA news reporter Marta Waller and legal analyst Al Deblanc begin a voice-over commentary as the sound from the courtroom is turned off. Simultaneously, the camera rests on the image of Judge Ito, Christopher Darden, Marcia Clark, Johnnie Cochran, F. Lee Bailey, and Robert Shapiro conferring about the court schedule. We no longer hear Lopez or her translator, and we do not see her either. The talk is about her, the conference is about her testimony, but she is utterly out of the picture.

Second, she is absent on the level of producing her own meaning of identity. Emptied of her own content, she stands in for something else, for a discourse about race, social hierarchy, and the integrity of American citizenship. As Judge Lance Ito said after having to extend the examination of Rosa Lopez, "This hearing has obviously taken on dimensions that go far beyond what we thought it would." The substantive issue of what Lopez witnessed or did not witness is displaced by a larger discussion and display of her work as a maid. Her stability in employment, her integrity in applying for unemployment insurance, and her honesty in claiming that she was leaving to go back to El Salvador are all presented as evidence of her loyalty to the United States or lack thereof. In this light, the test of Lopez's credibility as a witness is her trustworthiness as a Latin American immigrant in the United States, and the testimony becomes a narrative of allegiance. This media experience is a representational and discursive mechanism involving immigration, nationalism, and patriarchy, with a subtext of race, race relations, and miscegenation that is linked to the "guilt" of Simpson.

Lopez's alignment with O. J. Simpson made her an ally of a racial Other and an abettor of the supposed danger and crime of miscegenation that Simpson, with his white wife, represented. Already under a veil of suspicion as an immigrant who is not a U.S. citizen, she was rendered even more suspect because of her association with Simpson. The discourse of race, then, extended from one of

Latin immigrant identity to one of miscegenation and (the preservation of) white identity. Because the cultural subtext of O. J. Simpson's trial was his marriage to Nicole Brown Simpson, and because public opinion about the case was split along racial lines, Lopez chose to be on the side of O. J. rendered her guilty too. Her foreignness, marked by her appearance, her job, and her inability to speak English, worked against her.

As Flores and Yúdice discuss, language is a signifier of difference or belonging: "The attack on the perceived linguistic practices of Latinos is a vehicle for attacks on immigration, bilingual education, inclusion of Latinos in the services of the welfare state, and above all, a repudiation of the effect that Latinos are having in reshaping U.S. culture.... The language question then is a smoke screen for the scapegoating of Latinos on account of recent economic, social and political setbacks for the United States."[46] The representation of language, both in television programs and in lived experience, of people's ability to speak English in America, places people into different categories of Americanness. Are they able to speak English at all? If so, do they have accents? Are the accents connoted as pleasing and sonorous (French, for example) or as crude and cacophonous (Cantonese, for example)? Speaking English is seen as tied to nationalism and even patriotism. The stated principle of English-only legislation is that English should be declared the official language and other languages strictly curtailed or barred in order to protect a sense of national unity and identity.[47] The unstated motivation is to soothe the fears and insecurities of Anglos who speak only English and who may be aggravated by the presence of other languages in the public sphere. Because of her inability to speak English and because of her alignment with Simpson, the figure of Rosa Lopez—made visible in the temporary spotlight of the Simpson trial—unsettled and agitated many Americans. She was a "third term" that many did not want to incorporate into the racial calculus. As Angharad N. Valdivia writes, "In presence and erasure, Latina/os stand in for the imagined nation. They/we track the interstices and struggles of the contemporary identity crisis that face the United States, which formerly thought of itself as homogeneously white or binary in composition (i.e., black and white)."[48]

Conclusion: Suspicious or "Devious Maids"?

The envisioned story of the American Dream tends to be one of white faces and white families in predominantly white neighborhoods. But increasingly, these households and neighborhoods include a corps of Latina maids, house cleaners, and nannies, who overwhelmingly constitute the current domestic workforce. Isolated by language, disregarded as a low-paid toiler, and vulnerable, in some cases for her immigration status, the Latina domestic is in many ways invisible. Yet at the same time she is eminently viewable. She plays a major role in real-life social relations as well as in the production of race, class, and gender in visual culture.

The representation of Latina maids on television mediates the family, social space, and the law. This is notably the case with respect to the ongoing controversy over immigration law and policy. While not all Latina domestics are undocumented—immigration status, citizenship, and, more broadly, the question of who deserves inclusion in U.S. society has been a salient theme in the media representation of Latina maids. In *Watching Jim Crow: The Struggles Over Mississippi TV*, Steven Classen writes that "law has been and continues to be a key site for social and cultural conflict. What is deemed lawful, true, and trustworthy is defined as such within a particular discursive context."[49] The use of images as a way to engage larger social discourses yet still control them is one of the media's main functions.

In criticizing this discursive work, Ana López has developed the concept of "Hollywood as ethnographer." Films and television programs produced by Hollywood proffer descriptions of racial groups and enable a certain kind of interaction between viewers and "others" who are different from them. She writes, "Hollywood does not represent ethnics and minorities: it creates them and provides its audience with an experience of them."[50] Often a characterization of an ethnic or racial Other is not simply a gross caricature but rather a means to exorcise anxieties, creating a small space for negotiating fears such as the fear of difference, of intermarriage, and of a changing nationhood. Hollywood functions "not as a simple reproducer of fixed and homogeneous cultures or ideologies, but as a producer of some of the multiple discourses that intervene in, affirm and contest the socio-ideological struggles of a given moment."[51] We can see evidence of this in television portrayals of the Latina maid that display and expose their racial, linguistic, and cultural differences in order to make them less threatening.

From situation comedies to courtroom drama to television news, the "illegal alien" is portrayed as someone to laugh at, to fear, or to dismiss.[52] Arthur Petit argues about stories and narratives, myths and beliefs: "Fiction ... in such a fashion teaches us more about elitist racial fantasies than social realities. It describes more about what Anglo-Americans have wished to believe about themselves than what they actually were like; more about what they wished to happen than what actually happened; more about things as writers believed they should have been than things as they were."[53] While different racialized groups of women have replaced one another in the occupation of domestic service, the racialized domestic is still situated relative to her more privileged and usually white female employer. As Pierrette Hondagneu-Sotelo argues in *Doméstica*, "Women raised in another nation are using their own adult capacities to fulfill the reproductive work of more privileged American women, subsidizing the careers and social opportunities of their employer."[54] The story of the Latina maid is also a story about women and their relationships to one another within the literal as well as representational economy.

Creating characters in unexpected genres is one strategy for producing counter-stories. Though the figure of the racialized domestic has been employed staunchly and whether in a comedy, or a reality program (*Flipping Out*, featuring Zoila Chavez), or a dramedy-mystery (*Devious Maids*), she continues to signify doubt, guilt, and unease across genres. Is the image too loaded to be changed? This is a question of debate for the female-made, female-centered, *Devious Maids* (2013–2016), which aired on the female-targeted Lifetime network. Produced by actress (and political advocate[55]) Eva Longoria with Marc Cherry who created the nighttime soap, *Desperate Housewives* (2004–2012) in which Longoria costarred as an affluent suburban wife, there is a carryover campiness to *Devious Maids*. The series features four Latina lead characters, Marisol, Carmen, Rosie, and Zoila—as maids.

One critic lamented, "Because Latinas in leading roles on TV are rare, their images matter. A 2012 survey by the National Hispanic Media Coalition asked non-Hispanics how they view Latinos on TV and in movies. Sixty-one percent said that they saw Latinos as 'maids,' an answer beaten out only by 'criminal' and 'gardener.' That's a sad reflection of reality. Longoria would do far better to craft a TV show about a woman more like herself—independent, powerful and multitalented."[56] Longoria's rebuttal: "When we get any sort of backlash like that—'Oh, they're just playing the stereotypical maids'—my immediate response is, 'So you're telling me those stories aren't worth telling. That those people are lesser than. That their stories aren't worth exploring. That they have no complexity in their life because they're a maid?"[57] Another television critic asked, "Why does every Hispanic female character on this show have to be a maid? Thankfully, the maids themselves aren't stereotypes. But there are no Latina bosses here. The series barely shows the maids' homes or relatives who aren't servants. Even when these funny, charismatic ladies get together for lunch in a park, what do they talk about? Not their own families or interests; they talk about their bosses."[58] While the interactions with (and against) the wealthy white women who employ them are the sources for plot, humor, and drama, the maids are varied and individual, and each has her own backstory and motivation. While the marketing is sensationalistic, objectifying the "hot" housekeepers in tight dresses and high heels while holding mops, brooms, and dustpans as props, the success of the program is notable for employing four Latina actresses in lead roles as the main characters.

Moreover, a Mexican American executive produced the show, and Longoria knowingly and respectfully brought in Lupe Ontiveros for a role. Was it a wrong move to create a program focusing on Latina maids? While some critics thought so, many Latina/o viewers loved the program. They appreciated seeing smart, delightful, "devious" Latina characters—domestic workers, themselves, enjoyed the campy portrayals and seeing and hearing the perspectives (facilitated by the

FIGURE 33 The female-made, female-centered, *Devious Maids* starring Latina actresses (L-R) Edy Ganem, Judy Reyes, Ana Ortiz, Roselyn Sánchez, and Dania Ramirez.

script and camerawork) of Latina maids. *Devious Maids* can also be understood and appreciated as subversive. Similar to Raquel Gates's call to embrace the negative and eschew "respectability politics," perhaps *Devious Maids* gestures toward alternative models of representation of/for the maid in particular. Beverly Hills, where the characters work, is shown from the inside-out rather than the outside-in, thanks to the maids. They hold knowledge and do not hold their tongues. Still, because the major plot is a murder mystery about whether one of the women is the guilty one, and because the occupation for all four of the protagonists is that of a domestic, do they remain characters under suspicion?

Part of the project of this book is to look at how depictions of domestic servants help in understanding American culture and inequality. Much of American media—and U.S. race relations—is about the preoccupation with racial harmony and the struggle over integration. Because part of the job of the Latina maid in media culture is to discursively and intertextually mark the boundaries of race and class, of who is family and who is American, is integration possible?

The implications of this study also engage with production culture and practices. In her book, *Latino TV: A History*, Mary Beltrán conducts close analysis of programs with Latino leads, such as *a.k.a. Pablo* (1984, ABC) as case studies of representational practices. Considering factors such as star discourse and authorship as well as social contexts, Beltrán examines how limited the experiences of Latinos on television have been, and observes how television signals cultural citizenship. Key in her analysis is the notion of, "what works for TV," according to executives and producers. She writes in her opening, "I don't mean to imply that nuanced and appealing Latina/o narratives are necessarily only created by Latina/o writers and media makers, or that Latinas/os can only tell Latina/o stories."[59] At the same time, she argues later, "A homogeneous group of white male executives will more likely share a sense of cultural taste, which becomes codified as 'good TV'; when Latinas/os are excluded from executive ranks, it's less likely that a series like *a.k.a. Pablo* will be valued and given a chance to develop and draw a larger audience."[60] In her last chapter, Beltrán examines the rise of Latina writers and showrunners (in the 2010s), demonstrating that having Latinas in the lead is productive as well as innovative.[61]

Further, Beltrán finds proposed programs on what is called, "The Latinx TV List"[62] to have promising narratives; they are exciting and idiosyncratic (they are not what one has come to expect, and they have characters who are not maids or housecleaners). The description, idiosyncratic, is reminiscent of how filmmaker Renee Tajima-Peña has described Asian America as eclectic.[63] In her film, *My America* (1997), she tells multiple stories about how "America became its people, rather than how people have become American." We can also understand that television has the ability to show America as Latino, rather than struggle to portray Latinos as American.

While Mary Beltrán is concerned about Latino cultural citizenship, Arlene Dávila has written about Latinadad (cultural practices of pan-Latino communities) in particular relation to markets. In her book, *Latinos Inc.: The Marketing and Making of a People*, Dávila examines how Latino communities are homogenized and whitened in/for transnational markets as well as how Latino creatives are too often used as "cultural brokers." That is, "Corporate America consistently relegates Hispanics to community relations departments, where they advise the corporation about Hispanic issues of debates, or about the best activity or latest festival they should sponsor, but rarely have influence or the power to direct the development of original advertising executions."[64] She critiques the notion of corroborating mainstream inclinations about and conceptions of a "Hispanic market" in producing Latin images and argues against "the traps of corporate Hispanidad and its essentialist politics."[65] There remains a misunderstanding (or reluctance to understand) that the Latino audience and Latina/o representation in the United States is not addressed by Hispanic marketing. Instead, as Beltrán advocates for, there needs to be Latina/o access, self-representation, and creative agency.

Epilogue

Racialized domestics portrayed in television serve to idealize family dynamics and racial harmony. *Maid for Television: Race, Class, Gender, and a Representational Economy* shows that race and racial difference are defined in structures of work, family, class, and gender through the figure of the racialized domestic, and that these structures are intricately intertwined and rationalized. This book has discussed what Herman Gray identifies as "representational fields" formed through "images and their travels."[1] Fields to consider in the ultimate goal to expand the numbers and range of people of color on screen and behind the scenes include academic research, creative development in the television industry, the televisual portrayals or texts, employment (on both sides of the camera), and audience activity. While *Maid for Television* is an example of the first, an academic expression of concern, I also set forth suggestions in other realms as the figure of mammy or a subservient servant or the invisible-but-viewable domestica say more about their creators and consumers than about the person or community being characterized.

The Enduring Figure of the Maid

The figure of the servant continues to fascinate and evoke emotions. She continues to have a social presence and a media presence, inasmuch as the representation of family, motherhood, class identity, national identity, and race are part of the stories we wish to tell and strive to understand.

From the golden age of Hollywood's technicolored storytelling of our American history with a film like *Gone With the Wind* in which Miss Scarlett O'Hara is as iconic as Mammy is, whiteness together with Blackness comprised the way in which we read history. Twenty-five years earlier, the birth of cinema and cinematic language with *The Birth of a Nation* mapped out racialized characters (including a housemaid, Lydia), gender roles, race relations, narrative positioning, lighting, camera work, sound editing, set design, and more. And seventy years later, a film called, *The Help* replicated what I have called retrospective displacement in looking at America's past with only a partial sense of accountability in that "today" is always going to take credit for being better than "then." The problem with this is its facile (if not false) reliance on the passage of time to bring about change, and that these narratives (while somewhat sympathetic to structures of oppression) uphold white privilege, or more particularly, a privileging of white perspectives and authorship.

Self-determination—socially, politically, economically, and in the related realm of media culture—can come from self-authorship. Still, institutional recognition is needed to mark the independence. The powerless exist in the same world as the privileged, so a redistribution of power is necessary for change to happen. Television is a product of social power already in place as well as a producer of social power. In bringing this book to a close, after considering case studies across racial groups and demonstrating a variety of analytical theories about the function of representation as related to social discourses, I think that opening broader discursive practices concerning race is possible in and through television, and that we can identify strategies for making this happen.

Why Study Race?

First, to be better equipped to shift representational cultural practices we need to study race. Race matters—despite this becoming a contentious subject of debate, a certain reality remains: it is not possible to be color-blind, and espousing to be erases or ignores rather than seeks to acknowledge and understand difference. Difference can be positively mobilized, it does not have to mark anxiety or hierarchy as it has in traditional representational language (and attendant ideological meaning).

There are three false premises or misunderstandings about race in relation to television and film:

1) The misunderstanding that viewers cannot "identify" with characters of a different race than their own (this also ignores complex or mixed-race identities)
2) The misunderstanding that talking about race is a complaint (rather than a positive possibility)
3) The misunderstanding that being asked to improve diversity in production and media culture is limiting rather than creative

These misunderstandings underestimate the capacity of viewers, of television, and of the creative process.

Still, television has operated by what I call a representational racial economy, in which there isn't "too much" difference, and whiteness is kept in balance (i.e., dominant). A representational economy is one that manages how much difference, or diversity, is allowed in the system, and that benefits some more than others. Economy is about wealth and resources, expenditures and profit. Cultural and racial representation does not have to operate according to or be preoccupied by this model. Creating a new system of representation requires thinking about and opposing a racial capitalism in which some characters are endowed with more value. Jodi Melamed writes in relation to Cedric Robinson who first theorized this phenomenon: "Our dominant critical understanding of the term racial capitalism stays close to the usage of its originator.... Robinson develops the term to correct the developmentalism and racism that led Marx and Engels to believe mistakenly that European bourgeois society would rationalize social relations. Instead, Robinson explains, the obverse occurred: 'The development, organization, and expansion of capitalist society pursued essentially racial directions, so too did social ideology.'"[2] So how can race be represented in nonhierarchical terms? Seeing, intervening, and finding alternatives to a representational economy that disallows (or displays hesitancy toward) diversity is possible. We need to shift the representational economy and broaden its dimensions.

Maid for Television reveals the ways in which whiteness and Americanness coincide, in an effort to open up Other ways to comprehend who and what is American. The patterned, sometimes pat (and oftentimes unconscious), vision/version of America is outdated, even untrue (though there are those who have imbued the mythic America as "great" and want it "again"). America has been represented as "white" even when it was not. It has been represented as fully democratic and egalitarian even when it is not. Instead, we need racial stories, stories of struggle that are engaged in the present and which are delivered in broader genres than situation comedy. For Blackness or Asianness or Latina/oness to be represented in a new way, whiteness cannot be represented as prioritized. For "family" to be represented in new ways, the ways that women and mothers function narratively, visually, and ideologically need to expand and evolve. Americanness must be represented with specific stories of difference from the perspectives of people of color, of distinct class backgrounds, onscreen and behind the scenes.

Discourse of Diversity

On the one hand, casting and hiring have been managed to uphold whiteness, on the other hand, we have entered an era of what I see as a vexed discourse of diversity. In looking at DEI (diversity, equity, inclusion) within discourses of Hollywood itself, diversity is overplayed yet undernourished. #OscarsSoWhite has attempted (after a few years' delay) to address the problem by inviting scores of people of color into the Academy's voting body. Networks and film studios are rushing to show, and prove, that they agree politically with the call to have more diverse products/productions (and that they are not racist). These are sometimes self-congratulatory displays of awareness (at least an awareness of criticism and protest) with accompanying pledges; it has yet to be seen how they are meaningful. Moreover, a worrisome effect of performative allyship is that people will become overly reliant that the Industry will correct itself. I have written elsewhere about another fallacy: that change automatically comes with the passage of time, which is an utterly passive disposition.

The following are some concepts of diversity that can be applied in media criticism as well as in media practices:

- Diversity is a mode, not a mandate, it is a way to be creative not restrictive.
- It is about a pursuit of depth of character and story and background (not window-dressing or "coloring up," which methods have been used previously).
- It defies the underestimation of an audience's ability to "identify" with a character of color (which implies white-as-center) or with a character who is not "like" them.
- Counter-stories that are counter-hegemonic can be good stories; they are often unexpected and can bring unexpected pleasure.

Establishing diversity in representational culture is about, first, correcting and countering deeply embedded and unequal (disparaging and damaging) racial and gendered meanings, second, creating new stories and offering different perspectives, and third, intervening in the production of knowledge. It is also about employment opportunities and opening physical and symbolic doors. Diversity is both a principle and a practice; it requires time, thought, and effort to establish. And it comes from both the production side (institutional patterns) and the reception end (audience responses).

Race and Genre

Genre also matters. It is not a coincidence that the sitcom has been the main stage on which to display race relations. The significance of this is that laughter would diffuse tension and that a twenty-two-minute resolution would bring levity to gravity. The situation comedy genre, whether a family sitcom or one set in the workplace/school or among a group of friends/roommates, continues to be the most common structure and format to display "multiculturalism" because of the diffuseness of race. The representational racial economy allows for a diverse, integrated cast across an ensemble—with white characters as the lead and in the lead. In the larger landscape of televisual genres, comedies provide a kind of antidote but may also force a choice when it comes to the representation of race; representing race relations in drama, for example, changes the mood and mindset.

In the cases of programs with a predominantly Black cast, comedy has been the delivery system such that humor rather than anger or discontent is the mood. Timothy Havens has researched and written about *The Cosby Show* as a global sitcom (with complex viewership), which portrays a universal family as a "respectable" Black family. Racquel Gates has analyzed and written about rejecting and defying the "politics of respectability" as a method for seeing the Black image in popular culture.[3]

There are a handful of programs in television history that focus on a Latina/o cast, and there have been only a few that feature Asian Americans as the main cast: *All-American Girl, Fresh Off the Boat, Dr. Ken*, plus a limited reality series, *Bling Empire; Master of None, The Mindy Project*, and Mindy Kaling's *Never Have I Ever* feature Indian American protagonists who are comedic, imperfect, and self-deprecating. The generic patterns in U.S. television's representation of race and racial figures have tended to be as comic relief, as sports icons, as musical entertainment, and in specific racialized pairings. Certainly comedy is not in opposition to critique; there are numerous examples of stand-up comics in their own, literal voices expressing and exposing racist realities, often with quizzical and comical political sophistication and keen social insight. Margaret Cho, Dave Chappelle, Hasan Minhaj, sketch comedians Keegan-Michael Key and Jordan Peele, and Richard Pryor before them to name a few, but these voices and performances have mostly been off-center (or censored, in the case of Pryor's four-episode television series). The question is about the range of genres and characters for people of color in the media landscape, as well as in the cultural imagination.

A summary of key arguments from the previous chapters in *Maid for Television* includes the following: that in order for Blackness to be represented differently, whiteness needs to be represented differently; in television's depiction of family, comes the privileged power of whiteness to define what is American; Asian Americans need to be considered American, not as "perpetual foreigners"; Latina maids as a structuring absence must have that dynamic dismantled and their presence foregrounded. "Race" is, does, and causes many things. In this book, we think about race as a mode of perception and a frame of looking within representational practices that "economize" difference—and yet, we also understand that racial meanings are not fixed.

Cleaning as the Storyline and the Maid as Heroic

There are two recent programs that add intrigue to the discussion of women, race, class, and genre in television. *The Cleaning Lady* (2022–) on Fox has the protagonist's job as vital to her entrée into a crime drama and demonstrates how she utilizes or maximizes the stealth of being a cleaning lady, while the Netflix acclaimed hit, *Maid* (2021) portrays the protagonist having to resort to cleaning as part of her misfortune, setting up the narrative trajectory that she will get out of it in the end. For both, they need the work to survive, but *The Cleaning Lady* explores the circumstances of an undocumented immigrant, the vulnerability and limits in economic and personal security, while *Maid*, despite its title, focuses on a victim who escapes domestic violence for which working as a maid is something to also survive and move on from.

Maid is adapted from a memoir by Stephanie Land, *Maid: Hard Work, Low Pay and a Mother's Will to Survive*. The protagonist is admirable; Alex (Stephanie) struggles as a young mother with a daughter, and she triumphs in going to college and majoring in creative writing, gaining her independence and beginning her path to becoming a best-selling author. Housecleaning was temporary, character-building, and shown as not adequate for this working-class white woman.

Thony De La Rosa, a Cambodian woman trained as a surgeon also shows an overqualification for the job, along with her grit, determination, courage, and a fierce love for her child. She is in the United States seeking life-saving medical treatment for her son's immunodeficiency disorder. While cleaning hotels and buildings in Las Vegas, one night, she witnesses a murder, and in the moment that she is discovered and about to be killed, she states, "I'm just the cleaning lady, I can help you make this disappear." She then becomes "the cleaner" for the crime organization, saving herself, and saving the large sums of money she is paid to put towards her son's treatment. (There are also dramatic moments when her skill as a doctor saves lives.) Thony performs many layers of a working woman, a doctor, a sister-in-law, a wife, a mother, a maid, an FBI informant (who also informs her mob boss about what is going on), and an immigrant. *The Cleaning Lady* is the first U.S. television program to focus on a Cambodian-Filipino family, and to be created by and to star Asian women—actress Élodie Yung is French and Cambodian, producer and writer, Miranda Kwok, is Chinese Canadian.

In a postfeminist context, that is, when feminism as a direct political stance recedes with a presumption that the feminist concerns and demands of the 1970s have been met, programs like *Maid* and *The Cleaning Lady* elide feminism and keep the condition of women in service work fairly unchallenged. But there is a denaturalization of the role not seen in earlier depictions of women as domestic workers. Furthermore, the genres of memoir/drama and crime/thriller (with a touch of melodrama) stretch both the limits of story and of the viewer's imagination. These two examples redirect our understanding of why and how one comes to occupy the position of a person who cleans for a living, and they mark a shift for women as maids to take the lead on screen.

Maid for Television

In *Race and the Cultural Industries*, Anamik Saha advocates for a theory of cultural production that takes agency as well as structure seriously.[4] He wants to shift the question from how race is represented to how race is made. That is, to move (or connect) to the politics of production. He argues "that it is the process of commodification that steers the work of cultural producers into reproducing historical constructions of Otherness."[5] At the same time, he calls for and believes in the possibility of opening up representational practices. While Saha is looking for change to come from production practices, I would add the component of change and agency coming from audiences, from the viewer-consumer whose tastes and preferences are what producers are seeking to satisfy.

Race is visible, it is visual. Race is an aesthetic, though it is not immutable (whiteness as ideal beauty, Asianness as conditional beauty; it took a campaign for people to see that "Black is Beautiful" too, for example). Race relations happen on screen and off, the potential for social change through television and televisual discourse is strong. Racialized domestics live—in houses, in imaginations—we need their perspectives not just their passing images and deferential speech to tell stories about American life. What stories are we willing to tell, to hear, to share, and to learn from? The study of the maid of color in television is about how we, as a country and a culture, host difference in the home. I hope we will learn to be better, more informed, and more caring hosts.

The relationship between text and context is dialogic, diachronic, and co-constitutive. The maid mediates between family members, between public and private worlds, and between different racial, class, and gender positions. Focusing on the figure of the domestic servant enables us to see the relationship between cultural representation and social formation. In its promotion of a post–civil rights society, U.S. film and television represent racial disharmony as a thing of the past through the portrayal of African American domestics. White servants on television also make opaque the social reality of difference in obscuring class conflict. Television texts have been able to subsume subservience under the auspices of family or even of love and gratitude and to naturalize social hierarchies based on gender and nationality, as especially illustrated in the figure of the Asian servant. The figure of the Latina maid on television (in both fictional and nonfictional form) is an uncomfortable reminder that this country's declarations of democracy and equality exist alongside exploitation and economic, social, and political inequality. Still, the desire for equal opportunities in life, love, work, and education remains—both on and beyond television, manifest in fantasy worlds and grass-roots activism, in tangible and ephemeral ways.

Troy Duster has written that race is both structural and whimsical.[6] It is both entrenched and changeable. As we have come to understand how Otherness and whiteness are defined and determined in relation to each other, seeing how text and context are inextricably linked enables those of us who are critical yet hopeful to start to gain control of controlling images. Agency lies in different places, sometimes with producers, at other times with viewers. The case studies in this book span fifty years, reaching the millennium. The next century marks a new era in television culture, cultural practices, viewing practices, and media studies. Some of the changes underway give hope and inspiration for new and more flexible ways in which television may come to reflect and shape our understandings of race. As television, too, is structural and whimsical.

Acknowledgments

In bringing this book to publication there are people and programs who have advanced the project directly, or influenced its fruition indirectly, or fueled ideas encouragingly, or simply spoke about the endeavor positively—all have provided support. I am thankful to the following (and more).

At Smith College: government professors Dr. Walter Morris-Hale, Martha Ackelsberg, Philip Green, and my first film professor, Deborah Judith Linderman.

At UCLA: In the School of Theater, Film and Television professors Chon Noriega, Vivian Sobchack, John Caldwell, Teshome Gabriel, Nick Brown, as well as Dr. Walter Allen. Arts librarian, Raymond Soto. Members of my cohort (plus a few who were befriended during that era), Genevieve Fong, Gilberto Blasini, Luisela Alvaray, Anna Everett, Katherine Sarafian, Beretta Smith-Shomade, Teri Webb, Bambi Haggins, Miranda Banks, Jun Okada, Yeidy Rivero, Mary Beltrán. The collection and staff at the UCLA Film & Television Archive and the Archive Research and Study Center. Members of the Office of Affirmative Affairs and the Graduate Division, where I held a part-time position in outreach and mentoring for undergraduate students, and AAP (Academic Advancement Program), where tutoring students developed my desire to teach.

The Institute of American Cultures at UCLA offered me a postdoctoral fellowship in interethnic studies, and The Ralph J. Bunche Center for African American Studies hosted my stay. My thanks to then director Darnell Hunt, special programs coordinator, Alex Tucker, and then IAC chair Shirley Hune.

Other significant research experiences have been in connection to the Race and Independent Media Group convened at UCLA by Chon Noriega as director of the UCLA Chicano Studies Research Center; the Women of Color and Work Group convened at the University of Maryland by professors Elsa Barkley Brown and Bonnie Thornton Dill in The Harriet Tubman Department of

Women, Gender, and Sexuality Studies; and visits to The Library of Congress and The Wisconsin Center for Film and Theater Research (affiliated with the University of Wisconsin–Madison), specifically, the Ziv Television Collection.

At Northwestern University: Chuck Kleinhans was a mentor and friend, Mimi White, José B. Capino, Heon Seo, Nina Martin (and beyond Evanston), Anne Burton, Karla Rae Fuller, Julia Lesage, Barbara Katz, Michelle Hung, and special thanks to Jennifer A. White.

The Berkeley Chancellor's Postdoctoral Fellowship and the Film Program headed by Linda Williams provided valuable professional opportunities and returned me to the UC for the long-term.

At UC Santa Cruz: Many have been collegial and warm on this beautiful campus. In working on the book, I have appreciated the company and conversations with Stacy Kamehiro, Audrey Kim, Rui Li, Angela Gengler Dobkin, Alice Russell, and Anny Mogollón. I would like to acknowledge the institutional support through the EVC Fellows Academy and my writing group, Eva Bertram, Steve McKay, Alice Yang, along with colleagues who offered advice in my early years at UCSC, Margaret Morse, Amelie Hastie, and Herman Gray. The UCSC Arts Research Institute provided a completion grant, which helped with photographs/illustrations. Derek at Photofest helped secure the images in this book. The Center for Cultural Studies at UC Santa Cruz programs a stimulating speaker series and forum for discussion. Members of my department have shared their collegiality. The members and ethos of the UCSC Asian American Pacific Islander Faculty and Staff Group have given meaningful and sustaining motivation.

I would like to thank the readers who reviewed the manuscript in earlier stages and the editorial and production teams at Rutgers University Press, which has guided its authors through the dramatic past two years. I would also like to express my appreciation to Anne Jones at Westchester Publishing Services.

Finally and with long-standing as well as ongoing gratitude, I would like to thank my family, the Kims, Parks, and Greenfelds, with special acknowledgment for Eric, Jonah, and Jeremy Kim Greenfeld. My thanks to many who have made this book possible.

Notes

Chapter 1 Introduction

1. Patricia Hill Collins, *Black Feminist Thought: Knowledge, Consciousness, and the Politics of Empowerment* (New York: Routledge, 2000, 2009), 77.
2. Patricia Hill Collins, "Foreword," in *Emerging Intersections: Race, Class, and Gender in Theory, Policy, and Practice*, ed. Bonnie Thornton Dill and Ruth Enid Zambrana (New Brunswick, NJ: Rutgers University Press, 2009), vi.
3. Collins, viii.
4. Collins, x.
5. Collins, ix.
6. Bonnie Thornton Dill and Ruth Enid Zambrana, "Critical Thinking about Inequality: An Emerging Lens," in *Emerging Intersections: Race, Class, and Gender in Theory, Policy, and Practice*, ed. Bonnie Thornton Dill and Ruth Enid Zambrana (New Brunswick, NJ: Rutgers University Press, 2009), 1–21, 3.
7. Dill and Zambrana, 4.
8. *Critical Race Theory: The Key Writings That Formed the Movement*, ed. Kimberlé Crenshaw, Neil Gotanda, Garry Peller, and Kendall Thomas (New York: The New Press, 1995), xiv.
9. *Critical Race Theory*, xiv.
10. Consider: "Within this cramped conception of racial domination, the evil of racism exists when—and only when—one can point to specific, discrete acts of racial discrimination.... Given this essentially negative, indeed, dismissive view of racial identity and its social meanings, it was not surprising that mainstream legal thought came to embrace the ideal of 'color blindness' as the dominant moral compass of social enlightenment about race." *Critical Race Theory*, xv.
11. *Critical Race Theory*, xxv.
12. Lynn Spigel, "White Flight," in *The Revolution Wasn't Televised: Sixties Television and Social Conflict*, ed. Lynn Spigel and Michael Curtin (New York: Routledge, 1997).
13. Aniko Bodroghkozy, *Groove Tube: Sixties Television and the Youth Rebellion* (Durham, NC: Duke University Press, 2001), 3.
14. Darnell Hunt has asserted the idea of race-*as-representation* in his anthology, *Channeling Blackness: Studies on Television and Race in America*, and an example of

172 • Notes to Pages 7–11

the representation of race as that of race relations is explored in his book, *Screening the Los Angeles "Riots": Race, Seeing, and Resistance*.

15 The television program *Beulah* began as a radio show in which the voice of Beulah was performed by a white man, Marlin Hunt, lending another layer to the reading of this character.

16 Graham Allen, *Intertextuality* (New York: Routledge, 2002), 1.

17 Michael Omi and Howard Winant, *Racial Formations in the United States: From the 1960s to the 1980s* (New York: Routledge, 1994), 3–4.

18 Omi and Winant, 34.

19 The phrase "to express and form" comes from Stuart Hall, "New Ethnicities," in *"Race," Culture, and Difference*, ed. James Donald and Ali Rettansi (Thousand Oaks, CA: Sage, 1992), 253–254.

20 Tomás Almaguer, *Racial Fault Lines: The Historical Origins of White Supremacy in California* (Berkeley: University of California Press, 1994), 1. This is not to suggest that the different groups of people of color all banded together or were even at peace with one another. For example, though Native Americans and African Americans were both oppressed, and though they were involved in interracial relationships to a certain extent, they also assumed oppositional positions. After the Civil War, African Americans served in the Army in the West and were called "buffalo soldiers" because Native Americans thought their hair resembled buffalo fur. When a unit of these soldiers was sent to protect white homesteaders from Native Americans, the whites, especially those from the South, would often prefer the presence of the Native Americans to that of the African Americans. Furthermore, there has been a complex tension between African American and Asian laborers—both Asian Americans and immigrants—that extends to the present day. One manifestation is the so-called Black-Korean conflict, which contributed to the destruction of Korean-owned businesses in predominantly African American neighborhoods during the Los Angeles uprisings of 1992. Thus the process of racialization separates whites from nonwhites and at the same time creates schisms among people of color.

21 For elaboration on hooks's formulation of this patriarchy, see the video *Cultural Criticism & Transformation* (1997), produced and directed by Sut Jhally. Also see works by hooks: *Black Looks: Race and Representation* (Boston: South End Press, 1992); *Outlaw Culture: Resisting Representation* (New York: Routledge, 1994, 2006); *Talking Back: Thinking Feminism, Thinking Black* (Boston: South End Press, 1989); and *Feminist Theory: From Margin to Center* (Boston: South End Press, 1984; London: Pluto, 2000).

22 Herman Gray, *Watching Race: Television and the Struggle for Blackness* (Minneapolis: University of Minnesota Press, 2004).

23 Ruth Frankenberg, *White Women, Race Matters: The Social Construction of Whiteness* (Minneapolis: University of Minnesota Press, 1993), 6.

24 Aída Hurtado, *The Color of Privilege: Three Blasphemies on Race and Feminism* (Ann Arbor: University of Michigan Press, 2004), viii.

25 Hurtado.

26 David Katzman, *Seven Days a Week: Women and Domestic Service in Industrializing America* (New York: Oxford University Press, 1978), 72.

27 Mary Romero, *Maid in the U.S.A.* (New York: Routledge, 1992), 83.

28 Romero, 86.

29 It would be illuminating to know how many Latina and Latino immigrants are currently working in domestic service. Unfortunately, this information is difficult

30. Katzman, *Seven Days a Week*, 271.
31. See Charles Hirschman and Liz Mogford, "Immigrants and Industrialization in the United States, 1880 to 1920" (Department of Sociology and Center for Studies in Demography and Ecology, University of Washington, Seattle, 2007).
32. Romero, *Maid in the U.S.A.*, 75.
33. Romero writes, "As domestic service becomes increasingly dominated by women of color, particularly immigrant women, the occupation that brought women of different class backgrounds together in the woman's sphere is now bringing race relations into the middle-class homemaker's home," 69.
34. Romero, 79.
35. Judith Rollins, *Between Women: Domestics and Their Employers* (Philadelphia: Temple University Press, 1985), 48.
36. Quoted in Lynn Freed, "HERS: A Stranger in the House," *New York Times Magazine*, May 15, 1994, 34.
37. Nearly 77 percent of households owned a television set by 1955. By 1968, 95 percent of American family homes had a television.
38. Ella Taylor, *Prime-Time Families: Television Culture in Post-War America* (Berkeley: University of California Press, 1989), 3.
39. Lynn Spigel, *Make Room for TV: Television and the Family Ideal in Postwar America* (Chicago: University of Chicago Press, 1992), 2.
40. Spigel writes, "In this social climate, television was typically welcomed as a catalyst for renewed domestic values. In many popular sources, television was depicted as a panacea for the broken homes and hearts of wartime life; not only was it shown to restore faith in family togetherness, but as the most sought-after appliance for sale in postwar America, it also renewed faith in the splendors of consumer capitalism," 2–3.
41. In the year 1945, there were fewer than 10,000 sets in the country. By 1960, there were 52 million sets in American homes, which is one in almost nine out of ten households. This figure soared to 219 million in 1997, according to the *CIA World Factbook* for the U.S. (May 2007); the percentage of households with at least one television was 99 percent by 2007, according to Norman Herr, Television & Health, *Sourcebook for Teaching Science*, May 20, 2007.
42. J. Fred MacDonald, *Blacks and White TV: African Americans in Television since 1948*, 2nd ed. (Chicago: Nelson-Hall, 1992), 1.
43. MacDonald, 1–2.
44. These issues were discussed at a symposium I helped convene, "Race and TV: Where We Have Been, Where We Are Going, and Why Do We Care?" The June 10, 2005, event was sponsored by the Ralph J. Bunche Center for African American Studies at the University of California, Los Angeles, under the direction of Darnell Hunt.
45. As Almaguer writes in *Racial Fault Lines*, "The particular success of European-American men in securing a privileged social status was typically exacted through contentious, racialized struggles with Mexicans, Native Americans, and Asian immigrants over land ownership or labor-market position. These competitive struggles for valued social resources, in turn, had direct consequences for the invidious discourses that inscribed racial difference and provided popular ideological support for California's white supremacist origins," 3.
46. George Fredrickson, *White Supremacy: A Comparative Study in American and South African History* (New York: Oxford University Press, 1981), xi.

47 Almaguer, *Racial Fault Lines*, 7.
48 Angela Davis, *Women, Race & Class* (New York: Vintage Books, 1983), 227.
49 Quoted in Romero, *Maid in the U.S.A.*, 54.
50 Davis, *Women, Race & Class*, 238.
51 Indeed, the title of Judith Rollins's book is *Between Women*.
52 Rollins, *Between Women*, 158.
53 Elizabeth Clark-Lewis, *Living In, Living Out: African American Domestics and the Great Migration* (New York: Kodansha International, 1996), 109.
54 Clark-Lewis, 113.
55 Rollins, *Between Women*, 203.
56 In *Black Feminist Thought*, Patricia Hill Collins writes, "No matter how much they were loved by their white 'families,' Black women domestic workers remained poor because they were economically exploited," 81.
57 Collins, *Black Feminist Thought*, 68.
58 Collins, 72.
59 Mammy's body can be seen in American folk figurines such as cookie jars and salt and pepper shakers. A notable example is the Mrs. Butterworth's maple syrup bottle, described on the Pinnacle Food Group Web site as a "distinctive grandmother-shaped bottle." It has been modified over the course of a century to less blatantly resemble a Black slave.
60 See Darrell Y. Hamamoto, *Monitored Peril: Asian Americans and the Politics of TV Representation* (Minneapolis: University of Minnesota Press, 1994), and K. Sue Jewell, *From Mammy to Miss America and Beyond: Cultural Images and the Shaping of U. S. Social Policy* (New York: Routledge, 1993).
61 Evelyn Nakano Glenn, *Issei, Nisei, War Bride: Three Generations of Japanese American Women in Domestic Service* (Philadelphia: Temple University Press, 1986), 87.

Chapter 2 Domesticating Blackness

1 In writing about African Americans in early Hollywood film, Ella Shohat and Robert Stam argue, "Blacks appeared in these films, just as women still frequently do in Hollywood, as images in spectacles whose social thrust is primarily shaped by others: 'Black souls as White man's artifact' (Fanon)." *Unthinking Eurocentrism: Multiculturalism and the Media* (New York: Routledge, 1994), 187.
2 The domestic service performed by African Americans for white employers cannot escape its genesis in American slavery, nor are the chains of exploitation broken so definitively. A century and a half after the Emancipation Proclamation of 1863 freed the slaves, freedom remains a term in question as long as servants remain an integral part of the American economy and of the idealized American family.
3 John Caldwell's discussion about the news coverage of the 1992 L.A. Uprising (more popularly tagged "the L.A. Riots") as operating in "crisis mode" elaborates upon how "race" on television takes the form of racial conflict. Local news productions in Los Angeles struggled to take control in a period of social unrest and semiotic instability; within a few months, scripts for fictional television reflected a similar attempt to "make sense" out of the L.A. uprising through narratives that provided resolution through scenes that ultimately reached racial harmony. See John Caldwell, "Televisual Politics: Negotiating Race in the L.A. Rebellion," in *Televisuality: Style, Crisis, and Authority in American Television* (New Brunswick, NJ: Rutgers University Press, 1995), 301–335.

4 The famous television mini-series *Roots* (1977) was another memorable example of the representation of acknowledged racism and racial inequality. However, the program was not called "The Brutalities of Slavery," as Dr. Alvin Poussaint comments in Marlon Riggs's film *Color Adjustment*; it was called *Roots*. In telling the story of a former slave family, the program de-emphasized racism and played up the Horatio Alger, immigrant-striver aspects of the tale. The abuses and injustices perpetrated against African Americans were depicted as individual acts of cruelty rather than as an institutional American practice. And, like the representation of racial struggles within the framework of the struggle for civil rights, this story of post-slavery, post–Civil War America was set long ago and far away.
5 The series *American Dreams* (2002–2005, NBC), which offered a contemplative trip back to the 1960s, is another example of how representing changing race relations displaces or mutes a current-day discussion.
6 Both Viola Davis who played the role of the 1950s maid in the 2011 film and Bryce Dallas Howard who played one of the white women who employed an African American domestic, expressed their regret in contributing to the re-circulation/re-creation of this narrative, particularly because it was from a (nostalgic) white author's point of view.
7 Bambi L. Haggins, *Mad Laughter: The Black Comic Persona in Post-Soul America* (New Brunswick, NJ: Rutgers University Press, 2007).
8 Racial theory asks us to differentiate between race and racism. See Michael Omi and Howard Winant, *Racial Formation in the United States: From the 1960s to the 1990s* (New York: Routledge, 1994), 69–76.
9 Patricia Turner, *Ceramic Uncles and Celluloid Mammies: Black Images and Their Influence on Culture* (New York: Anchor Books, 1994), 45.
10 Turner, 47.
11 Tara Mcpherson interrogates the relationship between patterns of conventional narrative and social change. She believes that popular cultural narratives of the South can be reformed toward a new imagination. She writes that new narrative patterns might help to move "beyond nostalgia, guilt and white racial melancholia." *Reconstructing Dixie: Race, Gender, Nostalgia, in the Imagined South* (Durham: Duke University Press, 2003), 6.
12 Mammy characters sometimes bear similar-sounding names, such as Mamie, Mattie, or even Aunt Nellie. Beulah was often used in film roles, much as Maria or Rosa are used as the names of Latina maids in more contemporary film contexts.
13 Kimberly Wallace-Sanders traces the etymology of the word in *Mammy: A Century of Race, Gender, and Southern Memory* (Ann Arbor: University of Michigan, 2008), 4:

"The earliest use of the word *mammy* in reference to slave women caring for white children occurs in 1810 in a travel narrative about the American South. The *American Dictionary of Regional English* traces the etymological roots of the word to a blending of *ma'am* and *mamma*. There is evidence that the term was first used as a more common southern term for mother. The term *mammy* is not consistently linked to specific patterns of behavior before 1850, but by 1820 the word was almost exclusively associated with African American women serving as wet nurse and caretakers of white children.

"*Mammy* and *Aunt Jemima* are often used interchangeably today, but it is significant that the former predates the latter by almost a century. Aunt Jemima was introduced to the world at the 1893 World's Fair as a Reconstructionist alter ego to the mammy; the mammy's domain is the nursery, while Aunt Jemima's is the kitchen.

Aunt Jemima offered northerners the southern antebellum experience of having a mammy, without actually participating in slavery."

14 K. Sue Jewell, *From Mammy to Miss America and Beyond: Cultural Images and the Shaping of U.S. Social Policy* (New York: Routledge, 1993).
15 "Mammy" is part of the lexicon of antebellum mythology that continues to have a provocative and tenacious hold on the American psyche. Her large dark body and her round smiling face tower over our imaginations, causing more accurate representations of African American women to wither in her shadow. The mammy's stereotypical attributes—her deeply sonorous and effortlessly soothing voice, her infinite patience, her raucous laugh, her self-deprecating wit, her implicit understanding and acceptance of her inferiority and her devotion to whites—all point to a long-lasting and troubled marriage of racial and gender essentialism, mythology, and southern nostalgia. Wallace-Sanders, *Mammy*, 2
16 Jewell, *From Mammy to Miss America*, 39.
17 Wallace-Sanders, *Mammy*, 127.
18 It is worth noting that the character and actress are dressed nicely in the series. Lilly is not in uniform, nor does she wear drab clothing as a way to downplay the importance of her character, which occurs in other portrayals of servants. Rather, Lilly Harper, played by Regina Taylor, wears muted but colorful dresses and attractive cardigans paired with tailored skirts; on her birthday, she looks beautiful in a semiformal silk dress and jewelry, her hair and makeup done (notably, she dresses up for a party being held in her own home). This suggests that the character has a sense of her presentation of self and that the creators of the program (writers, costume designers, makeup artists) were invested in this character, treating the character (and the actress) decently.
19 Angela Davis, *Women, Race & Class* (New York: Vintage Books, 1983), 11.
20 Davis, 23.
21 "A round, black, shiny face is hers, so glossy as to suggest the idea that she might have been washed over with the whites of eggs, like one of her own tea rusks. Her whole plump countenance beams with satisfaction and contentment from under a well-starched checked turban, bearing on it, however, if we must confess it, a little of that tinge of self-consciousness which becomes the first cook of the neighborhood, as Aunt Chloe was universally held and acknowledged to be." Harriet Beecher Stowe, *Uncle Tom's Cabin* (New York: Barnes & Noble Classics, 2003), 24.
22 Turner, *Ceramic Uncles and Celluloid Mammies*, 47.
23 Turner, 48.
24 Turner, 49.
25 Tara McPherson, *Reconstructing Dixie: Race, Gender, and Nostalgia in the Imagined South* (Duke University Press, 2003). A topsy-turvy doll with which one flips the skirt to reveal one doll or another, as Kimberly Wallace-Sanders describes, also illustrates the connectedness between Black and white (they literally share a body), as well as the one-view-at-a-time lenticularity of seeing the Black nurse doll or the white girl doll, but not both faces at once.
26 Darnell M. Hunt, *Screening the Los Angeles "Riots"* (New York: Cambridge University Press, 1997), 16.
27 Patricia Hill Collins, *Black Feminist Thought: Knowledge, Consciousness, and the Politics of Empowerment* (New York: Routledge, 1991), 68.
28 In one of Oprah Winfrey's first forays into film she played the character Sophia in *The Color Purple* (1985). Sophia is a strong, "sassy" Black woman who is eventually punished, abused, and disabled by her white female employer for being self-assertive.

In more recent roles, Niecy Nash has taken up a character being seen more frequently and identified as becoming a new pattern, that of the Black Lady Therapist.
29 Turner, *Ceramic Uncles & Celluloid Mammies*, 51–53.
30 Donald Bogle, *Blacks in American Films and Television: An Encyclopedia* (New York: Simon & Schuster, 1989), 236.
31 Mamie's niece, Drucilla, represents the post–civil rights generation. She has subsequently become a major character, joining the glamorous cast of *The Young and the Restless* and the citizens of Genoa City. Still, Mamie allowed the growth of African American fandom for an otherwise "white" soap opera.
32 Bogle, *Blacks in American Films and Television*, 236.
33 Such images, made for whites, were also most often made by whites—the white producers and writers of Black characters. In *Blacks and White TV*, J. Fred MacDonald quotes a study of *Amos 'n' Andy* (1951–1953), which was one of the first television programs with African American characters: "Amos and Andy were only black on the outside.... Their birth, nurturing, and development—all of the inner 'machinations'—were white." J. Fred MacDonald, *Blacks and White TV: African Americans in Television since 1948*, 2nd ed. (Chicago: Nelson-Hall, 1992), 31.

Such "machinations" or creations are most often comedic, and the situation comedy is overwhelmingly the genre through which race and race relations are represented.
34 Darrell Hamamoto, *Nervous Laughter: Television Situation Comedy and Liberal Democratic Ideology* (New York: Praeger, 1989), 153.
35 The National Association for the Advancement of Colored People (NAACP) was active in monitoring media representations of African Americans and protested the depiction of the Mammy figure in Hollywood. The organization eventually succeeded in getting *Amos 'n' Andy* off the air.
36 It was rare in the 1950s for television screens to include integrated images of African Americans and white Americans. While Hollywood films maintained white subjectivity with characters of color in the background or in segregated productions, it was not easy to put Black faces on television, especially in nonsubservient roles. On his own television show, Nat King Cole was not allowed to be on stage alone with a white woman. The *Nat King Cole Show* (1956) was canceled within a year; despite the popularity of his beloved velvet voice, Cole's face was offensive to many viewers.
37 Tim Brooks and Earle Marsh, *The Complete Directory to Prime Time Network TV Shows, 1946–Present* (New York: Ballantine Books, 1992).
38 Donald Bogle, *Brown Sugar: Eighty Years of America's Black Female Superstars* (New York: Harmony Books, 1980), 74. For further information on McDaniel's life, see Carlton Jackson, *Hattie: The Life of Hattie McDaniel* (New York: Madison Books, 1990).
39 Hattie McDaniel is known to have said, "I'd rather play a maid, than be one."
40 According to the Internet Movie Database (IMDb, at http://www.imdb.com), when the date of the Atlanta premiere of *Gone With the Wind* (1939) approached, McDaniel told director Victor Fleming she would not be able to make it, when in actuality she wanted to avoid trouble in light of the virulent racism that was rampant in Atlanta at the time.
41 As I suggested earlier, Ella Shohat and Robert Stam (among others) also argue that within stereotypes, actresses and actors have forged moments of resistance. These authors also consult the work of Donald Bogle: "For Bogle, the history of Black performance is one of battling against confining types and categories, a battle homologous to the quotidian struggle of three-dimensional Blacks against the

imprisoning conventions of an apartheid-style system.... At their best, Black performances undercut stereotypes by individualizing the type or slyly standing above it. The 'flamboyant bossiness' of McDaniel's 'Mammy' in *Gone With the Wind*, her way of looking Scarlett right in the eye, within this perspective, indirectly translates into hostility toward a racist system." Shohat and Stam, *Unthinking Eurocentrism*, 195–197. Though I find Shohat and Stam a bit too optimistic, I agree with their belief that there are subtextual discourses and possibilities for resistance in the performances of actresses and actors of color.

42 According to IMDb, the studio forced Louise Beavers to eat extra servings of food so she could play the jolly Black mammy roles that were available to actresses of color at the time.

43 The Internet Movie Database lists Amanda Randolph as also having played the character of Beulah before she began playing the maid Louise, in *Make Room for Daddy*. But I have not found any existing episodes with her in them.

44 There is a hypervisibility of the Black domestic in contrast to the invisibility of the Latina domestica, who is also subordinated because often her primary language is other than English.

45 McDaniel appeared in episode 1.13 in 1949.

46 The character of Bill Jackson was played by three different actors: Buddy Harris, Ernest Whitman, and Dooley Wilson. Wilson is perhaps most famous for his role in *Casablanca* (1942) as the piano-playing Sam; his last work was in *Beulah*. Oriole was played by both Ruby Dandridge and Butterfly McQueen. Ruby Dandridge was the mother of Dorothy Dandridge, an actress who played famed roles in *Carmen Jones* (1959) and *Porgy and Bess* (1959) and was the first African American woman to be nominated for an Academy Award in a lead role.

47 Jewell, *From Mammy to Miss America*, 41.

48 To read more about the politics of the smile, see Brian Locke's chapter "The Dancing Itos" in *Living Color: Race and Television in the United States*, ed. Sasha Torres (Durham, NC: Duke University Press, 1998), 239–254. In this essay, Locke analyzes the racial dichotomy between Black and white and carves out a space for factoring in Asian Americans, specifically in the cultural zeitgeist surrounding the O. J. Simpson trial and its Japanese American judge, Lance Ito. Locke analyzes and critiques the broad, toothy smile of musician and racial sidekick Kevin Eubanks, who replaced Branford Marsalis (who refused to smile egregiously) on *The Tonight Show with Jay Leno*. This was the same program that regularly featured the Dancing Itos, a chorus line of men dressed to resemble Judge Ito, doing the can-can, kicking and exposing their bare legs underneath the judicial robes.

49 Butterfly McQueen played Prissy in *Gone With the Wind* and became famous for the hysterical line, "I don't know nothin' bout 'birthin' no babies!"

50 Alice Childress, *Like One of the Family: Conversations from a Domestic's Life* (Boston: Beacon Press, 1986), 2–3.

51 Musician Willie Wilson describes: "'I'll Fly Away' is a song that our forefathers traditionally sang during sad occasions like during slavery when the slave master would gather the Black slaves, take them to the trading blocks and divide and sell them to the highest bidder." *Chicago Defender*, February 2, 2002.

52 Vertamae Smart-Grosvenor's *A Domestic Rap* is another powerful personal account of domestic service from the servant's perspective. It contains many telling descriptions of the relationship between the maid and the employer's children. Among them: "White folks don't raise their children with no kind of manners. Slaps their hands when they should be cutting their asses. That brat I take care of

this most selfishest white bastard I ever took care of. Everytime I don't let him has his way, he scream I'm gonna tell my daddy and he'll fire you cause you a nigger and niggers are supposed to do what white people tell them. Also, I'm old enough to be his grandmother, and they allow him to call me by my first name. Now you tell me who taught that boy that—he must have overheard it from his parents. He sure didn't hear it from me. No. I'm telling you, white folks does not raise their children to respect other peoples." *Thursdays and Every Other Sunday Off: A Domestic Rap* (Garden City, NY: Doubleday, 1972), 32–33.

53 Turner, *Ceramic Uncles and Celluloid Mammies*, 54.
54 A story line develops in which Nathan begins to like one of the African American student activists, Claudia. See, in particular, the episode entitled "Commencement," first aired on January 29, 1993 (season 2).
55 The white woman who falsely (knowingly) accused Emmett Till, is still living; it was decided in 2022 not to press charges against her for lying.
56 Cobbs spoke at a tribute to *I'll Fly Away* presented as part of the Ninth Annual Television Festival of the Museum of Television & Radio (now the Paley Center for Media).
57 When an African American bystander or witness offers their opinion, it is usually framed in a way that portrays the individual as overly dramatic or suspect. In this way, the news program itself retains the power of authorship and controls the ideological boundaries of what is said or represented.
58 Though the producers shied away from owning that their program was about race, as illustrated in an interview in *The Washington Post* by Michael E. Hill dated September 15, 1991, in which Joshua Brand states that Lilly Harper "could be another nationality . . . it could be a person in Maine in 1991 talking to his housekeeper who is from a different part of the world, and a different color." The journalist writes, "Not likely. The story is essentially about a conflicted white Southerner sensing change in racial relations in the South before the dramatic outbreak of the civil rights movement in the '60s. And it is about his housekeeper, whose strength and dignity won't let him forget her name."
59 The three failed "quality" shows never achieved the type of audience allegiance won by intensely popular programs such as *The Waltons* (1972–1981) or *Little House on the Prairie* (1974–1983) that also revisited (and revisioned) America's earlier times. Furthermore, serious dramas that were successful in the 1990s tended to be police or hospital dramas, notably *NYPD Blue* (1993–2005) and *ER* (1994–2009), rather than those set in the home (one domestic drama, *My So-Called Life*, ran from 1994 to 1995, and there are other examples). PBS did, however, pick up a series that the major networks did not, *American Family* (2002–2003), which was about a Latino family set in Los Angeles.
60 John Caldwell, "Televisual Politics: Negotiating Race in the L.A. Rebellion," in *Televisuality: Style, Crisis, and Authority in American Television* (New Brunswick, NJ: Rutgers University Press, 1995), 301–335 (chapter 11).
61 The civil unrest is recorded as lasting 5 days, April 29–May 4, 1992.
62 Season 3, episode 2, "Will Gets Committed." Original Air Date: September 21, 1992.
63 Season 1, Episode 10, "Kiss My Butler. Original Air Date: November 5, 1990. Season 2, Episode 16, "Geoffrey Cleans Up." Original Air Date: February 20, 1992.
64 Geoffrey's accent is "posh," which is actually inaccurate.
65 Maya Gonzalez, PhD candidate in the History of Consciousness program, University of California, Santa Cruz.

66 Actress Isabel Sanford has another association with being a maid, in her role as Tillie, the family servant in the film, *Guess Who's Coming to Dinner?* (1967). Here, she is distinctly disapproving of the interracial relationship between the white young woman she presumably helped to raise, and Sidney Poitier's character who is her suitor.

67 See Robert Guillaume's interview as part of the Program of the Television Academy Foundation, sponsored by the Archive of American Television. http://www.emmytvlegends.org/interviews/shows/benson.

68 Guillaume won an Outstanding Supporting Actor Emmy Award in 1979 for the series *Soap*, and an Outstanding Lead Comedy Actor primetime Emmy Award in 1985 for the series *Benson*. He remains the only African American actor to have won as Lead Comedy Actor (Bill Cosby never won for the incredibly, globally popular, *The Cosby Show* (1984–1992).

69 Maya Gonzalez.

70 See the episode, "Inheritance" in Season 2.

71 The quoted line is from *Mad Men*, Season One, Episode 13, "The Wheel," airdate: October 16, 2007.

72 Air Date: October 17, 2010. Beginning at the 7:47 minute mark.

73 It is a missed opportunity to develop/to see a relationship between a Black woman and a white woman. The Lifetime series, *Any Day Now* (1998–2002) is notable in doing so. The program was about two women who met and grew up in the 1960s in the American South, providing a rarely seen interaction between Black and white: as friends.

74 Wallace-Sanders, *Mammy*, 5.

75 Wallace-Sanders, 8 and 134 (introduction and conclusion).

76 Collins, *Black Feminist Thought*, 68.

77 Programs such as *Insecure* and *Girlfriends*, and *Living Single* before them, feature fascinating, individual, varied Black women. These are important television series, and there are more that have recently premiered, such as *Harlem*, *Run the World*, Tyler Perry's *Sistas*, Lena Waithe's *Twenties*, and BET's *Leimert Park* (where a great deal of *Insecure* is set). There are scripts focused on Black female friendships, produced by African American creatives (out of a need for them). A question remains about how "mainstream" media production can create scripts with African American, white, and other characters without capitulating to racial hierarchies?

78 For further study of the representation of Black women and Black womanhood on television, see Beretta E. Smith-Shomade's *Shaded Lives: African-American Women and Television* (New Brunswick, NJ: Rutgers University Press, 2002).

79 Smith-Shomade, 177.

80 Niecy Nash also starred as Deputy Raineesha Williams in *Reno 911!* (2003–2009), an over-the-top character in an over-the-top spoof of *COPS*. Her full-of-attitude persona travels intertextually between the two programs. In the fall of 2008, Nash starred in a quickly canceled Fox sitcom, *Do Not Disturb*, set in a New York City hotel. Her character, Rhonda, who ran the hotel's human resources department, was described as "brash, fabulous and brutally honest."

81 bell hooks, *Art on My Mind: Visual Politics* (New York: New Press, 1995), 98.

82 "The Mammy was created by white Southerners to redeem the relationship between black women and white men within slave society in response to the antislavery attack from the North during the ante-bellum era, and to embellish it with nostalgia in the post-bellum period," Turner, *Ceramic Uncles and Celluloid Mammies*, 44.

83 Turner, 61.

84 September 15, 1991, *The Washington Post*, Michael E. Hill.
85 August 28, 1992, *The Washington Post*, Jacqueline Trescott.
86 Or worse, the mere mention of race gets read as racism, raising ire, so-called controversy, and inevitable disagreement. As MacDonald warns, "But let us not be naïve: the regressive forces of race prejudice still flourish in the United States. Racism makes money and it still generates votes," *Blacks and White TV*, ix.

Chapter 3   Shades of Whiteness

1 Ruth Frankenberg, *White Women, Race Matters: The Social Construction of Whiteness* (Minneapolis: University of Minnesota Press, 1993), 1.
2 Judith Levine, "White Like Me," *Ms.* Magazine Volume 4 (1994), 22.
3 Darnell Hunt writes about "chains of equivalence" illustrating positive connotations attached to whiteness and negative connotations attached to blackness, in his introductory chapter to *Channeling Blackness: Studies on Race and Television in America* (New York: Oxford University Press, 2005).
4 Matthew Frye Jacobson, *Whiteness of a Different Color: European Immigrants and the Alchemy of Race* (Cambridge, MA: Harvard University Press, 1999).
5 Jacobson, 9, 11.
6 Richard Dyer, *White: Essays on Race and Culture* (New York: Routledge, 1997), i.
7 One might be curious to know whether there are instances of white servants working for nonwhite families in television. I have found one example of this in a recent but short-lived program, *Kevin Hill* (1994–1995). In it, Taye Diggs plays an attorney and bachelor who gains custody of his cousin's baby daughter and then employs a gay white male nanny to assist him.
8 Frankenberg, *White Women, Race Matters*, 138.
9 Frankenberg, 229.
10 Michael Omi and Howard Winant, *Racial Formations in the United States: From the 1960s to the 1980s* (New York: Routledge, 1994), 1.
11 Jacobson, *Whiteness of a Different Color*, 10.
12 See John Fiske, *Media Matters: Race and Gender in U.S. Politics* (Minneapolis: University of Minnesota Press, 1996), 97–104, and Herman Gray, "Remembering Civil Rights: Television, Memory, and the 1960s" in *The Revolution Wasn't Televised: Sixties Television and Social Conflict*, ed. Lynn Spigel and Michael Curtin (New York: Routledge, 1997), 348–358.
13 See Justin Lewis and Sut Jhally, *Enlightened Racism: The Cosby Show, Audiences, and the Myth of the American Dream* (Boulder, CO: Westview Press, 1992).
14 The phrase "family values" came into popular usage during the George H. W. Bush administration in the late 1980s. It was used in political and social discourse to differentiate "good" versus "bad" Americans, especially after the uprising that took place in Los Angeles in 1992 around the Rodney King verdicts. The term is code for middle-class and upper-middle-class families, often white, who subscribe to a set of conservative "values," most notably heterosexual marriage, sometimes with a born-again Christian orientation.
15 Stuart Hall, "The Whites of Their Eyes: Racist Ideologies and the Media," in *Silver Linings: Some Strategies for the Eighties*, ed. George Bridges and Rosalind Brunt (London: Lawrence and Wishart, 1981), 39. Emphasis in the original.
16 Ella Taylor, *Prime-Time Families: Television Culture in Postwar America* (Berkeley: University of California Press, 1989), 19.
17 Taylor, 26.

18 I am using the term "linchpin" as Laura Mulvey does in her article about woman-as-Other, as object of the gaze; that is, the Other is what/who holds the whole apparatus—structure of looking, identification, pleasure—together. Mulvey's influential essay, "Visual Pleasure and Narrative Cinema," was first published in *Screen* 16 (Autumn 1975), 6–18.

19 A larger feminist critique and consideration is warranted in discussing niche programming such as those found on the Lifetime and Hallmark networks. For example, Lifetime (which has had female CEOs) sponsors nonfiction as well as based-on-true-stories about women's lives and women's issues. And while Hallmark is known to be a conservative brand, there have been moves to diversify its stories to include romantic leads of color.

20 Critics generally found the program mildly amusing, though some complained that it was often contrived and repetitive. Despite the mixed reviews of *Hazel*, the program was in the top 25 for the first three years of its five-year run. It ranked number 4 in 1961–1962, number 15 in 1962–1963, and number 22 in 1963–1964. It also held some value with a few network producers; after NBC dropped the show, CBS quickly picked it up.

21 Tim Brooks and Earle Marsh, *The Complete Directory to Prime Time Network TV Shows 1946–Present* (New York: Ballantine Books, 1992), 433. Hazel thus has more in common with Alice, the white housekeeper in *The Brady Bunch*, who is similarly unthreatening and well-intentioned, than with Nell, the Black housekeeper in *Gimme a Break!* (1981–1997), who is known for her intrusive and sassy manner. In moments, Nell is more caricature than character, even though this program is not based on a cartoon strip. A talented vocalist and Broadway performer, Nell Carter (as Nell Harper) sometimes had opportunities on the program to sing; however accomplished her singing, it was a form of othering and spectacle that disrupted the narrative, reminiscent of Hattie McDaniel's moments of spectacle in *Beulah*.

22 *Variety*, October 4, 1961.

23 This discussion of Hazel draws on an essay I wrote for *The Encyclopedia of Television*, ed. Horace Newcomb (Chicago: Fitzroy Dearborn, 1997; 2nd ed., 2004).

24 Marlo Thomas and Diahann Carroll and later Mary Tyler Moore (and her MTM production company) gained recognition in moving the representations of women into the arena of working women. Notable is that the women were single, unmarried (or widowed), and forging careers.

25 See George Lipsitz, "The Meaning of Memory: Family, Class, and Ethnicity in Early Television Programs," in *Private Screenings: Television and the Female Consumer*, ed. Lynn Spigel and Denise Mann (Minneapolis: University of Minnesota Press, 1992), 70–109.

26 Typically, in television and film, servants address their employers using a courtesy title in combination with a first name—seemingly familiar, but at the same time reminiscent of traditions from American slavery. Employers, on the other hand, most often call servants by their first names, even if the servant is older than the employer. There are a few significant exceptions, notably Mr. French and Mr. Belvedere (in *Mr. Belvedere*, 1985–1990), who are both British white male butlers, and Mrs. Livingston, with a name adopted in marriage to a Euro/Anglo husband.

27 There is a glorification of the white woman in these commercials, an idealization of her and a linking of white womanhood to the "best" car that would make the best addition to the happy family. Richard Dyer writes about one of the first film stars, Lillian Gish, who was famed director D. W. Griffith's muse: "There is, in other words, a special relationship between light and Gish: she is more visible, she is

aesthetically and morally superior, she looks on from a position of knowledge, of enlightenment—in short, if she is so much lit, she also appears to be the source of light." Dyer, "Lillian Gish: A White Star," in *The Matter of Images: Essays on Representation* (New York: Routledge, 1993), 151.

28 Though the suggestion is that the housewife/Dorothy drives the car, she does so for such purposes as taking Hazel to the grocery store, where Hazel does the shopping, or taking Harold to a sports game, where he soils clothing that Hazel will wash.

29 It is a conspicuous absence that in the program *The Cosby Show*, which features two working parents and five growing children in a rather large home, there is no maid to help. Apparently, the super-Huxtables have everything under control and need no assistance, as they have pulled themselves up by their bootstraps. Moreover, the presence of a household servant would disrupt the situation and make visible a class struggle, or would make their comfortable lifestyle a bit uncomfortable to digest, with a constant reminder that some enjoy comfort through the discomfort of others.

30 "Natural Athlete" aired November 29, 1962, season 2, episode 11.

31 "Everybody's Thankful but Us Turkeys" aired November 23, 1961, season 1, episode 9.

32 This is a common episode in most series with domestic helpers, in which the employee is shown to be indispensable and that the family cannot function without them.

33 Bill is an architect, interestingly, like the patriarchs in *The Brady Bunch* and *I Married Dora* (1987–1988).

34 Brooks and Marsh, *Complete Directory*, 288.

35 The British series *Upstairs, Downstairs* (1971–1975), set in early-twentieth-century England, foregrounds the traditional hierarchy among servants, all of whom are white. The head butler, who is usually older and always male, is in a revered position. He takes a leadership role among the other servants, giving an ironic turn to the phrase "head of the household."

36 This episode aired January 1, 1970.

37 In *The Courtship of Eddie's Father*, Mrs. Livingston is a mother figure for Eddie and at times a wife figure for Tom, but this is exactly the problem that the show struggles with. In *Family Affair*, by contrast, the arrangement is naturalized and accepted.

38 A common look for Alice in *The Brady Bunch*, however, is in her light blue bathrobe, with her hair in rollers; she is often seen wearing night cream, a bit of a scary sight. She thus contrasts to Mrs. Brady, who looks as lovely at bedtime as she does during the day.

39 The television program mimicked a popular 1987 film, *Three Men and a Baby*. It was the biggest box office hit of that year, surpassing *Fatal Attraction*. It is a remake of a French film, *Trois homes et un couffin* (Three Men and a Cradle), dated 1985.

40 For further discussion of television and masculinity, see Lynn Spigel's work, particularly the section "The Trouble with Fathers" in "Television in the Family Circle," chapter 2 of *Make Room for TV: Television and the Family Ideal in Postwar America* (Chicago: University of Chicago Press, 1992), and Lynne Joyrich, "Critical and Textual Hypermasculinity," in *The Logics of Television: Essays in Cultural Criticism*, ed. Patricia Mellencamp (Bloomington: Indiana University Press; London: BFI Books, 1990). Also see the work of Andreas Huyssen and Tania Modleski on mass culture and the notion of the "feminine."

41 Herman Gray argues, "As for fictional television, even the more cursory examination of commercial network programming in the 1950s and 1960s reveals the relative absence of blacks, never mind attention to civil rights issues. As illustrated by *Julia*,

Room 222, *The Bill Cosby Show*, *The Leslie Uggams Show*, and *The Flip Wilson Show*, the imaginary world presented by fictional television in the middle decades of the twentieth century was one of black invisibility structured by the logic of color blindness and driven by the discourse of assimilation." Gray, "Remembering Civil Rights," in *The Revolution Wasn't Televised: Sixties Television and Social Conflict* (New York: Routledge, 1997), 350.

42 A counterpoint to *The Brady Bunch* came in the form of the documentary television series *An American Family*, which aired on PBS in 1973. Since dubbed "television's first reality show," it showcased the real lives of the Loud family of Santa Barbara, California, whose initially perfect-seeming suburban life strays from the (supposed) norm through the course of the series. The parents separate, with Pat Loud asking her husband Bill for a divorce on camera. The children are caught up in the hippie movement (unlike the Brady kids, who merely dress the part). Lance Loud, perhaps the most memorable family member, is considered the first gay character on television. Billy Crystal acted in the role of "cross-dresser" Jodie Dallas in *Soap* (1977–1981), a spin-off from *All in the Family*, which featured a 1971 episode about Archie's friend, Roger, who Archie is surprised to learn is gay.

43 When she is introduced, the phrase "This is Alice" is used, while her gray-and-white maid's uniform speaks for itself. Introductions are rare, however, because people in the neighborhood already know who she is, and the Bradys live an insular, nuclear life in which there is little interaction with the world beyond their domestic sitcom home.

44 Both *Family Affair* and *The Courtship of Eddie's Father* have episodes about a troubled school friend whose parents are divorced. In the 1990s, there were two theatrically released films featuring the characters in *The Brady Bunch*, and in the second, *A Very Brady Sequel* (1996), Mrs. Brady's first husband and the girls' biological father returns, though he turns out to be a charlatan.

45 Aired October 17, 1969, it is among the first in the series. (Cindy, whose hairstyle changes later in the series, does wear curls in this episode as the lyrics of the program's theme song describe: "It's the story of a lovely lady, who was living with three very lovely girls. All of them had hair of gold like their mother, the youngest one in curls.")

46 Still, there are episodes in the *Family Affair* series that reify or reinstate Mr. French as belonging to the Davis household, rather than as being an independent entity. In "Go Home, Mr. French" (aired September 25, 1967), Mr. French has a romance that might take him to another house to work, and in "Mr. French's Holiday" (aired March 18, 1968), Mr. French has plans for a nice vacation—which the children end up coming along on.

47 Two interracial couples have had airtime in prime-time television with their relationship as sanctioned by marriage and as a sustained plot point: an African American woman and a white American man in the 1970s series *The Jeffersons*, played by Roxie Roker and Franklin Cover, and an Asian American woman played by Ming Na Wen and a white American man in the 1990s sitcom *The Single Guy* (they portrayed the married friends of the title character). When Roxie Roker was auditioning for *The Jeffersons*, a producer expressed his doubt about the possibility of her being married to a white man; Roker responded by producing a photograph of her real-life white husband, Sy Kravitz (father of musician Lenny Kravitz, grandfather of actress Zoe Kravitz).

48 The Netflix series, *Maid* (2021), received a great deal of attention and acclaim. It situates its young, white, female protagonist as heroic because of her occupying the

role of a maid; it is a position that is utterly temporary in her life's trajectory. She does struggle, but eventually becomes a published author who writes a best-selling book about being a maid, upon which the series is based. It is worth noting that much of the audience is aware while watching, that her identity is not that of a maid, but of a future writer.

49 IMDb describes the character of Daphne Moon as a "healthcare worker from England." Beulah is described as a "Negro domestic."
50 George Lipsitz, "The Possessive Investment in Whiteness: Racialized Social Democracy and the 'White' Problem in American Studies," *American Quarterly* 47, no. 3 (September 1995): 369. See also Lipsitz, *The Possessive Investment in Whiteness: How White People Profit from Identity Politics* (Philadelphia: Temple University Press, 2006). In the 2020s, Richard Wright's incisive statement rings again, with the polarization among those who understand the meaning and historical need of Black Lives Matter and those who see it as a problem. White privilege (re)asserts itself in the form of adjudicating, for example, whether critical race theory will be taught or banned in American schools.
51 Lipsitz, "The Possessive Investment in Whiteness," 372.
52 Lipsitz, 371. As Lipsitz argues, "Racism changes over time, taking on different forms and serving different social purposes in difference eras."
53 Ruth Frankenberg, "The Mirage of an Unmarked Whiteness," in *The Making and Unmaking of Whiteness*, ed. Birgit Brander Rasmussen, Eric Klinenberg, Irene J. Nexica, and Matt Wray (Durham, NC: Duke University Press, 2001), 74.
54 Howard Winant, "White Racial Projects," in Rasmussen et al., *The Making and Unmaking of Whiteness*, 99.
55 Winant, 101.

Chapter 4   Unresolvable Roles

1 Even a science fiction program set in the future, *Star Trek*, represents a white male–Asian female relationship as one of dominance and submission in an episode based on the tale of *The Taming of the Shrew*. The episode, "Elaan of Troyius," which aired on December 20, 1968, was written and directed by John Meredyth Lucas and guest starred France Nuyen.
2 Darrell Hamamoto speculates that the character of Mrs. Livingston is a war bride in *Monitored Peril: Asian Americans and the Politics of TV Representation* (Minneapolis: University of Minnesota Press, 1994). He writes, "As the soft-spoken, unassuming housekeeper in *The Courtship of Eddie's Father*, Mrs. Livingston, Umeki took care of widower Tom Corbett (Bill Bixby) and his inquisitive young son Eddie (Brandon Cruz). Although there is little direct evidence revealed in the program itself, on the basis of her Anglo-Saxon name it might be inferred that housekeeper Mrs. Livingston was a war bride at one point in her life. In any case, it was obvious that Mrs. Livingston was born and raised in Japan, given her accent, geishalike demeanor, and propensity for offering tidbits of 'Oriental' wisdom to her employer and his son" (11–12).
3 A version of this chapter was published, "'Serving' American Orientalism: Negotiating Identities in *The Courtship of Eddie's Father*," *Journal of Film and Video* 56, no. 4. (2004): 21–33.
4 Edward Said, *Orientalism* (New York: Vintage Books, 1979), 2.
5 Seeing this relationship in this way is based on Jacques Lacan's psychoanalytic theory of self-identity and the Other.

6 Said, *Orientalism*, 3.
7 For a reading on the various positions in postcolonial theory and criticism, see Bill Ashcroft, Gareth Griffiths, and Helen Tiffin, eds., *The Post-Colonial Studies Reader* (New York: Routledge, 1995).
8 Nakano Glenn, *Issei, Nisei, War Bride*, 65–66.
9 Hamamoto, *Monitored Peril*, 33.
10 Ronald Takaki, *Iron Cages: Race and Culture in 19th-Century America* (New York: Oxford University Press, 1990), 239.
11 James Moy, *Marginal Sights: Staging the Chinese in America* (Iowa City: University of Iowa Press, 1993), 23.
12 Quoted in Moy, *Marginal Sights*, 26.
13 Examples are films such as *Broken Blossoms* (1919) and *The Bitter Tea of General Yen* (1933), in which the Asian male is forbidden to be with the white woman. Even the "positive" characters that Bruce Lee has played show his energy directed toward his martial art, never toward a romantic relationship.
14 Prashad continues: "The word *coolie* operates, then, like the nineteenth-century English word for factory worker, *hand*.... But a 'coolie' is not quite the same as a 'hand,' because the former word applies more to those vilified by white supremacy as lesser beings, while the latter word is generally used for white labor." *Everybody Was Kung Fu Fighting: Afro-Asian Connections and the Myth of Cultural Purity* (Boston: Beacon Press, 2001), 71. The distinction he makes between terms is similar to my comparison between the words "domestic" and "nanny," or "houseboy" and "butler."
15 African American actor, Dennis Haysbert played the role of the president of the United States in the television series, *24*, starting in 2002, followed by a female president who joined the cast in 2004 played by Cherry Jones.
16 Lisa Lowe, *Critical Terrains: French and British Orientalisms* (Ithaca, NY: Cornell University Press, 1991), x; Gyan Prakash, "Orientalism Now," *History & Theory* 34, no. 3 (1995): 199–212.
17 Nakano Glenn, *Issei, Nisei, War Bride*, 5.
18 Chinese houseboys fit the description of what Darrell Hamamoto calls "controlling images": the objectification of subordinated groups is achieved through the application of controlling images that help justify economic exploitation and social oppression on the basis of an interlocking system comprising race, class, and gender. In sum, controlling images involve a process of objectification, subordination, and justification. Hamamoto, *Monitored Peril*, 2.
19 In *East Main Street: Asian American Popular Culture*, ed. Shipa Dave, Leilani Nishime, and Tasha G. Oren (New York University Press, 2005), 343.
20 I do not assume the categories of "masculine" and "feminine" to be fixed. Rather, I refer to their generalized connotations to illustrate gender as a construction and to acknowledge that there are ideological ideals.
21 See my book review of Hamamoto's *Monitored Peril* in *Amerasia Journal* 21, no. 3 (December 1995).
22 In 2001–2002, the character was revived in a television prequel, *Ponderosa*, that aired on PAX-TV. The depiction of Hop Sing was played by Gareth Yeun, and was quite different; specifically, the "glaring pidgin English was replaced with a softer, wise delivery," and Hop Sing was a trusted family counselor, according to Wikipedia.
23 Typically, the term "majordomo" refers to the highest (major) person of a household (domo) staff. Similar terms include concierge, chamberlain, seneschal, maitre d'hotel, butler, and steward.
24 Lisa Lowe, *Immigrant Acts* (Durham, NC: Duke University Press, 1996), 5.

25 In *Monitored Peril*, Hamamoto writes, "In the written history of the American republic, the often invoked phrase *the Westward movement* is fraught with deceptively benign meaning. It connotes a sense of historical inevitability, the realization of a higher destiny by the Euro-American executors of divine will. The phrase effectively masks the human and ecological depredation committed by 'explorers,' 'adventurers,' and 'settlers,' who, viewed through the eyes of the vanquished, might less sympathetically be considered brigands, pirates, and squatters" (32).

26 Season 1, episode 20, aired on CBS on January 30, 1960.

27 In episode descriptions, Jimmy Chang is referred to as a family friend of the Cartwrights rather than as the cousin of Hop Sing.

28 Because citizenship is a precondition of voting, immigrant Asian Pacific Americans did not vote in large numbers until after 1965, when the immigration and naturalization laws were changed. The Indian Citizenship Act of 1924 gave Native Americans the right to vote. In 1956 the State of Utah became the last state to grant that right. Many states, for example New Mexico, overtly prevented Native Americans from voting until 1962; New Mexico has a large Native population. For additional information about the history of voting rights, see: http://www.iwantmyvote.com/recount/history/.

29 *The Revolution Wasn't Televised: Sixties Television and Social Conflict*, ed. Lynn Spigel and Michael Curtin (New York: Routledge, 1997), 305–324.

30 As Classen notes: *The Clarion Ledger* "took the unusual step" of publishing a letter by Charles Evers, the state's NAACP field secretary. In it, Evers argues, "That these three men have indicated that they will not aid or abet 'age old customs in Mississippi' is not astonishing. It is astonishing, however, that the people of Mississippi continue to believe that they can expect to be treated with respect while they treat nearly 50 percent of their native Mississippians with disrespect." (317)

31 Philip Ahn, who played the role of Mr. Lee Chang, was billed below Amanda Ridley, who had the role of the sister of the young woman accidentally shot by her father; they engaged in a fight because she was attending to Jimmy after he was struck down by a white brute when Jimmy tried to defend her. Another note about the credit/cast list is that Hop Sing has no given last name, although his cousin and Uncle do (Chang).

32 Philip Ahn (born in 1905, died in 1978) was a Korean American actor. He was the first Asian American film actor to receive a star on the Hollywood Walk of Fame. Ahn was born Pil Lip Ahn in Highland Park, California. His parents emigrated to the United States in 1902 and were the first Korean married couple admitted; Philip Ahn is believed to be the first American citizen born in the United States of Korean parents. See Hye Seung Chung's *Hollywood Asian: Philip Ahn and the Politics of Cross-Ethnic Performance* (Philadelphia: Temple University Press, 2006).

33 It is worth noting that most of those who were active in the Montgomery, Alabama, bus boycott were African American women who worked as domestic servants.

34 White Americans also compared the Chinese immigrants to Native Americans. Governor Horatio Seymour of New York said in 1870, "We do not let the Indian stand in the way of civilization, so why let the Chinese barbarian? . . . Today we are dividing the lands of the native Indians into states, counties and townships. We are driving off from their property the game upon which they live, by railroads. We tell them plainly, they must give up their homes and property, and live upon corners of their own territories, because they are in the way of our civilization. If we can do this, then we can keep away another form of barbarism which has no right here" (quoted in Takaki, *Iron Cages*, 220).

35 Takaki, *Iron Cages*, 216.
36 Takaki, 217.
37 Takaki.
38 Takaki, 219.
39 Often Asian Americans come to socially, economically, and politically ally themselves with whites. This gives whites an excuse to claim "equal opportunity" and the absence of racism and allows Asian Americans to identify with dominant white America, severing ties with their "only slightly" darker cousins.
40 There is a phrase, "honorary whites," which has been applied to Asian Americans and which implies that it is a kind of reward (for passive, white-adjacent behavior) bestowed by white society.
41 Season 5, Episode 11, Air Date: December 5, 1961.
42 Though never ranked in the top 20 of the Nielsen ratings, the series lasted for three seasons, and all 73 episodes are available on DVD.
43 In *Family Affair*, the servant is also called by a courtesy title, and it could be argued that it is for distancing purposes, particularly in light of the male-male parental couple that is formed between Mr. French and his employer. However, Mr. French is given a courtesy title in a way that Mrs. Livingston, an Oriental housekeeper, is not, that is, out of respect for the air of formality that he exhibits as a British butler, a "gentleman's gentleman."
44 She was once married considering her English (sur)name while being Japanese-born, though no backstory is given; the 1940s, 1950s, 1960s constituted a historical period when military actions in Asia produced war brides, though Mrs. Livingston's previous and off-screen life is not revealed.
45 Miyoshi Umeki's intertextual film history includes an emblematic role in the Marlon Brando film, *Sayonara* (1957), for which she won an Academy Award for Best Supporting Actress. In *Sayonara*, which is set in Japan and features two interracial couples consisting of white American military men and Japanese women, the character of Katsumi is in a famous scene where she is scrubbing her husband's back in a hot bath and he comments that "this is the life." The film story takes up the issue of prejudice, specifically, the U.S. military is shown to frown upon "fraternizing with the locals" and more than that, formally advises against any interracial relationships. The newly married couple learn that Katsumi is not allowed into the United States. Katsumi and her husband, Kelly are devastated and contest such racism, but in the end, they commit double suicide.
46 The title alludes to a quote attributed to Welsh journalist Henry Morton Stanley, who upon finding medical missionary David Livingstone, who has been assumed missing in Central Africa, is alleged to have uttered, "Dr. Livingstone, I presume?"
47 Antimiscegenation laws that made interracial marriage illegal were finally found unconstitutional in 1967, when the last of them were eliminated from the books.
48 Unless a viewer spoke Japanese, they would only learn what "wakata" means by watching a later episode. In "Guess Who's Coming to Lunch," Tom, tellingly, says that he only knows two Japanese words, "domo arigato" and "wakata"—thank you and I understand.
49 Tom is even set up on a date by Eddie with his school friend's mother, played by Cicely Tyson in an episode called, "Guess Who's Coming to Lunch?" Once the two single parents see each other, it is clear to everyone in the text and watching the text that a relationship between them is impossible, presumably because he is white and she is Black. There is not even a moment of contemplation that she could be the next

Mrs. Corbett. Strangely, Mrs. Livingston has more potential to be Tom's spouse, though it is something that will also never happen.
50 Lowe, *Immigrant Acts*, 18.
51 Lowe.
52 Lowe, 23.
53 American Orientalism operates through a process that I call interracialization: it is less a colonialist, neocolonialist, or imperialist model than a kind of a parallel otherness, in which each person is an other to every other person. In this regard, whiteness is part of the process of racialization, and white identity, too, is racialized.
54 Said, *Orientalism*, 12.
55 Aniko Bodroghkozy makes this argument about the television program, *Julia*. By symptomatic text, she means that the television text/site demonstrated the same social problems that existed in its contemporaneous setting.
56 From Kimberly Wallace-Sanders, *Mammy: A Century of Race, Gender, and Southern Memory* (Ann Arbor, MI: University of Michigan Press, 2007), 3.
57 Pat Morita appeared in a Garry Marshall hit program, *Happy Days* (1974–1984), in a recurring role as the frenetic cook who speaks with a loud accent, Matsuo "Arnold" Takahashi; he starred in a short-lived program called Mr. T(akahashi) and Tina, considered the first network sitcom featuring an Asian American man family—and his white domestic helper, Tina. He performed in both films and television programs spanning several decades. He gained worldwide fame in the film series, *The Karate Kid* (1984, 1986, 1989), in which he taught a young white Italian American boy martial arts. Pat Morita's Mr. Miyagi has become a beloved character to many. In playing Mr. Miyagi, Morita spoke in an accent that the third-generation Japanese American did not actually have. Not being recognized (or able to play a role) as an American had been a profound experience since his childhood: after spending seven years in medical care as a child due to a serious illness, was escorted to an internment camp upon his release from the hospital.
58 This either/or dichotomy between being Asian *or* American is a theme in *All-American Girl* (1994–1995), the first television program about an Asian American family and their cultural experiences. It would be more than twenty years until there was another television program with Asian Americans as the main cast. *Fresh Off the Boat* (2015–2020), produced, created, and written by Asian Americans, was a series that finally (almost seven decades after broadcasting began) presented Asian Americans, as American. And it took over 100 years of Hollywood film culture before a major film featuring an Asian American (and Asian international) cast made it to the big screen, *Crazy Rich Asians* (2018); *The Joy Luck Club* (1993) directed by Wayne Wang, *Better Luck Tomorrow* (2003) directed by Justin Lin, and the screen adaption of the musical, *Flower Drum Song* (1961) are predecessors to the bona fide hit, *Crazy Rich Asians* marking one (semi-mainstream) film about Asian Americans every twenty to thirty years.
59 Joan Chen is a renowned actress who has directed and contributed greatly to both Chinese cinema as well as Independent Asian American projects.
60 Karen Eng, "The Yellow Fever Pages," *Bitch*, 12 (2000): 68–73.
61 See a heinous website such as the following: http://www.asianslave.biz/gallery_submissive.htm.
62 Professor Lisa Wade writes for thesocietypages.com, focusing on sociological images. One of her blogs is, "Marketing Asian Women to Anti-Feminist Men," in which she comments upon a website for anti-misandry, presumably about the

fight-back against the hatred of males, which features ads for dating Asian women. http://thesocietypages.org/socimages/2009/07/25/marketing-asian-women-to-anti-feminist-men/.

63 Kent Ono and Vincent N. Pham, *Asian Americans and the Media* (Cambridge, MA: Polity, 2009), 64.

64 For a historical overview and analysis of the representations of Asian Americans in U.S. television, see my article, "Be the One That You Want: Asian Americans in Television Culture, Onscreen and Beyond," *Amerasia Journal* 30, no. 1 (2004): 125–146.

65 The film *The Joy Luck Club* (1993) is significant in at least two ways. First, it is part of a pattern in film and television to ghettoize characters of color. In such works, ranging from the film *Stormy Weather* (1943) to the sitcom *Good Times* (1974–1979), an integrated world is not represented. Second, *Joy Luck Club* was supposed to mark a turning point not only for stories about Asian Americans but also in terms of jobs for Asian American actresses and actors. In neither case did it fulfill such expectations or hopes. Twenty-five years later, the huge financial success of and cultural interest in *Crazy Rich Asians* (some have called it wealth porn, a genre in which Asian characters are deemed appealing) has opened some doors.

66 Aniko Bodroghkozy, "Is This What You Mean By Color TV?" (reprinted) in *Equal Time: Television and the Civil Rights Movement* (Urbana: University of Illinois Press, 2013).

67 Simu Liu starred as a Marvel hero in *Shang-Chi: and the Legend of the Ten Rings* in 2021. Liu is Canadian, and while his character lives in San Francisco, Shaun/Shang-Chi travels to and spends most of the screentime in a mystical Chinese locale. Still, the film was considered a box office hit and a sequel has been announced; Simu Liu is a charismatic, talented, and popular rising star.

68 Cho makes this joke, statement, in her performance, "Revolution." Asian American actress, Lana Condor, was once given the direction, "to be more like Hello Kitty." Like Cho, Condor rebuffed: "Hello Kitty doesn't have a mouth. [So as] a woman, I'm like, 'One, you want me to be more like Hello Kitty, but she doesn't have a voice.'" https://variety.com/2020/film/news/lana-condor-hello-kitty-to-all-the-boys-2-netflix-1203468683/.

69 Reverend Laura Mariko Cheifetz, "Being Asian American means living in a country that treats you as a perpetual foreigner. That has to change," https://www.cnn.com/2021/03/20/opinions/asian-american-racism-violence-wellness/index.html.

70 Examples of anti-Asian violence are also examples of how race relations are intertextual. (Another example is the then president mislabeling the COVID-19 pandemic as "the China Virus," which allowed for and emboldened attacks against Americans of Asian descent.) Within a discourse of belonging (or blame) for Asians and Asian Americans in particular, race is gendered.

71 https://manaa.org/links/stereotype-busters.

Chapter 5   Invisible but Viewable

1 Chon Noriega, "El hilo latino: Representation, Identity and National Culture," *Jump Cut*, 38: 47.

2 Among other provisions, the Patriot Act (2001) expands the authority of law enforcement and immigration authorities to detain and deport immigrants on the grounds that they are suspected of terrorism-related acts.

3 Sociologist Pierrette Hondagneu-Sotelo, in her book on Latina domestic servants, asks why there has been an expansion of paid domestic work in recent decades. She cites four factors: (a) growing income inequality; (b) women's participation in the labor force, especially in professional and managerial jobs; (c) the relatively underdeveloped nature of day care in the United Sates; and (d) the mass immigration of women from Central America, the Caribbean, and Mexico. Hondagneu-Sotelo, *Doméstica: Immigrant Workers Cleaning and Caring in the Shadows of Affluence* (Berkeley: University of California Press, 2001).
4 Media scholar, Richard Dyer, explains that a *structuring absence* "refers to an issue, or even a set of facts or an argument, that a text cannot ignore."
5 Romero, *Maid in the U.S.A.*, 69.
6 Kathleen Anne McHugh, *American Domesticity: From How-to Manual to Hollywood Melodrama* (New York: Oxford University Press, 1999), 11.
7 McHugh, 6.
8 Stuart Hall, "New Ethnicities," in *Black Film/British Cinema*, ICA Documents 7, ed. Kobena Mercer (London: Institute of Contemporary Arts, 1988). Emphasis in the original.
9 Juan Flores and George Yúdice, "Living Borders/Buscando America: Languages of Latino Self-Formation," *Social Text: Theory/Culture/Ideology*, 24 (1990): 58.
10 Flores and Yúdice, 65.
11 Kathleen Anne McHugh, *American Domesticity: From How-to Manual to Hollywood Melodrama* (New York: Oxford University Press, 1999), 6.
12 Suzanne Oboler, *Ethnic Labels, Latino Lives: Identity and the Politics of (Re)Presentation in the United States* (Minneapolis: University of Minnesota Press, 1995), 12.
13 Oboler, 6.
14 Oboler, 14.
15 The Good Neighbor policy of President Franklin D. Roosevelt (1933–1945) represented a shift away from the armed intervention of the gunboat diplomacy era and toward more subtle means of maintaining U.S. hegemony in Latin America.
16 Chon Noriega, "Internal 'Others': Hollywood Narratives 'about' Mexican-Americans," in *Mediating Two Worlds: Cinematic Encounters in the Americas*, ed. John King, Ana M. López, and Manual Alvarado (London: BFI, 1993), 54.
17 Noriega, 53.
18 Noriega, *Shot in America: Television, the State, and the Rise of Chicano Cinema* (Minneapolis: University of Minnesota Press, 2000), xxx–xxxi.
19 Noriega, 29.
20 Noriega, 48.
21 For a study of Native American Indigenous women employed as domestic workers, see Caitlin Keliiaa's, *Unsettling Domesticity: Native Women and 20th-Century Federal Indian Policy in the San Francisco Bay Area*, forthcoming.
22 Stephen Neale and Frank Krutnik, *Popular Film and Television Comedy* (London: Routledge, 1990), 93.
23 Neale and Krutnik.
24 Arthur Pettit, *Images of the Mexican American in Fiction and Film* (College Station: Texas A&M University Press, 1980), 6.
25 The use of subtitles imposes another degree of separation in that they intermediate between what Marta says and what she means. Non-Spanish-speaking viewers must simply trust that the subtitles are accurate.

26 When Fred serves as a translator, he bridges two cultures yet also keeps them apart, on either side of him, much as Eddie does for his father and Mrs. Livingston in *The Courtship of Eddie's Father*.
27 Mireya Navarro, "Trying to Get Beyond the Role of the Maid; Hispanic Actors Are Seen as Underrepresented, with the Exception of One Part," *New York Times*, May 16, 2002.
28 Actress Lupe Ontiveros, in an NPR interview: https://www.npr.org/2012/07/27/157500677/lupe-ontiveros-proudly-portrayed-dozens-of-maids.
29 Quoted in Romero, *Maid in the U.S.A.*, 90.
30 Nor are such attitudes only in the past. Typing "Latina maid" into an online search engine promptly turns up dozens of pages of/links to pornography.
31 In *Down and Out in Beverly Hills*, the woman of the house (played by Bette Midler) states that she knows what her husband is doing and that this is the reason she hired Carmen—to give her husband some confidence. In an early scene, the man of the house, satirically named Dave Whiteman (played by Richard Dreyfuss), leaves his bed, where his wife "isn't in the mood." He sneaks down the stairway and enters the hallway leading to the maid's quarters. His short trip marks a journey from one world to another, from wealthy to working-class, from uptight to unrestrained, from nonsexual white to erotically racial. Unlike the cool, dark, and quiet of the upstairs, Carmen's room is flooded with light, loud Latin music is playing, and we see a sweaty Carmen lying on the bed, anxiously awaiting her visitor.
32 In this society, such a union is a symbolic "offense" in addition to being a federal offense, as the intertitle/disclaimer remarks.
33 In the series, *Will & Grace*, seventy-something Rosario Salazar works as a maid to the wealthy Karen Walker, who has her marry a thirty-something gay man, Jack, to prevent her deportation. (This is similar to the episode of *Designing Women* where the employer does not want to lose her housekeeper.) Jack later claims that they consummated their marriage. Rosario (played by Shelley Morrison) later leaves the marriage to pursue other romantic interests. The backstory for Rosario's character is that she is an undocumented worker, a former schoolteacher from El Salvador who was pursuing a master's degree but ended up in a job as a maid.
34 The so-called nanny tax actually consists of three federal employment taxes: Social Security, Medicare, and the Federal Unemployment, or FUTA, tax. Employers must pay these taxes for in-home employees whose annual wages are above a threshold amount ($1,600 in 2008). Employers may also owe certain state taxes.
35 See, among many other accounts, David J. Morrow, "Nanny Tax Tally of '95: Who Paid and Who Lied?" *New York Times*, April 21, 1996, F1; and S. J. Diamond, "Where Work Is Illegal, the Rules Confusing, the Fix Unsure," *Los Angeles Times*, February 18, 1993, E3.
36 Lynne Duke, "Activists Perceive Backlash from the Baird Affair," *Washington Post*, February 19, 1993, A13.
37 Huffington blamed his wife, Ariana, who he said did the hiring; he then began hurling similar accusations at incumbent senator Diane Feinstein. He also sought to place the blame on the immigrant worker, stating that "there are forgeries out there and we can't hold an employer responsible if he has what he thinks is a citizenship paper." *Los Angeles Times*, October 27, 1994, A42.
38 Ella Shohat and Robert Stam, *Unthinking Eurocentrism: Multiculturalism and the Media* (New York: Routledge, 1995), 227.
39 White male characters are conspicuously absent in this episode of *Designing Women* (as they later were in the real-life court hearing that featured Rosa Lopez). Reece,

Julia's boyfriend, only exists via telephone call, informing Julia that false representation is a federal offense. The state's governor is seen in the portrait on the wall of the immigration office, and the only white male character physically present at the swearing-in ceremony is the federal judge, who has no audible lines. Whereas the figure of the immigrant woman of color stands in for something else through her absence, the position of patriarchy and whiteness as embodied by white men stands firm; it is not so much absence as omnipresence.

40 There is a long tradition of representing African American men in drag. From Flip Wilson to Martin Lawrence (though Martin in some ways was self-reflexively speaking to past generations), Hollywood has created and accepted African American men as visual spectacle and farce. Highly successful and prolific writer/producer/director, Tyler Perry, created and performed a character in drag, Grandmother Madea. She is simultaneously funny and wise, and she speaks particularly to those in the Black community as a strong matriarch and a symbol of a struggle and resilience.

41 Tara McPherson, *Reconstructing Dixie: Race, Gender, and Nostalgia in the Imagined South* (Durham: Duke University Press, 2003), 184–185.

42 McPherson, 185.

43 McPherson, 183, 184.

44 The trial began in the California Superior Court in Los Angeles on January 25, 1995, and the not-guilty verdict came on October 3, 1995.

45 From KTLA channel 5 news coverage of the trial, Los Angeles, February 1995.

46 Flores and Yúdice, "Living Borders/Buscando America," 62. The passage continues:
"Anglo insecurity" looks to the claims of Latinos and other minority constituencies for the erosion of the United States' position in world leadership, the downturn in the economy, and the bleak prospects for social mobility for the next generation.
"In fact, now that dominant U.S. national rhetoric seems no longer able to project a global communist bogey, on account of political changes in the Soviet Union and against Eastern Europe, this rhetoric will increasingly consolidate its weapons against Latinos as the drug-disseminating enemy within. The War on Drugs will increasingly become a War on Latinos and Latin Americans."

47 It is no coincidence that such legislation has been pushed most vigorously in states like California, where whites are no longer the numerical majority and where the "threat" of people who speak different languages is considered high. One of the major sponsors of the English-only movement has been the National Eugenics Society, an organization that functions much like the Aryan Nation but with a veneer of science.

48 Angharad N. Valdivia. *The Gender of Latinidad: Uses and Abuses of Hybridity* (Wiley Blackwell, 2020), 5.

49 Steven Classen, *Watching Jim Crow: The Struggles Over Mississippi TV, 1955–1969* (Durham, NC: Duke University Press, 2004), 17.

50 Ana M. López, "Are All Latins from Manhattan? Hollywood, Ethnography and Cultural Colonialism," in John King, Ana M. López, and Manuel Alvarado, *Mediating Two Worlds* (British Film Institute, 1993), 68.

51 López.

52 In their 1994 study on Hispanic characters in television representation, S. Robert Lichter and Daniel R. Amundson report, "Latinos are less visible in prime time television than they were in the 1950s. Their portrayals have not improved markedly since the days of Jose Jimenez and Frito Bandito. Throughout television's history, Hispanics have been cast as heavies proportionately more often than either blacks or

whites. Their depictions are notable for the high proportion of criminals and violent characters like the 'Scarface' stereotype and the absence of starring roles and successful role models. In an age of heightened sensitivity to both the importance of ethnic diversity and the influence of popular culture in shaping social images, it is remarkable how little has changed in television's treatment of this growing segment of the population." Furthermore, they reveal that in science fiction and fantasy genres, Latinos are scarcely found—that in American television, we have imagined a future without Latinos. Lichter and Amundson, *Distorted Reality: Hispanic Characters in TV Entertainment* (Washington, DC: Center for Media and Public Affairs, 1994), 2.

53 Arthur Petit, *Images of the Mexican American in Fiction and Film* (College Station: Texas A&M University Press, 1980), xxi.
54 Pierrette Hondagneu-Sotelo, *Doméstica: Immigrant Workers Cleaning and Caring in the Shadows of Affluence* (University of California Press, 2007).
55 For example, Eva Longoria hosted the Democratic National Convention in the summer of 2020.
56 Raul Reyes, "'Devious Maids' Does a Disservice to Latinos" *USA Today*, July 9, 2013.
57 Jorge, Rivas, "Eva Longoria Defends New TV Series She's Producing on Latina Maids," April 16, 2012. https://www.colorlines.com/articles/eva-longoria-defends-new-tv-series-shes-producing-latina-maids.
58 "Can 'Devious Maids' Really Break Stereotypes About Latinas?" *Code Switch*, on NPR, June 27, 2013. https://www.npr.org/sections/codeswitch/2013/07/02/196204084/Can-Devious-Maids-Really-Break-Stereotypes-About-Latinas.
59 Mary Beltrán, *Latino TV: A History* (New York University Press, 2022), 4.
60 Beltrán, 121.
61 The case studies focused on *Cristela* (ABC), *One Day at a Time* (the reboot was broadcast on three different, successive networks, Netflix, Pop TV, and CBS), and *Vida* (Starz), along with creators and executive producers Cristela Alonzo, Gloria Calderón Kellett, and Tanya Saracho.
62 https://www.nalip.org/latinxlist.
63 Renee Tajima-Peña, "No Mo Po Mo and Other Tales of the Road," in *Countervisions: Asian American Film Criticism*, ed. Darrell Y. Hamamoto and Sandra Liu (Philadelphia: Temple University Press, 2000).
64 Arlene Dávila, *Latinos Inc.: The Marketing and Making of a People* (University of California Press, 2012).
65 Dávila.

Epilogue

1 Herman Gray, *Watching Race: Television and the Struggle for "Blackness"* (Minneapolis: University of Minnesota Press, 1995, 2004), xv.
2 Jodi Melamed, "Racial Capitalism," *Critical Ethnic Studies* 1, no. 1 (Spring 2015): 76–85. Melamed refers to Cedric Robinson, *Black Marxism: The Making of the Black Radical Tradition* (1983; Chapel Hill: University of North Carolina Press, 2000). Racial Capitalism describes the process of extracting social and economic value from a person of a different racial identity, typically a person of color.
3 See Timothy Havens, "'The Biggest Show in the World' Race and the Global Popularity of *The Cosby Show*," in *The Television Studies Reader*, ed. Robert C. Allen and Annette Hill (New York: Routledge, 2004). See Racquel J. Gates, *Double*

Negative: The Black Image & Popular Culture (Durham, NC: Duke University Press, 2018).

4 He writes, "A theory of race and cultural production recognizes that racism is a powerful structural force but there is always the potential for contestation and disruption." Anamik Saha, *Race and the Cultural Industries* (Cambridge: Polity Press, 2018), 51–52.

5 Saha, 23.

6 Troy Duster, "The 'Morphing' Properties of Whiteness," in *The Making and Unmaking of Whiteness*, ed. Birgit Brander Rasmussen, Eric Klinenberg, Irene J. Nexica, Matt Wray (Durham, NC: Duke University Press, 2001), 113–137.

Bibliography

Allen, Graham. *Intertextuality*. New York: Routledge, 2002.
Almaguer, Tomás. *Racial Fault Lines: The Historical Origins of White Supremacy in California*. Berkeley: University of California Press, 1994.
Beltrán, Mary. *Latino TV: A History*. New York: New York University Press, 2022.
Bodroghkozy, Aniko. *Equal Time: Television and the Civil Rights Movement*. Urbana: University of Illinois Press, 2013.
———. *Groove Tube: Sixties Television and the Youth Rebellion*. Durham, NC: Duke University Press, 2001.
Bogle, Donald. *Blacks in American Films and Television: An Encyclopedia*. New York: Simon & Schuster, 1989.
———. *Brown Sugar: Eighty Years of America's Black Female Superstars*. New York: Harmony Books, 1980.
Brooks, Tim, and Earle Marsh. *The Complete Directory to Prime Time Network TV Shows, 1946–Present*. New York: Ballantine Books, 1992.
Caldwell, John. *Televisuality: Style, Crisis, and Authority in American Television*. New Brunswick, NJ: Rutgers University Press, 1995.
Childress, Alice. *Like One of the Family: Conversations from a Domestic's Life*. Boston: Beacon Press, 1986.
Chung, Hye Seung. *Hollywood Asian: Philip Ahn and the Politics of Cross-Ethnic Performance*. Philadelphia: Temple University Press, 2006.
Clark-Lewis, Elizabeth. *Living In, Living Out: African American Domestics and the Great Migration*. New York: Kodansha International, 1996.
Classen, Steven. *Watching Jim Crow: The Struggles Over Mississippi TV, 1955–1969*. Durham, NC: Duke University Press, 2004.
Collins, Patricia Hill. *Black Feminist Thought: Knowledge, Consciousness, and the Politics of Empowerment*. New York: Routledge, 2000, 2009).
Collins, Patricia Hill. "Foreword." In *Emerging Intersections: Race, Class, and Gender in Theory, Policy, and Practice*, ed. Bonnie Thornton Dill and Ruth Enid Zambrana, vii–xiii. New Brunswick, NJ: Rutgers University Press, 2009.
Crenshaw, Kimberlé, Neil Gotanda, Garry Peller, and Kendall Thomas. *Critical Race Theory: The Key Writings That Formed the Movement*. New York: The New Press, 1995.

Curtin, Michael, and Lynn Spigel. *The Revolution Wasn't Televised: Sixties Television and Social Conflict.* New York: Routledge, 1997.
Dave, Shipa Leilani Nishime, and Tasha G. Oren. *East Main Street: Asian American Popular Culture.* New York: New York University Press, 2005.
Dávila, Arlene. *Latinos Inc.: The Marketing and Making of a People.* Berkeley: University of California Press, 2012.
Davis, Angela. *Women, Race & Class.* New York: Vintage Books, 1983.
Duster, Troy. "The 'Morphing' Properties of Whiteness." In *The Making and Unmaking of Whiteness*, ed. Birgit Brander Rasmussen, Eric Klinenberg, Irene J. Nexica, Matt Wray, 113–137. Durham, NC: Duke University Press, 2001.
Dyer, Richard. "Lillian Gish: A White Star." In *The Matter of Images: Essays on Representation*, 151. New York: Routledge, 1993.
———. *White: Essays on Race and Culture.* New York: Routledge, 1997.
Fiske, John. *Media Matters: Race and Gender in U.S. Politics.* Minneapolis: University of Minnesota Press, 1996.
Flores, Juan, and George Yúdice. "Living Borders/Buscando America: Languages of Latino Self-Formation." *Social Text: Theory/Culture/Ideology*, 24 (1990): 58.
Frankenberg, Ruth, "The Mirage of an Unmarked Whiteness." In *The Making and Unmaking of Whiteness*, ed. Birgit Brander Rasmussen, Eric Klinenberg, Irene J. Nexica, and Matt Wray, 72–96. Durham, NC: Duke University Press, 2001.
———. *White Women, Race Matters: The Social Construction of Whiteness.* Minneapolis: University of Minnesota Press, 1993.
Fredrickson, George. *White Supremacy: A Comparative Study in American and South African History.* New York: Oxford University Press, 1981.
Freed, Lynn. "HERS: A Stranger in the House," *New York Times Magazine*, May 15, 1994.
Gates, Racquel J. *Double Negative: The Black Image & Popular Culture.* Durham, NC: Duke University Press, 2018.
Gray, Herman. "Remembering Civil Rights: Television, Memory, and the 1960s." In *The Revolution Wasn't Televised: Sixties Television and Social Conflict*, ed. Lynn Spigel and Michael Curtin, 348–358. New York: Routledge, 1997.
———. *Watching Race: Television and the Struggle for Blackness.* Minneapolis: University of Minnesota Press, 2004.
Haggins, Bambi L. *Mad Laughter: The Black Comic Persona in Post-Soul America.* New Brunswick, NJ: Rutgers University Press, 2007.
Hall, Stuart. "New Ethnicities." In *Black Film, British Cinema*, ed. Kobena Mercer, ICA Documents 7, 27–31. London: Institute of Contemporary Arts, 1988).
———. "The Whites of Their Eyes: Racist Ideologies and the Media." In *Silver Linings: Some Strategies for the Eighties*, ed. George Bridges and Rosalind Brunt, 28–52. London: Lawrence and Wishart, 1981.
Hamamoto, Darrell. *Monitored Peril: Asian Americans and the Politics of TV Representation.* Minneapolis: University of Minnesota Press, 1994.
———. *Nervous Laughter: Television Situation Comedy and Liberal Democratic Ideology.* New York: Praeger, 1989.
Han, Benjamin M. *Beyond the Black and White TV: Asian and Latin American Spectacle in Cold War America.* New Brunswick, NJ: Rutgers University Press, 2020.
Havens, Timothy. "'The Biggest Show in the World' Race and the Global Popularity of *The Cosby Show*," in *The Television Studies Reader*, ed. Robert C. Allen and Annette Hill, 442–456. New York: Routledge, 2004.
Herr, Norman. Television & Health, *Sourcebook for Teaching Science*, May 20, 2007.

Hill Collins, Patricia. *Black Feminist Thought: Knowledge, Consciousness, and the Politics of Empowerment*. New York: Routledge, 2000, 2009. (Originally published Boston: Unwin Hyman, 1990.)

Hondagneu-Sotelo, Pierrette. *Doméstica: Immigrant Workers Cleaning and Caring in the Shadows of Affluence*. Berkeley: University of California Press, 2001.

hooks, bell. *Art on My Mind: Visual Politics*. New York: New Press, 1995.

———. *Black Looks: Race and Representation*. Boston: South End Press, 1992.

———. *Feminist Theory: From Margin to Center*. Boston: South End Press, 1984; London: Pluto, 2000.

———. *Outlaw Culture: Resisting Representation*. New York: Routledge, 1994, 2006.

———. *Talking Back: Thinking Feminism, Thinking Black*. Boston: South End Press, 1989.

Hunt, Darnell. *Channeling Blackness: Studies on Television and Race in America*. New York: Oxford University Press, 2005.

———. *Screening the Los Angeles "Riots": Race, Seeing, and Resistance*. Cambridge University Press, 1997.

Hurtado, Aída. *The Color of Privilege: Three Blasphemies on Race and Feminism*. Ann Arbor: University of Michigan Press, 2004.

Jackson, Carlton. *Hattie: The Life of Hattie McDaniel*. New York: Madison Books, 1990.

Jacobson, Matthew Frye. *Whiteness of a Different Color: European Immigrants and the Alchemy of Race*. Cambridge, MA: Harvard University Press, 1999.

Jewell, K. Sue. *From Mammy to Miss America and Beyond: Cultural Images and the Shaping of U.S. Social Policy*. New York: Routledge, 1993.

Joyrich, Lynne. "Critical and Textual Hypermasculinity." In *The Logics of Television: Essays in Cultural Criticism*, ed. Patricia Mellencamp. Bloomington: Indiana University Press; London: BFI Books, 1990.

Katzman, David. *Seven Days a Week: Women and Domestic Service in Industrializing America*. New York: Oxford University Press, 1978.

Keliiaa, Caitlin. *Unsettling Domesticity: Native Women and 20th-Century Federal Indian Policy in the San Francisco Bay Area*. Forthcoming.

Levine, Judith. "White Like Me." *Ms.* Magazine Volume 4, 1994.

Lewis, Justin, and Sut Jhally. *Enlightened Racism: The Cosby Show, Audiences, and the Myth of the American Dream*. Boulder, CO: Westview Press, 1992.

Lipsitz, George. "The Meaning of Memory: Family, Class, and Ethnicity in Early Television Programs." In *Private Screenings: Television and the Female Consumer*, ed. Lynn Spigel and Denise Mann, 70–109. Minneapolis: University of Minnesota Press, 1992.

———. *The Possessive Investment in Whiteness: How White People Profit from Identity Politics*. Philadelphia: Temple University Press, 2006.

———. "The Possessive Investment in Whiteness: Racialized Social Democracy and the 'White' Problem in American Studies." *American Quarterly* 47, no. 3 (September 1995): 369–387.

Locke, Brian. "The Dancing Itos." In *Living Color: Race and Television in the United States*, ed. Sasha Torres, 239–254. Durham, NC: Duke University Press, 1998.

López, Ana M. "Are All Latins from Manhattan? Hollywood, Ethnography and Cultural Colonialism." In *Mediating Two Worlds*, ed. John King, Ana M. López, and Manuel Alvarado, 67–80. British Film Institute, 1993.

Lowe, Lisa. *Critical Terrains: French and British Orientalisms*. Ithaca, NY: Cornell University Press, 1991.

———. *Immigrant Acts*. Durham, NC: Duke University Press, 1996.

MacDonald, J. Fred. *Blacks and White TV: African Americans in Television since 1948*, 2nd ed. Chicago: Nelson-Hall, 1992.

McHugh, Kathleen Anne. *American Domesticity: From How-to Manual to Hollywood Melodrama*. New York: Oxford University Press, 1999.

McMillan, Uri. "Mammy-Memory: Staging Joice Heth, or the Curious Phenomenon of the 'Ancient Negress.'" *Women & Performance: A Journal of Feminist Theory* 22, no. 1 (2012): 29–46.

McPherson, Tara. *Reconstructing Dixie: Race, Gender, Nostalgia, in the Imagined South*. Durham, NC: Duke University Press, 2003.

Melamed, Jodi. "Racial Capitalism," *Critical Ethnic Studies* 1, no. 1 (Spring 2015): 76–85.

Moy, James. *Marginal Sights: Staging the Chinese in America*. Iowa City: University of Iowa Press, 1993.

Mulvey, Laura. "Visual Pleasure and Narrative Cinema." *Screen* 16 (Autumn 1975): 6–18.

Nakano Glenn, Evelyn. *Issei, Nisei, War Bride: Three Generations of Japanese American Women in Domestic Service*. Philadelphia: Temple University Press, 1986.

Neale, Stephen, and Frank Krutnik. *Popular Film and Television Comedy*. London: Routledge, 1990.

Noriega, Chon. "Internal 'Others': Hollywood Narratives 'about' Mexican-Americans." In *Mediating Two Worlds: Cinematic Encounters in the Americas*, ed. John King, Ana M. López, and Manual Alvarado. London: BFI.

———. *Shot in America: Television, the State, and the Rise of Chicano Cinema*. Minneapolis: University of Minnesota Press, 2000.

Oboler, Suzanne. *Ethnic Labels, Latino Lives: Identity and the Politics of (Re)Presentation in the United States*. Minneapolis: University of Minnesota Press, 1995.

Omi, Michael, and Howard Winant. *Racial Formations in the United States: From the 1960s to the 1980s*. New York: Routledge, 1986, 2004, 2014.

Ono, Kent, and Vincent N. Pham. *Asian Americans and the Media*. Cambridge, MA: Polity, 2009.

Prakash, Gyan. "Orientalism Now." *History & Theory* 34, no. 3 (1995): 199–212.

Prashad, Vijay. *Everybody Was Kung Fu Fighting: Afro-Asian Connections and the Myth of Cultural Purity*. Boston: Beacon Press, 2001.

Rivero, Yeidy M. *Tuning Out Blackness: Race and Nation in the History of Puerto Rican Television*. Durham, NC: Duke University Press, 2005.

Robinson, Cedric. *Black Marxism: The Making of the Black Radical Tradition*. Chapel Hill: University of North Carolina Press, 2000.

Rollins, Judith. *Between Women: Domestics and Their Employers*. Philadelphia: Temple University Press, 1985.

Romero, Mary. *Maid in the U.S.A.* New York: Routledge, 1992.

Saha, Anamik. *Race and the Cultural Industries*. Cambridge: Polity Press, 2018.

Said, Edward. *Orientalism*. New York: Vintage Books, 1979.

Shohat, Ella, and Robert Stam. *Unthinking Eurocentrism: Multiculturalism and the Media*. New York: Routledge, 1994.

Smart-Grosvenor, Vertamae. *A Domestic Rap Thursdays and Every Other Sunday Off: A Domestic Rap*. Garden City, NY: Doubleday, 1972.

Smith-Shomade, Beretta E. *Shaded Lives: African-American Women and Television*. New Brunswick, NJ: Rutgers University Press, 2002.

Spigel, Lynn. *Make Room for TV: Television and the Family Ideal in Postwar America*. Chicago: University of Chicago Press, 1992.

———. "White Flight." In *The Revolution Wasn't Televised: Sixties Television and Social Conflict*, ed. Lynn Spigel and Michael Curtin, 47–72. New York: Routledge, 1997.

Tajima-Peña, Renee. "No Mo Po Mo and Other Tales of the Road." In *Countervisions: Asian American Film Criticism*, ed. Darrell Y. Hamamoto and Sandra Liu, 245–262. Philadelphia: Temple University Press, 2000.

Takaki, Ronald. *Iron Cages: Race and Culture in 19th-Century America*. New York: Oxford University Press, 1990.

Taylor, Ella. *Prime-Time Families: Television Culture in Post-War America*. Berkeley: University of California Press, 1989.

Turner, Patricia. *Ceramic Uncles and Celluloid Mammies: Black Images and Their Influence on Culture*. New York: Anchor Books, 1994.

Valdivia, Angharad N. *The Gender of Latinidad: Uses and Abuses of Hybridity*. Hoboken, NJ: Wiley Blackwell, 2020.

Wallace-Sanders, Kimberly. *Mammy: A Century of Race, Gender, and Southern Memory*. Ann Arbor: University of Michigan, 2008.

Winant, Howard. "White Racial Projects." In *The Making and Unmaking of Whiteness*, ed. Birgit Brander Rasmussen, Eric Klinenberg, Irene J. Nexica, Matt Wray, 97–112. Durham, NC: Duke University Press, 2001.

Index

Numbers in italic represent figures.

ABC (network), 30, 31, 38–39, 92, 147
Academy Award, *26*, 33, 35, 56, 90–91
accent, 33, 71, 85, 98–99, 130, 139, 154
Adventures of Ozzie and Harriet, The, 142
advertising, 72, 137
affirmative action, 37, 60
African American domestic servants, representation of, 4, 11, 23–25, 79, 84, 97, 105–106, 132; Beulah, 30–37; Lilly, 37–47; male domestic servants, 47–50, 52–54; representation of, 21–60
African American family, 6, 48–52, 66, 84–85, 129
African Americans, representation of: and Black womanhood, 16, 17, 29–30, 138, 160; and black maid as stock character, 1, 17, 32, 35, 41, 58, 95, 98, 128; in media, 21–60, 129, 132, 138; and performative Blackness, 32, 35, 57, 74, 97, 150–152; and sassy trope, 22, 33, 56; and stereotypes, 17, 25–28, 56, 58, 150
Ahn, Phillip, 102, 103, 187nn31–32
All-American Girl (1994–1995), 189n57
Allen, Steve, 30
All in the Family, 51, 184n42
Almaguer, Tomás, 9, 14, 117
American Domesticity, 133, 136
American Dream, the, 7, 29, 68, 85, 142, 154

American Family, An, 184n42
Americanness: and racialized domestics, 66, 148–149; and whiteness, 19, 63–64, 84, 145, 162. *See also* citizenship; discrimination; language; perpetual foreignness
American Orientalism, 92–94, 103. *See also* Orientalism
American South, the, 38–40, 45, 46, 47; and domestic workers, 15, 16; as origin of mammy trope, 21, 25–28, 33, 36
amnesty, 147
Amos 'n' Andy, 30, 67
Andy Griffith Show, The, 6, 7
"Angry Asians and the Politics of Cultural Visibility," 97
anti-Asian violence. *See* violence, racial
Any Day Now, 180n73
As Good as It Gets (1997), 142
Asian American women, representations of, 92, 102–103, 138, 165. *See also* Asians and Asian Americans stereotypes
Asian men as desexualized, 19, 95, 97
Asians and Asian Americans stereotypes, 29, 98, 130; as Chinese houseboy, 94–96, 98–111, 127, 186n18; as exotic, 17, 121; as hyperfeminized, 26, 95, 114, 125; as subservient, 84, 90, 93–95, 97, 111, 107, 113, 115, 125–127
assimilation, 4, 8, 19, 48, 75, 102, 135–136

Atlanta spa shootings, 138
audience: African-American, 30, 33, 39, 46, 129–130; domestic workers as, 156–158; and gender, 72, 130, 139; identification with characters, 41, 141, 161, 163; Latino, 159; and portrayal of Blackness, 52–53, 56, 58, 60, 62, 164; and role in racial representation, 30, 32, 160, 166–167; white (and non-Black), 22, 33–34, 39, 129

Bachelor Father (1957–1962), 5, 6, 19, 78, 79, 90, 91, 97–98, 105–111, *106*, *110*; as referent, 118, 119
bachelors, 53–54, 68, 75, 94–95, 102–103, 109–110, 113. *See also* "missing mother" theme
Baird, Zoë, 148–149
Baker, Julia, 70
Banks family, 48–50
Baxter family, 69, 70–74, 81
Beavers, Louise, 32–34
Bedford family, 39–44, *40*, *43*, 45
Bel Air, 48–50
belonging. *See* perpetual foreignness of Asian Americans
Beltrán, Mary, 158–159
Belvedere, Mr., 82
Benson (1979–1986), 22, 52–54, *53*
Beulah (1950–1953), 5, 7, 18, 30–37, *31*, 46, 57; as referent, 68, 70, 71, 78, 110, 141, 142
Beulah (character), 20, 21, 26, 29, 30–37, *31*, 41; as referent, 76, 77, 140, 142. *See also* McDaniel, Hattie
Beverley Hills, 107, 158
Birth of a Nation, 21, 29, 46, 161, 162
Bixby, Bill, *112*. *See also* Corbett, Eddie
Black Lives Matter, 185n50
Blacks in American Films and Television, 29
Blake, Whitney, 72
Blocker, Dan, 99. *See also* Hoss
Blonde Venus (1932), 35
Bodroghkozy, Aniko, 6, 129
body type and African American women, 17, 29, 33, 35, 42, 56, 97, 123; and Asian American women, 29, 123, 127; and men, 79; and white women, 71, 114
Bogle, Daniel, 29, 30, 32
Bombshell (1932), 32
Bonanza (1959–1973), 2, 98–105, *99*, *104*; "The Lonely Man," 103–104

Booth, Shirley, 69, *69*, 72. *See also* Burke, Hazel
Bouvier, Anthony, 149–151, *151*. *See also* Taylor, Meshach
Bower, Angela. *See* Light, Judith
Brady Bunch, The (1969–1974), 5, 7, 16, 19, 66, 67, 70, 75, 79–84, 141, 142; "Alice Doesn't Live Here Anymore," 81
Brady family, 80–83
Brand, Joshua, 59
Brent, Linda, 28
Bringing Down the House (2003), 58
Bristol, Dudley, 139–142
British culture, 48–49, 50, 73, 75–76, 78, 85, 139
Broken Blossom's (1919), 103, 104, 186n13
Brooklyn Bridge, 38–39
Brooks and Marsh, 75
Burke, Hazel, 68–75, 77
Bush, President George H., 48
butler, 48–50, 52–54, 183n35

Cabot, Sebastian, 76. *See also* French, Giles
Cairo (1942), 32
Calderón, Dora, 76, 145–147, *144*, *146*. *See also* Peña, Elizabeth
Caldwell, John, 48
California, 14, 95, 108, 113, 117, 131, 132, 193n47
camerawork, 34, 46, 103, 152–153, 156–158, 161
capitalism, 9, 14, 89, 87; and immigration 135–136; and race, 12, 13–15, 117, 162
Carmen (in *Down and Out in Beverley Hills*), 145, 192n31. *See also* Peña, Elizabeth
Carroll, Diahann, 70, 129. *See also Julia* (1968–1971)
Carter, Nell, 56–57, *57*
Cartwright, Ben, 99, 100, 103, 104–105
CBS, 38–39, 69
Ceramic Undies and Celluloid Mammies, 24
Chang, Jimmy, 101–103
Charles in Charge (1984–1985, 1987–1990), 6, 7
Chen, Joan, 126, 127. *See also* Packard, Josie
Chicanos, 137–138
Childress, Alice, 37
Chinese Exclusion Act (1882), 94, 131
Chinese immigrants, 94, 96, 98, 100, 107, 111

citizenship, 97, 131–132, 133, 137, 149, 152–154, 155, 187n28. *See also* Americanness
civil rights movement, 39–40, 62, 102, 112, 123, 137–138, 166; and non-fiction media, 45–46, 138; and racial discourse on television, 21, 44–45, 79, 84, 92, 101–102, 105, 111, 118
Clark, Marcia, 153
Clark-Lewis, Elizabeth, 15
class, 8, 12, 56, 61, 136; and black male domestics, 48, 49, 52–53; and domestic servants, 5, 15, 49, 95, 132, 133, 154–155, 160, 166; and white servants, 61–89; and whiteness, 74, 75, 85–86, 95–96
Classen, Steven, 102, 155
class mobility, 48, 50, 51, 71, 131
Clean House (2003–2011), 29, 58
Clinton, Hillary Rodham, 148
Clinton, President Bill, 48, 134, 148–149
Cobbs, Bill, 46
Cochran, Johnnie, 150, 152, 153
Collins, Patricia Hill, 1, 17, 28, 29, 56
colonialism, 92, 128
color blindness, 4, 64, 161
colorism, 87–88. *See also* skin color
comedy, stand-up, 24, 129, 164. *See also* humor
controlling images, 17–18, 23–25, 29, 167; and racialized domestics, 23–25, 56, 96, 128, 150
coolie, trope of, 95–96, 98
Corbett, Eddie, 92, 93–94, *112*
Cosby, Bill, 66
Cosby Show, The (1984–192), 48, 65, 68, 164, 183n29
Courtship of Eddie's Father, The (1969–1972), 6, 16, 19, 59, 75, 78, 91, 97–98, 111–125; as referent, 127, 128, 130, 141, 142
Crazy Rich Asians, 189n58, 190n65
Crenshaw, Kimberlé, 3
critical race theory (CRT), 4, 171n10
Cruz, Brandon, *112*. *See also* Corbett, Eddie

Danza, Tony, *87*. *See also* Micelli, Tony
Darden, Chris, 150, 152, 153
Dávila, Arlene, 158–159
Davis, Angela, 14, 15, 27–28
Davis, Ann B., *83*. *See also* Nelson, Alice

Davis, Bill, 75–79
Davis children, 77–78
de Havilland, Olivia, 32
democracy, ideal of, 12, 17, 75, 166, 101, 117
deportation, 131, 145–147, 149
desexualization, 17, 53, 82, 114–116, 118–118
Designing Women (1986–1993), 19, 134, 149–153, *151*
Desperate Housewives (2004–2012), 143, 156
Devious Maids, 156, *157*
Dill, Bonnie Thornton, 3
discrimination, 12, 64, 79, 117; against African Americans, 46, 87–88; against Asian Americans, 94, 96, 100–101; against Latinos, 13, 14, 131–132, 138. *See also* oppression; racism
displacement, 7, 36, 79, 101, 128, 136, 161. *See also* retrospective displacement
diversity, 161, 162, 163
divorce, 81, 124, 184n44
documentary film, 45–46, 131, 143–144
Doméstica, 155
domesticity, 14, 60, 92, 133, 136
domestic servant as surrogate wife, 113–125, 123, 147
Down and Out in Beverley Hills (1986), 145
Downton Abbey (2001–2015), 68
dragon lady, trope of, 115, 129
drama (genre), 2, 7, 22, 38–39, 41, 46–47, 164
Drescher, Fran, *88*. *See also* Fine, Fran
DuBois, Benson, 52–54, *53*, *54*. *See also* Guillaume, Robert
Dudley (1993), 6, 19, 134, 139–144
Duster, Troy, 166
Dyer, Richard, 62

East, the, 90, 92
education, access to, 71, 85, 87–88, 52, 135, 165, 166
Ed Wynn Show, The (1949–1950), 34
El Norte (1983), 142
El Salvador, 145, 152, 146–147
emasculation, 95, 97–99, 103–104, 105, 107, 109–110
Emmy Awards, 30
employment laws, 132, 148–149, 152–154. *See also* immigration law
employment of domestic workers by women, 5, 15, 16, 44, 91, 127

ethnicity, 8, 11, 66, 94, 128, 135–136
Ethnic Notions (1986), 135
Everybody was Kung Fu Fighting: Afro-Asian Connections and the Myth of Cultural Purity, 95–96

Falsey, John, 59
Family Affair (1966–1971), 6, 19, 66, 70, 75–79, *78*, 118, 141; "The Girl Graduate," 77
family ideal, nuclear, 70, 80, 93–94, 124–125; white, 13, 64–65, 68, 79–80, 91–94, 101, 114, 154
family values, 148, 181n14
Farrell, Peter, 145
fatherhood, 54, 70–71, 73, 76, 113, 119–120, 124–125, 142
Father Knows Best, 68, 70
femininity and Asian American characters, 90–91, 94, 100, 111–112, 114, 118, 125, 127–128, 193n40; defined in contrast to servant, 26–28, 71, 112, 136
feminism, 6, 10, 79, 80, 84, 127–128, 165. *See also* women's movement
Fibber McGee and Molly (1944), 30
film industry, 13, 17–18, 21, 58, 129, 139
Fine, Fran, 67, 85, *88*
Fiske, John, 65
Flipping Out (2007–2018), 6, 156
Flores, Juan, 135–136, 141, 154
Floyd, George, killing of, 138
Frankenberg, Ruth, 10, 61, 63, 89
Frasier (1993–2004), 6, 85
Fredrickson, George, 14
French, Giles, 67, 75–79, 82, 97, 110, 142
Fresh Off the Boat, 97, 164, 189n58
Fresh Prince of Bel-Air, The (1990–2006), 6, 19, 22, 48–51, *49*, 52, 53, 65, 78, 82; "Kiss My Butler," 50, "Geoffrey Cleans Up," 50
From Mammy to Miss America and Beyond, 25–26

Gates, Raquel, 158, 164
gender and relationship to race, 9, 63, 78, 129. *See also* gender hierarchy; gender roles
gender hierarchy, 8, 14, 16, 72, 95–96, 129, 105, 161, 166
gender roles, and domestic labor, 10–11, 14, 27–28, 76, 83–83, 111–112, 133–134, 146; and television, 61, 71–72, 164–165. *See also* gender roles

gender subordination. *See* sexism
Geoffrey the Butler, 19, 48–51, *49*, 82, 85. *See also* Marcell, Joseph
"ghetto, the," 48, 52
Gibbs, Marla, *51*. *See also* Johnston, Florence
Gimme a Break! (1981–1987), 6, 16, 22, 30, 56–58, *57*
Gish, Lillian, 103, 182–183n27
Goldberg, Whoopi, 56
Gone With the Wind, 7, 21, *26*, 29, 32, 33, 35, 37, 160
Gone With the Wind (novel), 27
Gonzalez, Maya, 50, 54
Good Neighbor Policy, 137
Good Times (1974–1979), 30
Gray, Herman, 9, 47, 160
Great Gildersleeve, The (1955), 30
Great Wok Cookbook, The, 105
Greene, Lorne, 99, 102
Green Hornet, The (1966–1967), 90, 107, 109, *109, 110*
Guillaume, Robert, 52–54, *53, 54*

Hall, Stuart, 66, 67, 71, 135
Hamamoto, Darrell, 17, 30
Harper, Adlaine, 42–44
Harper, Lewis, 46, 47
Harper, Lilly, 27, 37–47, *38, 40, 43*, 56, 59, 60. *See also* Taylor, Regina
Harper, Nell, 56–57, 182n21
Harper, Lewis Jr., 47
Harte, Bret, 95, 98
Havens, Timothy, 164
Hazel (1961–1966), 19, 66, 68–75, 80, 83; "Natural Athlete," 71–72; "Everybody's Thankful But Us Turkeys," 73
Help, The (2011), 161
Hemsley, Sherman, 51. *See also* Jefferson, George
Henderson, Donnie, 34–35, 36, 58
hierarchy of servitude, 75, 77–78, 183n
Hill, Kevin, 181n7
Hispanic market, 132, 159
Hollywood, golden age of, 5; and racial representation, 26, 32–33, 90, 116, 129–133, 137, 155, 160–162; and retrospective displacement, 36, 98
homosexuality, 50, 78, 150–152
Hondagneu-Sotelo, Pierrette, 155
Honeymooners, The, 13

hooks, bell, 9, 58
Hop Sing, 19, 78, 79, 82, 85, 90, 97, 98–105, *99*, 107, 108, 128. *See also* Yung, Victor Sen
Hoss, 99, *99*. *See also* Blocker, Dan
housewife, ideal of, 6, 14, 27, 54–55, 70, 72, 81, 162
Howard, Bob, 30
Hugh-Kelly, Daniel, 145
humor: and African American servants, 32, 33, 34, 38; and critique, 47, 51–52; and racial representation, 9, 39, 164, 60, 107, 108, 113–114
Hunt, Darnell, 29, 169, 171n14, 181n51
Hurtado, Aída, 10
hypersexualization, 91, 114, 125–128, 129

I'll Fly Away (1991–1993), 6, 18, 22, 27, 33, 37–47, 56; "All God's Children," 43–44; *I'll Fly Away: Then and Now*, 47
"I'll Fly Away" (hymn), 40, 178n51
I Married Dora (1987–1988), 19, 78, 134, 144–148
immigrants, 9, 8, 13, 134–135, 137; Asian and Chinese, 17, 94–96, 107; Latin American, 5, 19–20, 131–133, 145–147, 152–154; non-white, 11, 75; undocumented, 132–135, 149–152, 154–155, 165; and whiteness, 11, 12, 13–14, 62
Immigration and Naturalization Service, 149
immigration law, 94, 100, 131–132, 145–147, 148, 150, 155
Immigration Reform and Control Act of 1986, 148
Indians (native US), 98, 100
integration, 4, 44, 177n36. *See also* segregation
intersectionality, 3–4
intertextuality, 4, 7, 8, 9; and actors, 33, 90, 105, 116; and Latina maids, 19, 158; and race, 20, 29, 62, 89, 133, 135–136, 138
invisibility, 132, 133, 149–151, 153, 154–155, 178n44
Ito, Judge, 152, 153, 178n48

Jack Benny Show, The (1950–1965), 30, 79
Jackson, Bill, 35, 58, 178n46
Jacobson, Matthew Frye, 62
Japan, 62, 94, 117, 119
Japanese war bride. *See* war bride, Japanese

Jefferson, George, *51*, 51–52
Jefferson, Louise, 51. *See also* Sanford, Isabel
Jeffersons, The (1975–1978), 6, 19, 22, 51–52, 184n47
Jetsons, The (1962–1963), 5, 6
Jewell, K. Sue, 17, 23
Jezebel trope, 56, 58
Jim Crow laws, 40, 44–45
Johnston, Florence, 19, *51*, 51–52
Joy Luck Club, 189n58, 190n65
Julia (1968–1971), 70, 129

Karla (*Mad Men*), 54–55
Kato, 90, 107, 109, *109*, *110*. *See also* Lee, Bruce
Katzman, David, 10–11
King, Dr. Martin Luther Jr., 45, 47
King, Rodney, 47–48
Korea, 62
Korean War, 93

Landon, Michael, 99, 102, 103. *See also* Little Joe
language: child as translator of, 120, 123; and difference, 71, 113–116, 131, 135–136, 139–141, 145–147, 152–154
Latifah, Queen, 58
Latina maid, 1, 19–20, 85, 132–159, 166
Latin American immigrants, 5, 12, 131–159, 166
Latino identity, 135–136
Latinos, Inc.: The Marketing and Making of a People, 158–159
Latinos, representation of, 1, 154–156, 158, 159, 162, 164, 193–194n52
Latinos, stereotypes of, 136–139, 156; as fiery, 17, 138–139, 145, 150; as maids, 1, 11, 19–20, 85, 95, 131, 154, 156
Latino TV: A History, 158
law and public policy, 4, 25–26, 39, 95; immigration, 131–132, 134, 138, 145, 148–149, 152, 155. *See also* immigrants
lead roles, actors of color in, 102–103, 107–108, 111, 129, 130, 142–144
Leave It to Beaver, 16, 68, 70
Lee, Bruce, 90, 107, 109, *109*, *110*, 186n13. *See also* Kato
Lee, Guy, 101. *See also* Chang, Jimmy
Leigh, Vivien, *26*, 26–27, 32. *See also* Scarlett O'Hara

Lifetime, 68, 156
Light, Judith, *86*
Lipsitz, George, 87, 88
Little Joe, 99, 103
Living In, Living Out: African American Domestics and the Great Migration, 15
Living Single (1993–1998), 58, 180n77
Longoria, Eva, 143, 156, 194n57
López, Ana, 155
Lopez, Jennifer, 131
Lopez, Rosa, 19, 134
Los Angeles Rebellion. *See* Los Angeles Uprising
Los Angeles Riots. *See* Los Angeles Uprising
Los Angeles Uprising, 47–48, 174n3
lotus blossom trope, 29, 95, 121
Lowe, Lisa, 100, 117
Lydia (*Birth of a Nation*), 161
Lynch, David, 127

Mad Men (2007–2015), 6, 54–55
Maid in Manhattan (2002), 129, 131
Maid in the U.S.A., 133
Make Room for Daddy (1953–1964), 5
male domestic servants, African American, representation of, 47–50, 52–54
Mama, 13
Mammy, 7, 21, *26*, 160, 161
mammy: Beulah as, 30–38; in foundational stories of slavery, 21–22, 25–28, 29–30, 97, 160, (see also *Gone With the Wind*; McDaniel, Hattie); as trope of Black womanhood, 17, 25–28, 42, 55–60, 97, 100, 123, 128; and white womanhood, 26–27
Marcell, Joseph, *49*
marriage, 53–54, 118–119, 120–123; interracial, 62, 68, 75, 91, 103, 121–123, 144–148 (*see also* miscegenation); and white servants, 11, 80–81, 85–86, 89
Marta, 139–143. *See also* Ontiveros, Lupe
masculinity, 183n40; of male servants, 50, 75–76, 79, 87, 97 (*see also* emasculation); and race, 90, 97, 98–99, 103, 126, 128, 150–152; of women, 27, 36, 82
Maude (1972–1978), 6, 16, 30
McDaniel, Hattie, 7, 21, *26*, 29–37, *31*, 56, 58, 91, 177n40. *See also* mammy: Beulah as; *Gone With the Wind*
McDonald, Jeanette, 32
McDonald, J. Fred, 13

McHugh, Kathleen Anne, 133, 136
McPherson, Tara, 28, 150
McQueen, Butterfly, 36, 178n49
Media Action Network for Asian Americans, 130
Melamed, Jodi, 162
meritocracy, myth of, 4, 48, 49, 53, 131
Mexico, 98, 100, 132
Micelli, Tony, 67, *87*, 97. *See also* Danza, Tony
middle-class women, 5, 14, 17, 20, 72, 78, 133–134
miscegenation, 17, 95, 114, 115–116, 137, 153. *See also* marriage: interracial
"missing mother" theme, 6, 12, 15, 16, 19, 134; and white domestic servant, 74, 75–78, 80–82; and African American domestic servant, 53–54, 55, 56–57; and Dora, 144, 147; and Asian American domestic servant, 27, 42, 45, 98, 100, 93–94, 111–125; and Latina domestic servant, 134, 141–142
Mizz Alice, 33–34, 36, 70, 77
model minority, myth of, 19, 93, 105–106, 107, 111, 118, 124, 129
Moon, Daphne, 85
Moore, Dudley, 139
motherhood, 55, 70, 80–82, 114, 123, 136, 160, 162; and feminism, 14, 118, 133, 144
Motion Picture Academy, The, 163
Moy, James, 95
Mr. Belvedere (1985–1990), 6, 16
Mr. French. *See* French, Giles
Mr. Harry (in *Beulah*), 34, 36
Mrs. Livingston, 19, 75–92, 97, 128, 142. *See also* Umeki, Miyoshi
multiculturalism, 163
My Three Sons, 6, 16, 18

Nakano Glenn, Evelyn, 18, 94
Nanny, The (1994–1999), 6, 16, 19, 67, 85
Nannygate, 19–20, 134, 144, 145, 148–149
narrative power, 59–60, 77, 102, 138, 161; and African Americans, 34–36, 41, 43, 45–46, 54–55, 56, 59
Nash, Niecy, 29, 58, 176–177n28, 180n80
National Domestic Workers Alliance, 138
National Hispanic Media Coalition, 156
national identity, and race, 19, 20, 47, 92, 97, 98, 111, 117; and whiteness, 63–64, 78–79, 87, 160, 162

Nava, Gregory, 142
NBC, 38–39, 69, 142
"Negro Problem, The," 87
Nelson, Alice, 5, 7, 16, 19, 67, 70, 75, 79–84, *80*, *83*, 141
Nervous Laughter, 30
"New Ethnicities," 135
news: and Latina domestic servants, 131, 134–135, 148, 152, 155; and racism, civil rights, 2, 21–22, 45–46, 47, 48, 93
non-traditional family, 6, 16, 75–76, 80–82, 93–94
Noriega, Chon, 131, 137

Oboler, Suzanne, 136–137
Omi, Michael, 8, 9, 64, 89
Ono, Kent, 128
Ontiveros, Lupe, 139, *140*, 142–144, *143*, 156, 192n28. *See also* Marta
oppression, 96, 89, 161; class, 17, 56; gender, 17, 27, 56, 92; racial, 9, 17, 27, 39, 46, 56, 64, 92
Oren, Tasha, 97
Orientalism, 19, 92–94, 19, 102–103, 117–118
Oriole (character in *Beulah*), 36, 37
#OscarsSoWhite, 162
Other, 12, 62, 64–65, 162, 166; and identity, 12, 92–95, 144, 162, 165–166; people of color as, 17, 48, 85, 100, 119, 123, 125, 133, 155

Packard, Josie, 125–128, *126*
Page Law, 94
patriarchy, 9, 75, 78, 152, 153; and domestic service, 6, 72, 75, 97, 127; and race, 10, 18, 75, 89, 92, 95–96, 97; and women of color, 9, 10, 54–55, 70, 72, 96–97
Patriot Act, 131–132
Peña, Elizabeth, 145, *144*, *146*
perpetual foreignness of Asian Americans, 90, 103, 129, 130, 164
Petit, Arthur, 138, 155
Pham, Vincent, 128
Pinky (1949), 35
politics, 101, 131, 135, 138, 135, 147–150
"Possessive Investment in Whiteness, The," 87, 88
post–WWII economic boom, 39, 5, 11, 68
Prashad, Vijay, 95–96
private world of domestic servants, 21, 41, 43, 50, 59; lack of, 68–69, 70, 73, 100,

102–104, 114, 119–120; and romance, 81, 82, 113, 118–121
Production Code Administration, 137
Proposition, 187; 1994 (California), 131–132
protest, 6, 38, 40, 44, 111, 118, 137–138, 163
public television, 47

Queens, 85

race, definition of, 61–62, 64
Race and the Cultural Industries, 166
race relations, 7, 21–22, 29, 45, 37, 111, 133, 135–136
racial anxiety, 89, 117, 132, 136, 137, 150–152, 154, 155
racial difference, 8, 9, 14, 20, 160, 161–162; and Asian Americans, 97, 113, 123; and Latinos, 139, 146, 155; and white domestic servants, 61–63, 67
racial discourse, 2, 5, 9–10, 33, 38, 55–56, 59, 96–98, 128
Racial Fault Lines: The Historical Origins of White Supremacy in California, 9
racial formation, 8–10, 89, 136
Racial Formation in the United States from the 1960s to the 1990s, 8, 9
racial harmony, ideal of, 7, 16, 21–22, 26, 28, 30, 160
racial hierarchy, 22, 56, 64, 85–86, 92–93, 95–96, 100, 111
racialization, 1–2, 8–10, 14, 88–89, 107, 117–118; and change over time
racism, 4, 28, 64, 66, 91, 117; in Bonanza, 101–102, 111; representations of, 18, 21–25, 37, 39–42, 45–46, 129, 133, 145, 150; structural, 4, 8–10, 22, 29, 41, 43, 52, 60, 166
radio, 13, 30
Reagan, President Ronald, 48
Reconstructing Dixie: Race, Gender, and Nostalgia in the Imagined South, 28, 150
religion, 11, 13
representational economy, 7, 9, 105–106, 134, 154–156, 162
retrospective displacement, 16–18, 22–23, 59–60, 101–102, 161, 166; and period pieces, 38–39, 54–56
Reverend Henry, 46, 47
Riggs, Marlon, 135, 174n4
Robinson, Bill "Bojangles," 35
Robinson, Cedric, 162

roles for people of color, limited, 90–91, 96, 105, 142–144, 163; supporting roles, 79, 98, 132, 163, 164–165
Rollins, Judith, 12, 15
Romero, Mary, 11, 133
Rosario (*Will & Grace*), 6, 192n33
Roseanne (1988–1997), 16, 60
Rosie the Robot, 156

Saha, Anamik, 166
Said, Edward, 92–93, 97, 117
Sanford, Isabel. *See* Jefferson, Louise
"sass," 22, 33–34, 38, 42, 56, 57, 107
Sayonara (1957), 90, *91*, 116, 121
Scarlett O'Hara, 26–27, 35, 160, 161
segregation, 9, 40, 44–45, 47, 48, 52, 87, 188, 102, 177n36. *See also* integration
September 11, 2001 attacks, 131
sexism, 15, 55–56, 91, 95, 97, 118, 129, 138–139
sexuality, 57, 91, 97, 115, 125–127, 146
sexualization of domestic servants, 137, 138–139, 145–146, 156
sexual subjugation, 121
shades of whiteness, 62, 71, 75, 85–86, 89
She Done Him Wrong (1933), 32
Sheffield family, *88*
Shohat, Ella, 149
Shot in America: Television, the State, and the Rise of Chicano Cinema, 137
Simpson, O.J., trial of, 19, 134, 149, 150, 152–154, 178n48
sitcoms, 2, 7, 16, 18, 37, 46, 47, 67–68, 118; immigration in, 118, 155; race in, 22–23, 30, 37, 41, 56, 134, 138, 150, 162–164
skin color, 28, 44, 61–63, 67, 75, 87–88
slavery, 22, 174n2, 182n26; legacy in domestic service, 12, 27–28, 30, 33–36, 40, 42–43, 50, 58, 82; and role in mammy trope, 26–28, 58;
slaves, 33, 35, 45, 90, 100
Smart-Grosvenor, Vertamae, 178n52
Smith, Will (actor), 48, 129. *See also* Smith, Will (character)
Smith, Will (character), 48–50. *See also* Smith, Will (actor)
Smith-Shomade, Beretta, 58
social change, and Asian American characters, 112, 118, 128; outside of show, 59–60, 68, 79, 80, 84, 111; on television, 45, 166
Sound of Music, 68
South, the. *See* American South, the

South Central Los Angeles, 48, 52
"Southern Discomforts: The Racial Struggle over Popular TV," 102
Spanish-American War, 93
Spielberg, Steven, 142
Spigel, Lynn, 5, 13
sports, 2, 16, 164
Stam, Robert, 149
Stanwyk, Barbara, 32, 33, 98
Star Trek, 118, 185n1
Star Trek: The Next Generation (1987–1994), 56, 118
stereotypes, 95, 117, 124, 130, 137–138, 155
Stowe, Harriet Beecher, 28
structural racism, 8, 9, 10, 52, 60, 63–64, 87–89, 97
structuring absence, 2, 132, 134, 138, 149, 164, 191n4
suburbs, 5, 21, 65, 71, 132; family in the, 5, 67, 70, 156; homes in the 4, 11, 36, 144
Sugarbaker, Suzanne, 149–150
Sullivan, Ed, 30–31
supermoms, 6, 144
supporting roles, people of color in, 2, 6, 34, 55, 85, 107–108

Tajima-Peña, Renee, 158
Takaki, Ronald, 95, 107
talking back, 33, 37, 38, 42, 51–52, 60, 158
Taylor, Meshach, *151*. *See also* Bouvier, Anthony
Taylor, Regina, *38*, *40*, 41, *43*, 56, 59, 176n18. *See also* Harper, Lilly
television industry, 5, 12, 13, 20, 29, 64, 166; Latinos in the, 132, 137–138, 156–159; and race, 17–18, 29, 58, 160, 161, 163
Till, Emmett, 45, 179n55
Tong, Peter, 78, 79, 90, 97, 105–108, *106*, *108*, 128
Tong, Sammee, 90, 105, *106*, *108*. *See also* Tong, Peter
Truth, Sojourner, 28
Tubman, Harriet, 28
Turner, Patricia A., 25–26, 28, 29, 44, 59
Twin Peaks (1990–1991), 91, 125–128, *126*

Umeki, Miyoshi, 90–91, *91*, 92, *112*, 116, 121, *122*, 128, 129. *See also* Mrs. Livingston
Uncle Tom's Cabin, 7, 28
Unthinking Ethnocentrism, 149
upper class culture, 76, 78, 132, 133, 145

Upper East Side, New York, 51–52
Upstairs Downstairs (1971–1975), 68

Valdivia, Angharad N., 154
Valverde, Consuela, 149–150
Veronica's Closet (1997–2000), 142
Vietnam War, 62, 80, 92, 93, 112, 117, 118
Viola, 54–55
violence, racial, 93, 129, 190n70
voting, 36, 44, 96

Wallace-Sanders, Kimberly, 27, 55
war bride, Japanese, 19, 91–96, 118, 185n2, 188n44
Watching Jim Crow: The Struggles Over Mississippi TV, 155
Waters, Ethel, 31–33, 35
Waterson, Sam, 42
welfare mother, trope of, 56
Wells, Ida B., 28
Welter, Barbara, 14
West, the, 90, 92
west, the (region of US), 98–105
Western (genre), 98
Western United States. *See* west, the
West Philadelphia, 52
westward expansion, 98, 100, 107, 117
white domestic servants, 10–11, 63–65, 77–78, 82, 85–86, 134, 166
white family ideal and domestic servant, 2, 29, 37, 63, 84–85, 82, 132, 142, 144
white male hero, 98–99, 103, 126–128
whiteness: as culture, identity, 11, 52, 75, 84, 95, 103–104, 125, 154; definition of, 61–64; and television, 46, 64–68, 84–89, 162; representation of, 21–23, 39, 52, 61, 164, 166
Whiteness of a Different Color, 62

white privilege, 7, 8, 10–11, 15, 39–42, 64, 85, 87–88; and domestic servants, 41–42, 45, 52–53, 55, 56, 81, 155
"Whites of Their Eyes: Racist Ideologies and the Media, The," 66
white supremacy, 12, 13–15, 63–64, 89, 172n20; and ethnic immigrants, 14, 93, 96, 129
white womanhood, 10, 12, 15, 72, 107
White Women, Race Matters: The Social Construction of Whiteness, 61, 63
white women and relationship to domestic servants, 16, 26–27, 58, 95, 70, 154–155
Who's the Boss (1984–1992), 6, 16, 19, 67, 86, 87
widowers, 52, 57, 81, 92, 127
Will & Grace (1998–2005), 6, 192n33
Wilson, Governor Pete, 149
Winant, Howard, 8, 9, 64, 89
Winfrey, Oprah, 29, 58, 176–177n28
Women, Race, & Class, 27–28
women's movement, 5, 19, 78, 80, 82, 112, 118, 123, 165. *See also* feminism
women working outside the home, 10–12, 39, 80–81, 116, 133–134, 148–149, 152, 156
Wood, Kimba M., 148–149
working class, 7, 14, 51, 17, 133
"World the Coolies Made, The," 95–96
World War II, 39, 93, 94, 118
Wright, Richard, 87

Your Maid from Mexico, 145
Yúdice, George, 135–136, 141, 154
Yung, Victor Sen, 90, 98, *99*, 102, 105. *See also* Hop Sing

Zambrana, Ruth E., 3

About the Author

L.S. KIM is an associate professor in the Department of Film and Digital Media at the University of California, Santa Cruz. She graduated from Smith College with a major in government and a minor in film, and earned her MA and PhD degrees in the Department of Film and Television at UCLA. She serves on the *Ms.* Committee of Scholars and on the American Film Institute Awards Jury.